acknowledgments

compiled and written
by Tuppy Owens

designed by Animage

background colour images
by Kirk Woolford

editing and proofing by Christopher,
proof reading by Phil Adams,
astrology by Adrian Smart

printed by Grafo in Spain

published by Tuppy Owens
PO Box 4ZB, London W1A 4ZB

distributed to the gift trade by
Powerfresh
3 Gray Street,
Northampton NN1 3QQ
☎ (01604) 30996 fax 21013

distributed to the book trade by
AK
22 Lutton Place,
Edinburgh EH8 9PE
☎ (0131) 667 1507
and
PO Box 40682
San Francisco CA 94140-0682, USA
☎ (415) 255 7350 fax 923 0607

Thanks go to my wonderful
personal correspondents
(and you are very welcome to
become one) and the listings in
many magazines and guidebooks,
acknowledged below:

Tahanga for his continual stream of
information and support; Dag
Örland International on Rio; Jan-åke
Siljeström; *S&M News*; Stewart
Parkinson on Amsterdam; James
Phallus on Ipoh; Bob Sullivan;
Picture; Grant Lauden and Peter
Hassall on New Zealand; Norman
Reynolds and Danny Varney on
Australia; Stewart Parkinson on
Africa, UK and Holland; Craig Allen
on Africa; Justin Keeble; Miles A
Way; Rick Thomson; Bob Shaw on
Scotland; Scotland Chris who sent
info from many countries; Richard
Goss; Billy Peacocke on Ireland;
David O'Sullivan on Ireland and
elsewhere; Mike Warriss on
Hungary; Michele Capozzi and
Michele Santini on Italy; Momo on
Japan; Marrianna Botey on Mexico;
Eugene Seymour on Nebraska; Carol
Queen and Robert Lawrence for
performance inspiration; Mistress
Clare on enemas; *The Trust
Handbook* on handballing; *The
Spectator*; *Hustler*; Fiona Pitt-
Kethley and *Forum*; *The Black Pages*,
Third World Traveller; *Mentertain-
ment*; *American Sex Scene*; *Climax
Times*; *Screw*; *Sex Havens*; *Loisirs
2000*; *International Directory of
Swing Clubs and Publications*;
Business Traveller; *Australia & New
Zealand After Dark*; and *Asia File*.

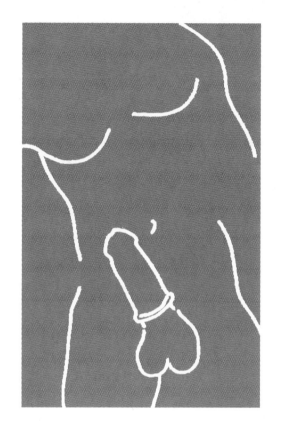

LOVE THE ONE YOU'RE WITH...

(SAFELY)

A PUBLIC SERVICE ANNOUNCEMENT OF THE KEITH MEDICAL GROUP
AND HOLLYWOOD COMMUNITY HOSPITAL

1

**the
sex world is open
to *everybody***

...

for this
HANDBOOK

This book is the sequel to **The Sex Maniac's Bible** which was written in 1990 and enjoyed by enthusiasts around the world. Because it was a Bible, it began with these 10 Sexual Commandments:

▶ **1** Keep your mind open to variety and diversity

▶ **2** Devote time to your desire, sexual pleasure and satisfaction, giving, taking and exploring without exploiting others

▶ **3** Defend sexual freedom without shame

▶ **4** Explore Safer Sex so you can't spread diseases

▶ **5** Stand by those friends who are condemned because of their sexual tastes

▶ **6** Attempt to deal with jealousy

▶ **7** Brighten the world by letting your sexuality shine through

▶ **8** Resist playing with your neighbour's lover behind their back

▶ **9** Be compassionate towards those who are unlucky in sex because of their physical or mental inelegance

▶ **10** Never forget that people who hate sex, journalists who make money out of 'titillating' defamation, and hypocrites who pretend to be 'above' it, will superciliously attempt to restrain, and maybe even ruin you. So: **DON'T GET CAUGHT!**

The Bible's devoted readers sent in information in wafts of mail, phone calls and friends reported back after trips. Thus, the contents of this Handbook reflect who my readers are, and what they enjoy.

Many of them are young white heterosexual males — these do make up the vast majority of clients at sex establishments and clubs, but I try to consider everyone. The sex world is open to *everybody*, more so as time progresses. There are black swingers, fetish people and groovers, as well as every other colour. Women, who don't always enjoy the same sort of sexual entertainment as men, are now setting up their own sex shops, clubs and societies, to establish their own sexual identity. Their effect is beneficial because women are instilling a certain degree of quality, sometimes taking away the sleaze aspect and sometimes enhancing it. Older people have always been accepted at most swing clubs, and they are certainly not shunned at fetish clubs. Older people can be very sexy: in streets in Marseilles, for example, prostitutes in their 70's and 80's ply their trade to an appreciative clientele.

Neither are disabled people excluded. I have been delighted to receive letters from sex clubs about exciting experiences with disabled guests. **The Planet Sex Diary** which uses symbols to describe the clubs, has symbols for wheelchair access and "welcomes disabled people", making it the best resource for such information. Prostitutes often tell me happy tales about their work with disabled people too, although sex parlours tend to have many steps leading up to them. The organisation **SAR** in Holland specialises in disabled clients.

I do omit the enormous gay scene because gays have so many excellent guides of their own. Some gay places get included to offer choice, especially when they offer things heteros might enjoy and cannot get elsewhere.

I make no judgements about my readers. Business men go to fetish clubs, punks visit whores, women read porn, naturists have kinks, most people like a little sleaze and a little glamour.

I would need ten large volumes to do justice to the wonderful things that are happening in the world of sex today. Travellers will be glad it's small enough for your pocket and you can tear the relevant pages out and put them in your filofax. What I have tried to do is to provide is at least the entré to everything.

I wish to be jubilant about erotic opportunities, but much of what you read here is the result of hard struggles for freedom. Moralists who attempt to ruin so much of our sexual fun, have seldom even tried half the things they want to to stamp out! Nowdays, sex enthusiasts are fighting back. Offer your support, the organisations are listed below.

In such fights, sex enthusiasts have been brought together and it's important that we do not alienate ourselves from one another. Respecting other people's sexual tastes is fundamental and I hope this book will broaden your tolerance. The sex world is changing fast. Strippers and whores are beginning to cherish their work, and are creating a whole new genre of erotic performance and art from it. The fetish scene has spilled out into high fashion. Outrageous tranny clubs have become so fashionable that women try to out-camp the men, and there is an explosion of dressing-up sexily and posing in night clubs. Much of the erotic enjoyment of today is Safer Sex: showing off, flirting, watching, S/M sexplay and fetishism.

I've enjoyed sitting here in my ocean of porn, putting all this together for you. I hope I will inspire you to dance around the pages, learning a bit here and a bit there, coming back for more when you're ready. Then, when you go out, either in your own locality or abroad, I hope you'll have a fabulous time!

Tuppy Owens

directions

ACLU
132 W 43rd Street, NY NY 10036, USA.
Publishes guides to the rights of minorities and groups

Adult Video Association (AVA)
8599 Venice Blvd, Suite J, Los Angeles CA 90034, USA.
Porn industry defence group involved in First Amendment legal battles in the USA

Adult Businesses In the State of Florida And Abroad
☎ (305) 779 1700

The All Kerala Penfriends and Philatelic Association
XIII/600 Pallippadam-Polpakara, PO 679 576 Kerala, India.
Serious efforts to bring sexual freedom to India. Send small donation to receive publication

American Library and Freedom to Read Foundation
50 E Huron Street, Chicago IL 60611, USA.

ASSERT
PO Box 2601 Lane Cove, NSW Australia.

Association of Libertarian Feminists
POB 20252 London Terrace, New York NY 10011, USA.

British Fetish Clubs Against Harrassment
c/o BCM Box 9253 London WC1N 3XX, UK.
A new group (its name is yet to be decided) of fetish clubs and businesses protecting themselves against the authorities

CAL-ACT! (Californians Against Censorship Together!)
California ☎ (510) 548 3695.
Political activist group to protest free expression. Meets quarterly

Campaign Against Censorship
25 Middleton Close, Fareham, Hants, UK
☎ (01329) 284471
Campaigning group

Censorship News
NCAC, 275 Seventh Avenue, New York NY 10001, USA

Committee to Preserve Our Sexual and Civil Liberties
PO Box 422385, San Francisco CA 94142-422385, USA
Weighty editors produce a well-researched newsletter Journal of Sexual Liberty *which only costs $10 a year*

Computer Professionals for Social Responsibility
POB 717 Palo Alto, CA 94301, USA.
Freely reprint, distribute, display, fax and upload information

Dutch Society of Sexual Reform (NVSH)
PO Box 64 The Hague, Holland.
Long-standing organisation protecting the rights of minorities and pressurising for improvements in the law

Eros Foundation
PO Box 3079 Canberra 2601 ACT Australia.
The Australian sex industry's freedom campaign group

The Erotic Party (Nezávisla Erotická Iniciativa)
Mikojanova 379, 109 00 Prague, Czech Republic

Feminists Against Censorship
BM Box 207, London WC1N 3XX, UK.
☎ (0181) 552 4405.
Monthly meetings for women, with campaigns and talks. Men may also join

Feminists for Free Expression
2525 Times Square Station, New York NY 10108, USA ☎ (212) 713 5446.
A group of women including lawyers and professionals from the industry who campaign, hold seminars, do lecture tours and help people understand how great pornography can be and how censorship hurts women

The Freedom to Read Foundation, Frank Zappa Memorial Fund, and **ALA Office for Intellectual Freedom**
50, Huron Street, Chicago IL 60611, USA.
Provide legal and defence assistance to

< wherever they burn books, they will also, in the end, burn people. >
Heine

publishers, libraries, authors, booksellers and librarians who face charges in America for seizures and threats from conservative and right wing pressure groups. Accepting donations

Gauntlet — Exploring the Limits of Free Expression
309 Powell Rd, Springfield, PA 19064, USA.
Publishes paperbacks devoted to specific interests, and often available in Books Etc

Index on Censorship
FFE 485 Fifth Avenue NY NY 10017, USA

Information Services
PO Box 82 Blackheath, NSW 2785 Australia.
A private, non-profit organisation dedicated to sexual equality, freedom and exploration

International Society for Individual Liberty
1800 Market Street, San Francisco CA 94102, USA.
Publishes Index on Liberty, an international guide to groups

The Lesbian Avengers
208 W 13th Street, New York NY 10011, USA ☎ (212) 967 7711 ext. 3204.
A civil rights organising project fighting anti-queer initiatives in America

Libertarian Alliance
25 Chapter Chambers, Esterbrooke Street, London SW1P 4NN, UK.
Publishes pamphlets on relevant topics and lobbies politicians

Love and Attraction
Pergamon Press, London
Papers of an international conference of 1977 in which topics were discussed by professionals on a level which would be considered taboo today.

NCROPA (National Campaign for the Reform of the Obscene Publications Acts)
David Webb, 15 Sloane Court West, London SW3 4TD, UK.
Active in lobbying and defending sexual freedom in all areas. They produced an excellent critique of the Criminal Justice and Public Order Bill, available to all members. Membership is £5 per year

NW Feminist Anti-Censorship Taskforce
13510-A Aurora North #229, Seattle WA 98133, USA.

Open Forum
PO Box 8343 Athens, Greece 10010.
Little magazine covering world issues

Outrage!
5 Peter Street, London W1V 3RR, UK
☎ (0171) 539 2381.
A broad-based group of gay people committed to radical non-violent action and civil disobedience to assert the dignity, pride and human rights of lesbians and gay men, so they may enjoy sexual freedom, choice and self-determination, in a world without homophobia

Outsiders
PO Box 4ZB, London W1A 4ZB, UK
☎ (1071) 739 3195
Campaigns for the rights of sexual freedom for people with physical and social disabilities through The Integration Trust and provides a self-help group

Reseau Voltaire
Annabelle Faust 8 rue August Blancqui, 93200 St Denis, France ☎ 48 09 22 10.
A new group campaigning against crackdowns on S/M in France and references to S/M in the French press

Sexual Freedom League
PO Box BOS 33681 Phoenix Arizona 85067-3681, USA.
A re-launch of the League of the 60's, planning to have a library and polyamorous group

Sexual Liberties
c/o Iskender Savasir, Hersey Yayinlari, Dostluk Yurdu Sok, 10/7 Sultanahmet, 34400 Istanbul, Turkey.
An encyclopaedia on the subject

Spanner / SM Pride
c/o Central Station, 37 Wharfdale Road, London N1, UK.
Campaigning organisation dedicated to upholding the rights of consenting sadomasochists and overturning the infamous "Operation Spanner" verdicts

Spirit of Stonewall
c/o Gayne Magazine, PO Box 15645, Boston, MA 02215, USA ☎ (617) 695 8015, fax 266 1125 and BM Box 207, London WC1N 3XX, UK.
An outcry by those at the bottom and on the margins of society against puritanical self-righteousness and bigotry.

Spunk - Journal of Free Expression League
The Free Expression League PO Box 436, New Philadelphia, Ohio 44663, USA.
From ROC Out Censorship

▶ Groups for prostitutes and particular sexual minorities are listed in the Reaching section ◀

SAFER SEX and *where* it is **TAKING** *US*

You don't have to be a prude to remain HIV negative, just practise safer sex at all times. Many people think they are "safe" because they are white, heterosexual and don't mix with druggies. This is insane: you don't know who your partner has been with, and you may have contracted HIV yourself in the past, and be passing it on without knowing it. People will always try and sweet-talk you into unsafe sex, and temptations are always with you. The choice is yours.

Women

Globally, women's share of HIV infection rose from 20% to 40% between 1980 and 1992, and is still rising. ▶ *See listings below for info addresses* ◀

Swinging

Swingers have got more into voyeurism and exhibitionism, dressing up, putting on shows, sometimes using camcorders and photography, and using hands only when playing with different partners. Some use bondage and power exchange to enhance their erotic enjoyment. Becoming more sexually aware often means that *less is more*. Going out to a swingers' dance and flirting in the highly sexually charged atmosphere can be more of a turn-on than getting involved in a full-blown orgy in which the sex is mindless and perfunctory. The safer sex Jack 'n Jill-Off parties of San Francisco, have not caught on elsewhere, because many swingers believe that they are immune to HIV.

Fetish

Parading around in leather and rubber, exposing nipples and erogenous zones (which may be pierced) and getting into little bondage or flagellation scenes with friends or strangers offers people a new sexual dimension, fascinating their minds and stimulating their groins. Women generally take on the dominant stance, which makes them feel safer and in control.

Tranny

Transgressing gender boundaries and transforming your appearance to portray multi-sexual extremism opens up incredible fantasies. The fashionable clubs attract as many women as men, the transvestite men inspiring the women to flirt outrageously and provocatively and

Safer sex has made a considerable contribution to the many interesting changes in the way we enjoy ourselves sexually in the 90's

in a way which would be considered prick-teasing in any other situation. Women can become sexually more expressive without feeling vulnerable.

New Age Sex

Not having sexual intercourse but finding other ways to reach ecstasy has led many people to Tantric sex. Massage enhances the feelings people have between them. These techniques also allow people to share intimacy outside conventional partnerships and expand their sexual boundaries safely.

Prostitution

Professional women use safer sex but some still rely on condoms rather than using alternatives to intercourse. However, many are refusing to have intercourse with clients, offering fantasy role play instead, and New York is full of fantasy parlours where everyone has a great time. The big problem lies with the HIV+ junkies who whore to support their habit and don't bother with precautions.

Sexual expression & art

Performance art, writing, photography, collage and every visual medium is counteracting disillusionment with conventional commercial pornography and conventional sex. Making artistic statements about your sexuality helps you heal old wounds, gain strength through voyages of discovery and realize your own erotic world.

Condoms

Many people equate condoms with safer sex. The problem is that they aren't that safe. Epidemiologist Dr Susan Weller from the University of Texas Medical School has recently published the results of her studies on how effectively condoms have prevented the spread of HIV. She found that condoms had a failure rate of 31% among heterosexual couples. If you must fuck, use superior condoms. These are available from condom shops or mail order companies *(see listings, below)*. Best brands are **Gold Circle Coin**, **Trojan Enz**, **Sheik Elite**, **Ramses Sensitol** and **Harmony**. When travelling abroad, don't rely on local brands, especially in Eastern Europe, the East and Africa. Take plenty: in Uganda, for example, even soldiers at the road blocks hassle you for condoms, as theirs have perished in the heat. Local brands are badly made, and imported condoms are often defective rejects.

Non-latex condoms for men are on their way in Britain and elsewhere. The female condom is called **Femidom** in the UK and **Reality** in the States. These do not protect you from HIV infection through the urethra, so need to be used with care. **Eros Veil Shields** for disposable plastic barriers that lessen the risk of STD and HIV infection during oral sex. They come in various styles, six in a pack. *(See listings below).*

▶ *Groups for people who are HIV+ are listed in the Reaching section* ◀

Women and AIDS Clinical Resource Guide
c/o San Francisco AIDS Foundation
333 Valencia St, 4th Floor, San Francisco
CA 94103.

Condomania
Unit 5, Rivermead, Pipers Way, Thatcham, Berks RG1 4EP

Personal Necessities Inc.
138 Prospect Street, Newburgh NY 12550.

Eros Veil Shields
552 Fourteenth Street, San Francisco
CA 94103.

SWINGING

directions

People swing because they find it unnatural to stay faithful to one partner all their lives and would rather share sex together than apart. They would rather be open about their desires than sneaky.

Swingers make up a large but hidden population. As they tend to be middle class married couples with conventional jobs and children at school, they find it very difficult to be open about their lifestyle. This is a shame. It makes it difficult for would-be swingers to find out what is available, and people who are not part of the lifestyle remain ignorant about just how "normal" swinging is. Questioned on why they do it, swingers usually answer: why not? The fun is there to be had and there's no reason to stop having fun once you're married or settled down. Some have been in relationships torn apart by sneaky affairs, and don't wish to repeat the experience. They decide to have sex openly and honestly, together, in the future, and find sex partners through ads or at clubs.

Swing clubs have been going for over twenty years and older clubs established traditions which other clubs have followed. The scene is conventional and does not attract very radical players, except for a few ex-hippies who swing on idealistic grounds.

Some swingers decide that they like their swinging friends so much that they want to mix with them all the time, and this is called *social* swinging. They feel more relaxed than having to make the big divide between their swinging activities and other social commitments. Swinging is a non-lookist activity and non-swingers might look at the various swing magazines and be horrified that people parade themselves in sexual poses when they are fat and old and seemingly unattractive. They miss the point. Swinging sex is to do with being with "like-minded" people who don't restrict themselves to one partner but relax to enjoy the possibilities around them in an open and honest way. It involves the thrills of adventure, tasting new partners and watching your own partner in the throws of ecstasy in a light-hearted romp. There's a generosity in it. Putting yourself in a situation where you can see your partner having the time of their life without being jealous is an accomplishment that many swingers value. Sometimes there's more to it than that. Some men get off on watching and don't enjoy sex with their wives

directions

unless some other man has been there. Other men may not get hard, and want to see their wives being shafted by a stiff prick. Some women find that they want more sex than one man can supply, or that being gang-banged is a sexual urge that needs satisfying on occasion. The emotional detachment during swinging is sometimes an important factor. This attracts many single men to the swinging scene, which works well where there are insatiable women who like being ravaged, although some husbands don't like the way they swarm around their women without offering anything in return.

Swinging enhances trust in a relationship. If trust and love are not there to begin with and the relationship is shaky, swinging will definitely not cure it: it will precipitate a rapid break up.

putting yourself in a situation where you can see your partner having the time of their life without being jealous is an accomplishment that many swingers value

A strong relationship can thrive on swinging because it brings an added sexual dimension and a great deal of fun.

Clubs vary a great deal, from those that simply provide the opportunity to chat about sex, to full orgy facilities. Throughout this book, the best clubs in each area are described. Couples are advised to find out as much as possible in advance. Before you set out, decide on any limits you want to set for yourselves, and promise to keep to them. Jealousy is usually a problem to begin with, until you have become experienced and secure about swinging. Don't jump in at the deep end. What often happens is that the woman is apprehensive but goes along with the man. Then, as the evening progresses and the man has come so much he's sleepy, he discovers she has developed an unexpected appetite and is enjoying every man (and woman) in the place.

Nearly all swinging women get into same-sex play, but this is taboo with the men, except in the most liberated groups. However, bisexual swing clubs are beginning to be all the rage in America.

Swing conventions are held annually all over the US, providing people with the chance to enjoy sex with new people and attend workshops to learn more about the lifestyle.

▶ *Swingers' magazines are listed in the Reaching section – swing videos (currently very popular) are listed in the Looking section* ◀

FETISH S/M
and

Fetish clubs are all the rage but the scene is
far more than designer clothing.
It is a form of radical sexuality which involves
not only a different approach to sex,
but also to life in general, often defying
marriage, gender roles, and heterosexuality.
As Pat Califia so rightly states,
"being radical means being defiant
as well as deviant".

Glancing through the Reaching section will give you some idea of the range of sexual tastes that are encompassed under 'fetish'. Many people fail to realise that the variations are endless. The more you get to know this scene, the more there is to know. For example, there are submissives who are masochistic and find pain ecstatic, others who get off on being humiliated but hate pain. Their needs may be quite specific, e.g. being paddled, being forced to eat shit, being led around on a leash. Some like rubber and leather, others do not. Most people want affection in an S/M situation, but others want ritual role play that is dramatic and distant. Most people want to feel safe, since they are exposing and revealing emotions that make them feel vulnerable, releasing tension in a way that many straight people fail to understand. It is the same for dominants. Often, doms say that it's essential to have experienced submission themselves, to be a good dominant, to know the submissive's needs, and vice versa. Within each preference, some people like to exhibit their fetishism at clubs and others would find this an embarrassment. To study the scene is endlessly fascinating, as is your study of your own particular quirks, preferences, fetishes and desires, especially as they change as you mature and go through phases. Entering this world is like opening Pandora's box, hopefully not a shady box of shame but a box of what Pat Califia defines as defiant people who know that the 'straight' people outside the box have got to be made to understand.

Fetish clubs are heart-rendering places where gender, class, age, lookist and many other of the

**entering
this world
is like opening
Pandora's box**

normal restrictions found in society are lacking. Commercial mistresses, hard core fetishists as well as the fashionable experimentalists interact. An essential trust is usually struck up, so it's rare to find people misbehaving like they do in normal clubs. **New York** clubs are far more commercial and less fashion oriented than those in the UK. Mistresses dress up but the subs trail round in their trainers, dicks out and jerking off. **California** is also less dressy, leather being more predominant than rubber. More than anywhere, American clubs are a means to find more interesting private parties. **Germany**'s fetish clubs are divided between the rubber fashion scene, initiated by *Marquis*, where husbands parade their wives in latex suits, and the non-commercial clubs where outfits are more makeshift and skimpy and action takes place. The **Scandinavian** clubs have always been rather serious: discussions, self-help and perhaps a little demonstration if you're lucky but raucous summer camps and disco nights are now beginning. In **Japan**, the fashion for fetish has subsided although **Azzlo** still put on dazzling nights. Their underground scene is mostly men dominating women, using them as horses on race tracks and whipping tied-up bodies in secret venues.

Fetish clubs have an erotic buzz: the rubber, leather and chains, together with bound breasts, dicks and heads in harnesses look bizarre and mysterious. People come to clubs for many reasons: to hang out with people in the scene, meet new lovers, play out erotic rituals in public (which feels quite different to doing it in private), show off, observe, experience S/M pleasures,

lick boots, find new clients, promote their wares, network, or just be in a place where they can wear their fetish clothes and be accepted. In general. There's always a preponderance of male subs and not enough dom women for them, sadly. There are also rarely any submissive women who aren't already shackled to a dominant man or woman. The Spanner Case in Britain made it illegal to mark or be marked for pleasure, either by whipping, piercing or other means. Thus there are never any heavy scenes in **British** clubs and clubbers are angry that their clubs are being raided by the police. **New York** law now forbids penetration and oral sex in clubs for health reasons (mainly to prevent the spread of HIV) but no rules about S/M. **French** laws have always been strict on S/M and that's why there's no big scene there. Anything is allowed in the **Dutch** clubs and that's why **Club Doma** in The Hague can have such heavy shows where guests get strung up by the nipples and the whipping tends to be competitive! Clubs are important learning grounds. Public domination offers newcomers the chance to learn, so it's extremely important that you administer your punishments immaculately. If you see anyone floundering or whipping stupidly, or doing something dangerous, do intervene and show them how to improve their skills. This is especially true right now because so many people are experimenting with S/M because of exposure in the media and most of them have no idea what it's about. Apart from these situations, never attempt to control someone else's slave without permission, and don't join in a scene or ritual without first being invited.

photo housk randall

Bear in mind that some slaves have been instructed not to talk. The fetish club is a place where all kinds of dynamics exist and nobody wants to be left out. But the best doms choose the best subs and many male subs are starved of partners. If you're a lonely neglected submissive male, here's how to be chosen. Learn how to be humble and submissive without being a dull wimp. Approach doms as *people*, offering to serve them in a way they will enjoy, i.e. usefully, amusingly, beautifully, or erotically. Making yourself useful will always get you accepted, especially if you carry out your tasks well, not trying to get punished for doing them wrong. Providing interesting conversation, not always about S/M, will make you popular — doms need to take a break from dominating all the time. Looking beautiful, adorning a dom will always be appreciated — so make yourself look lovely in rubber or some exotic gorgeous outfit. Finally, the domination must be an erotic experience for the dom, so think of that first and your kicks second. Ask the dom what *their* fantasies are first before stating your own. Never go home alone with a dom you do not know, and never take more punishment than you enjoy just to impress those around you. Women these days are using the fetish scene as a chance to dress sexy yet be in charge. They strut exuding power but, deep down, they may be just as submissive as their mums were. However, you can train people to enjoy domination (and submission). Don't take things at face value. You can say, "How may I be of service?" but asking people what they are into at clubs is really boring. Most people are looking for adventure.

directions

...tone up the body and mind, storing and augmenting

NEW AGE psychic energy

Improved love for one another and inner peace can be gained through Tantra and age-old techniques and knowledge, much of which come from the age-old teachings of Taoist masters and Tantric adepts of Eastern and European priestesses and priests.

Tantra involves using the regulation of breathing to connect sexual energies through your body. Linking with another who breathes in time with you, you can enter orgasmic states. It also involves the flow of sexual energy through the seven chakras of the body. The first, the root chakra is in the perineum, between the vagina/testicles and the anus, deep inside the muscle. The second is in the penis/vulva and these are the primary chakras. The goal is to move sexual energy up through the heart and the throat, to the chakra at the top of your head. This brings your brain in touch with your genitals, a very important link to achieve in sex. Men are encouraged to orgasm not through shooting semen but by using Kundalini, taking the orgasm up from the base of the spine to the top of the head. The ideal is prolonged orgasm without ejaculation and the conservation of semen is believed to tone up the body and mind, storing and augmenting psychic energy. Men who find normal masturbation uninspiring can get more positive feelings and even a brighter outlook on life as a result of using of using this method. It can feel as if two conflicting halves of themselves are being brought together.

Tantric couples practice Karezza. The goal of Karezza is to transform the penis and vagina into instruments for nourishment. The man barely moves his penis inside the vagina and the vagina milks it. This is called pompoir. You stay at a low level of arousal but practitioners find it thrilling, inspiring, ecstatic, regenerating, spiritual and transcendental. Naturally, these days, a condom is used.

▶ *addresses:*

Maithuna
Maithuna teach Tantric Kriya Yoga, seminal retention, G-Spot work for men and women, erotic visualisations and increasing your capacity to love. $27 for 12 monthly lessons by post from:
Maithuna Lessons, PO Box 108, Torreon, New Mexico 87061, USA.

Head
Head is a new age erotic magazine, anti-religion/pro philosophy from:
BM Uplift, London WC1N 3XX.

Body Electric
Now run by Colin Brown, holds workshops in San Francisco with Jwala and Annie Sprinkle, at the Atininous Institute in Berlin and the New Ancient Sex Academy in Amsterdam.
6527A Telegraph Avenue, Oakland, California CA 96409-1113 ☎(510) 653 1594 fax (510) 653 4991.

TRANSGENDER
and
GENDER *euphoria*

Fashionable clubs are making tranvestitism fun for some, but beneath this is a maze of intricate identity scenes, conflicting ideals and often confusing personal dramas.

Men have been forced to wear boring clothes, be shut off from their emotions and inhibited from being flamboyant and overtly sexual, for so long, that many are breaking out. Similarly, some women, having felt pressurised to look pretty and act cute, are rebelling, wearing trousers and exploring their virility. It can be enough just to go to the appropriate club and groove out in your chosen apparel but, for the less exhibitionist, the process may be more furtive and challenging.

For many men, dressing up in women's clothing might be a purely fetishistic activity which aids masturbation and/or sex. How much women do this is less talked about but I know I've got a kick from wearing a boyfriend's father's underpants! With both genders, there may be more of an identity crisis when they need, for certain periods of their life at least, to feel like a different gender and be recognised as such.

Such needs appear to be more common in men at the moment, and there's a new trend in transformation salons like **Miss Vera's Academy for Boys who Want to be Girls** in New York. Women, both wives and friends, are

becoming receptive, being 'girlie' with transvestites for fun, going shopping and clubbing. For all these lucky men, there are thousands of closet trannies who might, if they are brave enough, dress up in feminine clothing and go to a gathering, mix with other men, forget that they are social outcasts and enjoy disco dancing and femming it up.

For many transvestites, dressing up is their ideal, but others might feel they want to move on. They may join the group of people who are uncomfortable as the gender they were assigned to at birth.

Women, both wives and friends, are becoming receptive, being 'girlie' with transvestites

Wanting to change sex is an urge that many people experience and it can be a long, painful process of convincing doctors to perform operations, especially if you don't have any money and are relying on the National Health Service. Tales of British male trannies attending the Charing Cross Clinic, not fitting into the idea of what a "proper" woman should be, and getting rejected for the operation, are legendary. ▶ *See listings below for contact addresses* ◀

Almost as many women want to become men, but their plight is normally more sympathetically received by doctors. The journey may, nevertheless, be equally confusing and the organisations offer help for them too.

Some transsexuals want the right to live as their re-assigned gender with equal civil rights, having birth certificates reissued. A contrary view is that your birth certificate is part of your history and you should be issued with something else which shows that the new gender is now legally recognised.

Many male transvestites use their newly-found female erotic personas to earn money on the game to pay for private operations. The popularity of transvestite and transsexual professionals in recent years has been astounding. It's a tradition in Italy, where there's a lack of cultural gay identity amongst men and a fondness for dicks, but the craze is now everywhere. Of course, being confronted with a beautiful face and boobs, an assured sexual exuberance, plus the

uncertainty of what exactly is under the skirt and inside the panties is a turn-on for any male who is into adventure and the unknown.

With the recent bad press that plastic surgery is getting on the boob front and some bizarre experiences being reported by operated transsexuals, the trend has now swung back to staying a pre-op tranny. That way, men get to keep their dicks, even if they don't get erect due to hormone injections. They can, if they are lucky, make the best of both worlds.

Some transgenderists might find all of the above clichéd and superficial. There are many different journeys which are being trodden in the tranny scene. Some people are into becoming totally androgynous and, fortunately for them, other people seek androgynous partners. Conferences, magazines and forums are springing up, including the Transgender Board on Internet, where men and women can discuss breaking the traditional boundaries of their own gender.

▶ *The Reaching Section of this book aims to put people in touch with places where they can get suitable support and advice* ◀

▶ **addresses:**

The Gender Dysphoria Clinic
counselling

TV/TS Help Group
London (0171-729 1466)
might point you in other directions.

Transgender Board
on Internet

PROSTITUTES
and their *clients*

> "After pleasuring me, she stayed and chatted while I dressed — which, in my mind, is one of the things that makes a John feel like a person."
> *Irwin Garfield*

The working relationship between the prostitute and client can be wonderful. Each session can be enjoyable, leaving the client satisfied and the whore with pride. Sadly, this ideal is not often reached. Clients tend to approach workers with so much guilt and lack of human warmth, that the workers' defences go up. If you treat the whore like a human being, have a laugh and offer fair returns for their work, you will find that services improve no end.

The business of clients finding a prostitute and vice versa is frustrating for both of you, because of the laws surrounding prostitution. Be patient and kind with each other. You are both probably feeling paranoid in your attempts to overcome the legal situation, so comfort each other when you do make contact.

The professional is working for money. It might not be their chosen profession. Single women with kids may find that it is the only way they can make ends meet. Money is the first consideration so pay up front, having negotiated what services you require. Things other than straight hand-jobs or blow jobs cost more. Stick to the things you asked for, and treat her respectfully throughout.

Pay cash. Never haggle. Tipping is standard practice.

Professionals make their own limits on what they will and will not do, so don't try to persuade them to do things they say they won't. No intercourse means that, but pros who use safer sex usually have some pretty exciting alternatives. Believe it or not, many idiot men still try to negotiate intercourse without a condom.

be patient and kind with each other

Don't insult a professional by expecting sex if you haven't recently washed. If they wish to inspect your genitals before playing, be happy in the fact that they care about their health and yours.

If you are in your car, be careful not to look as if you are curb crawling in areas that are filmed or watched by the police. Turn into a side-street when you see a street girl you like, negotiate through a partly open window and, when the agreement is set up and the prostitute gets into your car, don't leave your wallet on the dashboard.

Girls working in the street should team up and keep the registration

directions

numbers of the cars you see your pals go off in.

If negotiating over the phone, clients should not be sexually explicit unless asked specific questions. On the other hand, do specify any special needs — a disability, for example. Professionals are used to catering to people of all kinds, but like to know what to expect in advance.

Whether you're a client or whore, if you make an appointment, arrive on time and phone to cancel if you cannot turn up. Treat this business like any other. Like seeing a doctor or lawyer, the client is paying for a service. More important to the professional, you are paying for their time. While the professional should not have one eye on the clock, the client must realise that time is important. Don't expect to hang around after sex. If it takes you longer than the agreed time to reach a climax, compensate by paying a little extra.

Not all escort agencies provide hookers but those that do will ask for information, to check you out and make sure you are bone fide. Renting a call-out girl means you pay for her travelling time as well as the service.

The fantasy parlour attracts actresses and performers, who enjoy creating scenes which allow them the freedom to try out new things on their clients. Offering the professional scope to improvise will improve the session.

A professional provides an erotic entrée, to make the client horny. You can ask them to display themselves in particular ways and do things to turn you on. They may, or may not like you making advances on them, like attempting to give them an orgasm.

Even if you have a disability or find forming relationships difficult for any reason, it seems a shame to rely on prostitutes, if a relationship is what you crave for. Your sex drive will encourage you to go out and find a partner but, if you always satisfy your libido by seeing a professional, you may find you never seem to get off with anyone "for real". The professional can help you to learn how to seduce someone, and teach you how to initiate sex, if that's what you find difficult. Whatever sort of help you need, ask for it.

▶ *Places to find prostitutes and prostitute groups, many of which campaign for the decriminalisation of their trade, are listed in the Reaching section* ◀

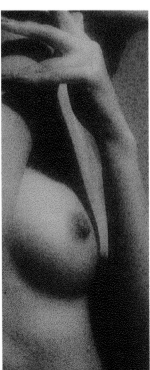

DOGGING

directions

This British tradition of enjoying sex with strangers in car parks and open air spaces is quite extraordinary. The French, Italians and Belgians do it too but not so obsessively.

Furtive and anonymous, using secret dogging spots, doggers have codes to deter outsiders from spoiling the fun. The individuals know each other solely by their car number plates, genitalia and nick names.

Dogging involves exhibitionism and voyeurism. The voyeurs are mostly men and the exhibitionists are couples. Sand dunes, country parks and a few naturist club grounds are the *al fresco* sites. Traditionally, a couple who want to be watched will make love in the known spot while voyeurs wank at the side. Occasionally, group scenes develop. Safer sex is the norm.

Certain car parks are used for dogging in vehicles. On arrival, you wait to see if any of the other vehicles are "active" and seeking attention. This will become obvious from signals: flashing interior lights or other secret codes invite the voyeurs to wander over silently, or park their cars next to them. The standard scene is for the exhibitionists to make love while voyeurs wank over the car windows, or even over the limbs of the woman as they poke out of the car. Adventurous couples stand up and screw with their heads through the sunroof, or get out and make love on the bonnet.

When couples dog together in cars, they sometimes park side-by-side, put blankets up, blocking all the windows except those facing the other car, so they can just watch each other while in action. Other times, one couple will get into the back of another couple's car.

The voyeurs will do anything to see what is happening: climb trees, use

...flashing interior lights or other secret codes...

pencil — or infrared torches. Although most peeping is done with the full knowledge of the exhibitionists, it is not unheard of for courting couples to be unknowingly watched too. The professional dogger is skilled at doing this without anyone having any clue. All kinds of motor vehicles pitch up, from Rollers to Robin Reliants. CB radios are sometis used to communicate on the road to let other doggers know where the action is. Doggers have to be devoted, since so much of their time is spent searching and waiting. Of course, the anticipation whets the appetite, and a good show keeps their spirits high for weeks.

running

a SEX CLUB

Running a sex club isn't like running anything else because, paradoxically, unless you live in an unusually liberated part of the world, the more you try to give people a good time, the more likely you are to be breaking the law.

The hard-nosed rip-off clubs survive while the enthusiasts get busted. This was particularly true when Whiplash got busted in London in October 1994. Robin had always worked hard to make sure everyone enjoyed themselves and low and behold, he was the one who the police went for.

There are ten basic rules to obey when running a club. They are easy to forget when you're trying to organise something that will attract the crowd in the face of competition. But remember:

▶ **1** Don't break the law unnecessarily. Many club owners think they are above the law when it comes to licensing and normal club regulations. Make sure you get all the licences and stick to the regulations

▶ **2** Don't provide services which break the law. Showing illegal porn, allowing prostitutes to solicit, allowing illegal acts to take place might excite your guests but they won't be excited on the night of the bust

▶ **3** Introduce guests to one another. Many people are shy and just need a little encouragement. Spend time with them, find out what they like about your club and what they dislike. Sex is a human activity and people don't want to feel isolated in a social vacuum

▶ **4** People who seem nervous or shy should get special encouragement. Just by asking a regular to go over and chat to them will make all the difference. Make your club accessible to people with disabilities, both physically and socially. It's only fair to them and, anyway, people like to think that everyone can get in, no matter what their bodies are like

people go crazy if you provide them with a playground to flirt and experiment

5 Ask regulars to be on the look-out for unsafe sex practices. These may be people screwing without condoms or getting into domination which is being administered without care or knowledge. Clubs are places where people learn about new kinds of sex. They find out how to play from people who are exhibiting themselves. This is a very important aspect of sex clubs and your responsibility is to make sure that the sex people see at your club is exemplary

6 Spice up the atmosphere up with flamboyant, stunning-looking, sexy and flirtatious characters. Your guests don't need to know they have been paid (or somehow otherwise encouraged) to be there, but will feel elated by their presence. This secret formula has been the making of some of the most successful clubs. These hired hands encourage guests to dress up and look sexy, and guests mimic the style they exude. Fetish and swing clubs might employ professionals to initiate play, get everything moving, and include people who otherwise might get ignored. Also, people go crazy if you provide them with a playground to flirt and experiment

with intriguing toys. The Planet Sex Ball is a very good example of this. Buy a copy of the video to see what we do (advertised at the end of this book).

7 All clubs wax and wane. They may become cliquey with new people arriving, feeling left out. Your job is to discourage cliques and make sure newcomers get admired and encouraged

8 Let it be known to everyone that, should they encounter a new member or guest who seems suspiciously like a prying journalist or snoopy police officer, they should inform you immediately. Even if their suspicions turn out to be unfounded, it's worth the effort, just in case

9 Have a newsletter which involves your members so they feel part of a family

10 Form a support group with the other people in your area who run similar clubs. Find legal advisors who will assist and advise you. Ideally there should be a fund to help anyone who gets into legal difficulties. Contact your local campaigning and sexual freedom groups for their co-operation

directions

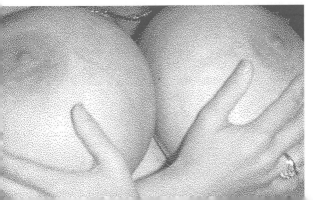

ZODIAC SIGNS
&sexual
compatibility

directions

▶ **search for the male sign**
in the vertical bar,
then look for the female sign
in the column opposte...

aries ♂ +

aries:	too hot to handle: sex, sex and more sex
taurus:	a head-on collision, exhaustion after the first night
gemini:	her seductive talk will make him come in his pants
cancer:	he runs like hell from her talk of babies and mortgages
leo:	this could set the world on fire
virgo:	her carping criticism will leave him impotent
libra:	tie her up and she won't want to escape (he might)
scorpio:	should whip up a frenzy
sagittarius:	just for once, she 'll get on top
capricorn:	if he pays the bill, sex will be smooth
aquarius:	a cordial encounter, nothing serious
pisces:	his fiery thrust overcomes her dreamy indecisiveness

taurus ♂ +

taurus:	you'd want a ringside seat for this bullfight
gemini:	her flirtatiousness makes him insanely jealous
cancer:	satin sheets and sweet music will wet the crab's crotch
leo:	fur will fly as the lion scratches at the bulls eyes
virgo:	his big willy in her loud mouth should keep her quiet
libra:	her knees go weak at his rampant advances
scorpio:	wonderful, but talk falls flat after sex
sagittarius:	wild, animal sex
capricorn:	could scale the heights of ecstasy
aquarius:	boresville
pisces:	69 will give these two multiple orgasms
aries:	sex and violence don't mix

virgo ♂ +

gemini:	verbally exciting and creative
cancer:	he wants to go out, she wants to stay in
leo:	let her do the work and she'll make him happy
virgo:	heartbreak Hotel
libra:	probably the best lovers in the world
scorpio:	he'll want oral when she wants anal
sagittarius:	the thrill of the chase swells his prick
capricorn:	down to earth with a bump
aquarius:	should teach each other a few new tricks
pisces:	a square peg in a round hole
aries:	extroverts who enjoy showing off their sex life
taurus:	nervous breakdown time

cancer ♂ +

cancer:	passionate when they're in the mood
leo:	the crab will sidestep the lion's charge
virgo:	a thoroughly respectable middle-class marriage
libra:	she has lovely shoulders to cry on
scorpio:	get the kinky gear out
sagittarius:	his moods will put out her fire
capricorn:	great sex, morning after a let-down
aquarius:	her unusual ideas will bring him out of his shell
pisces:	oral sex and watersports will keep them high
aries:	he wants it when he feels like it: she wants it now
taurus:	she'll keep him too busy sexually for him to get depressed
gemini:	his possessiveness will turn her off

leo ♂ +

leo:	two purring pussies, can't leave each other alone
virgo:	wham, Bam, Thank You Ma'am
libra:	glorious sensual pleasures
scorpio:	spilling blood is not Safer Sex: a jealous hell
sagittarius:	can we come to the party, too?
capricorn:	he gives: she takes
aquarius:	variety is the spice of this relationship
pisces:	pisces' natural wetness will put out Leo's fire
aries:	only a crowbar might separate them
taurus:	bulls and Lions will devour each other if left alone for more than one night
gemini:	fun, fun, fun !
cancer:	tears before bedtime, then kiss and make up

directions

virgo ♂ +

virgo:	technical proficiency, emotional death
libra:	he might bore her pants off
scorpio:	a union where he learns the secrets of sex
sagittarius:	he'll be appalled by her spending habits
capricorn:	down-to-earth, no nonsense shagging
aquarius:	produces some interesting variations
pisces:	publicly respectable, privately… Wow!
aries:	don't bother
taurus:	wedding bells
gemini:	emotional suicide
cancer:	he'll teach her every trick in the book
leo:	good for screwing but not much else

libra ♂ +

libra:	stop talking about it: do it
scorpio:	a real ball-bruiser
sagittarius:	delight in their sex show
capricorn:	his vanity will get her goat
aquarius:	group groping will get them horny
pisces:	just good friends
aries:	pin him down for some serious fun and games
taurus:	before he's made up his mind she's elsewhere
gemini:	should share their secrets in a manual
cancer:	may appreciate each other's finer points
leo:	her claws will hurt his sensitive parts
virgo:	could run a brothel togther

scorpio ♂ + scorpio

scorpio:	strange things lurk in dark corners
sagittarius:	no way
capricorn:	these could make money out of sex
aquarius:	shouldn't plan a holiday together, as they won't be able to get on for that long
pisces:	both too deep to let it all hang out
aries:	weighty Scorpios will not be impressed by flighty Arians
taurus:	the kinks in the Scorpion's tail will fall foul of the Bull's straight charge. Violently incompatible
gemini:	intense Scorpios will scare them silly
cancer:	drowning in the sea of love
leo:	violent sex, Leo is too cruel for Scorpio's taste
virgo:	a good time, Virgo having the upper hand
libra:	balanced Libra can't match Scorpio's passion

sagittarius ♂ +

sagittarius:	it's firework night all over again
capricorn:	the irresistible force against the immovable object
aquarius:	a good match, with a touch of spice
pisces:	all right for brief encounters
aries:	phew! What a scorcher!
taurus:	a Horse and a Bull: farmyard noises
gemini:	would last forever and a day
cancer:	bit of a damp squib
leo:	putting out fire with gasoline
virgo:	he won't appreciate her fussy ways
libra:	she'll be swept off her dainty feet
scorpio:	her sting could scar him for life

directions

capricorn ♂ +

capricorn:	too busy trying to get on top of each other to have a really successful sex life
aquarius:	hell on earth
pisces:	what a way to go!
aries:	the devil of a fight
taurus:	a truly horny Ram-Goat encounter
gemini:	she'll clean out his wallet
cancer:	strictly business
leo:	she 'll eat him for breakfast
virgo:	lots of depravity and lust
libra:	he'll be gone before she's made up her mind
scorpio:	lick her to ecstasy
sagittarius:	making love with the grace of horses

aquarius ♂ +

aquarius:	weird and wonderful
pisces:	weird and wretched
aries:	come fly with me (can't sheep fly?)
taurus:	not on the same planet
gemini:	both bisexual, there could be jealousy
cancer:	water and air mix - a wet dream
leo:	will tire quickly
virgo:	a thoroughly kinky relationship
libra:	a change is as good as a rest
scorpio:	he won't know what's hit him
sagittarius:	...and they rode off into the sunset
capricorn:	will end in a bankruptcy court

pisces ♂ +

pisces:	oil on troubled waters
aries:	a good fling
taurus:	water and earth makes mud (sticky, with a little wrestling perhaps?)
gemini:	geminis shouldn't expect too much praise
cancer:	stroke her big boobs to wet her knickers
leo:	should try sex in the bath, sea, etc.
virgo:	while he's in the pub, she's at the kitchen sink
libra:	if they ever get round to it....
scorpio:	could get very inventive in bed
sagittarius:	a great time in bed — terrible otherwise
capricorn:	occasionally exciting, usually dismal
aquarius:	great if they're both as high as kites

2 PLAYING

Kat Sunlove

< **getting off** is **not** my purpose in *erotic activity.*

I am more interested in **getting** it *on,* **and** *on* **and** *on* >

safer SEX PLAY

The gay Jack-off parties that gay men enjoy in many cities of the world and the multi-persuasional Jack'n'Jill-off parties thrown in San Francisco are living proof that you can combine promiscuous, anonymous fun and kinky, crazy sexplay with the realities of HIV infection today. Risk-taking as an act of intimacy does not include health risks. Obey the rule:

on me, not in me

Avoid infection by becoming highly aware of your skin and where it might be broken because of knocks, cuts or eczema. Always keep these areas covered and/or away from other people's genitalia or love juices. Bleeding gums means unhealthy gums which also puts you at risk. See a dental hygienist regularly and floss every day. A healthy diet, with muesli in the morning, prevents the bleeding bum syndrome.

playing

a-z safer SEX PLAY

Here is a list of various types of sex play, with clues on what places you or your partner(s) at risk of passing on HIV:

Anal Sex
is risky and should never be attempted by anyone who cannot open their arse easily, otherwise you will put too much stress on the condom. Strong condoms should always be used

Bathing Together playing with water, ice and soap are safe

Bondage is safe as long as you can trust the person who's tying you up not to penetrate your vagina or arse without a condom. Rope can

cause abrasions to the skin so take care, especially if the rope is to be cut later on

Cleavages can be used for "penetration" by the penis between the breasts, buttocks, arm-pit or behind the knee, all of which are safe so long as the skin isn't broken

Dildos vibrators and butt plugs are safe but should not be shared. If you're borrowing or sharing one, thoroughly clean it before use and put a condom on it

Dirty Talk is safe

Docking shunting inside each others' foreskins or clit hood, is rather unsafe because pre-come and come could get up each other's urethras

Dressing Up in uniforms, frilly undies, cling film and fetish clothing or simply in your lover's clothes is, of course, not risky

Drugs sharing needles for injecting drugs is one of the most common ways HIV is passed on. Recreational drug use impairs your immune system and so accelerates your illness if you're HIV positive. The other major problem is that drugs and alcohol can make you forget about Safer Sex altogether

Dry Humping — a combination of kissing and grinding your pelvis and other sensitive areas into your partner's sensitive areas whilst clothed — is safe

Enemas and Douching are safe. They are only unsafe if you have intercourse afterwards or if you share unsterilised equipment

Feathering — using feathers is safe and sensual

Fingering Inside The Vagina Or Rectum Is safe so long as you have no cuts on your fingers

Fisting is risky if the penetrator has cuts on the arm. Always use non-latex, waterproof gloves if you are going to use lubricants which are not water soluble

Kissing is safe

Love Bites/Hickeys are safe because they don 't break the skin

Massage is safe. Beautiful oils are available in most New Age stores. They enhance the massage

experience: jasmine, rose, patchouli, sandalwood, clary age, ylang ylang and myrtle are favourites. To obtain a tingling sensation, try tiger balm,

a tingling sensation

Metholatum or Witch Hazel

Masturbation is absolutely safe, whether you do it to yourself alone, in front of the mirror, with your lover watching or playing with him/herself at the same time, or whether you do it to each other (so long as there are no cuts on your fingers). But don't use each other's genital juices as lubricants

Nipple Play is safe, with your mouth, hands or genitals

Oral Sex is only likely to be risky if you have cuts in the mouth and/or infected gums

Piercing, Shaving, Tattooing And Branding are not risky so long as sterile disposable needles and blades are used. Wrap sharp objects before throwing them away, and wipe the skin with antiseptic. Marking another person's body for sexual pleasure is illegal in Britain

Playing with candle wax, nettles, electric batteries and other S/M devices is safe with regard to HIV but can be hazardous in other respects, Electricity should never be used above the waist. Make sure you know what you are doing

enjoy the warmth, aroma and visual pleasures

Rimming and Scat are not safe if you get faeces in your mouth. Use cling film, microwave saran wrap or latex to cover your mouth - you can still enjoy the warmth, aroma and visual pleasures, but don't get smothered and suffocate (too much!)

Testicle Fondling is safe

Touching all over with Fingers is safe and it's therapeutic to home in on the sensation of where fingers meet skin, whether you are the one being touched, or doing the touching. Many people who find this difficult but who learn to do it will heighten their sexual experience. You can vary the touch from light tickling to stroking and kneading, moving slowly or hardly at all. Choose a time when you won't be interrupted and take a nice long time to explore

moving slowly or hardly at all

Vaginal Intercourse is risky without a condom and even then, condoms can fall off or split. Even just putting a dick in or against the vagina without coming is risky, as the pre-come (the liquid that emerges out of the end of the dick when it is aroused) might contain the virus and could enter up the urethra

marking someone is against the law in the uk

playing

Watching other people make love, watching videos and exhibiting yourself (taking turns to perform in front of an audience) are all safe

Watersports there's no risk at all in pissing on healthy, unbroken skin or taking it in the mouth although the latter could transmit CMV, Hepatitis or salmonella, all of which might be serious, especially if you are HIV+

Whipping and Spanking are safe. If sharing whips and canes, sterilise them first and avoid drawing blood. Remember that marking someone for pleasure is illegal in the UK. Never strike where internal organs could be damaged and remember the kidneys are just above the buttocks

< I wish there were more places on your body to touch, that each time we made love I would find a nerve not known before. >
William Levy

SEX GAMES

T&T: *tantalisation and teasing are erotic alternatives to shagging. These games are designed to get you off whilst keeping you safe. There are games to play on our own (just ourselves or with the World Outside), games to play with new people, and games to get the party swinging and help people get to know each other. Then there are the popular swing club games. If you have an exclusive partner, Variety Spinners will add new dimensions to your sex play.*

Send me your favourite games, readers, and remember…
no cheating!

You with someone new

Rude Pool

Take your new-found friend to a bar where you can get a game of pool. Before each game decide, in hushed tones, what the winner will have as a prize. The prizes may be as sexually provocative as you like and take place in specific locations but be sure to restrict your treats to Safer Sex. You might glimpse the bewilderment on the faces of your spectators as you sigh with desire or sexual nervousness when one or the other of you gets close to winning.

> **people prejudge each other from past experience**

Blank Face

This game is ideally played in the privacy of your home, with someone for whom you have an unconsummated sexual desire. One of you stays silent and expressionless whilst the other tries to seduce them using any method other than kissing and caressing. It's even better if you have no idea what the other is into but are prepared to make wild guesses. Note how people prejudge each other from past experience.

Tantric Sex

Lie down together in a cosy spot and breathe in each other's breath, staying perfectly still with your arms around each other. You might want to look at each other or close your eyes. After about ten minutes, begin to move your hips back and forth together in time with the breathing. Gradually, you may be overcome with full body orgasmic convulsions. If not, after half on hour or so, take a break. This might be difficult with someone new, but it's exhilarating Safer Sex when you make it

Limits
As well as Safer Sex limits, agree on your others. Each writes down three things they definitely *don't* want to do or have done to them. They might be your most or least favourite things, or things that are currently boring you. Then you can relax into enjoying yourselves within the confines of your 'pact'. You'll remember from your teens that putting limits on sex can create a certain edge.

Household Sex Toys
One person lies down blindfolded and naked, or with as few clothes on as they feel comfortable with. The other person caresses them with various items from around the house. Can you guess what they are? Then reverse roles.

Fantasy Marriage
This game was devised by psychologist Chris Gosselin. It allows two players who have never met to conduct a relationship by post. You won't be encumbered by your normal limitations as the deal is that you relate as your fantasy selves. You can find a partner through an ad, a penpal agency or through mutual friends. It is a game often played on the bulletin boards (discussed in the

you could even change the era or dimension of your existence

Talking section), although letters can provide more suspense. Neither of you will quite know what your fantasy personalities will become: you can initiate them by choosing which gender you'll be, with a name and a general idea of the type of person - you could even change the era or dimension of your existence. Things will mature, moulded by your own private and innermost yearnings and your "fantasy partner's" own tastes and desires. There may come a time when the two of you will feel you ought to meet but this will probably put a quick end to your game. Unless . . .

I Know That My Receiver Liveth
I'm talking about your telephone receiver! There's somebody you speak to regularly on the phone, whom you never meet (the person on a switchboard ?) with whom you could start a telephone affair. Make sure they're willing and slowly does it. Sex couldn't be safer! Simply finding out their bodily shape and what pleases them, can lead to more interesting secrets. Eventually, you can send each other underwear, vibrators and souvenirs, as the sex gets hotter and the calls become more creative and crazy.

playing

You and the World

X-Ray Specs
Take a pair of dark glasses and inscribe X-Ray Specs on the rims. Wear them out to a place where you'll find some groovy people. Knowing looks will unnerve those who don 't wish you to see them naked and turn on those who do.

Menu T-Shirt

Write your Safer Sex specialities on the back of a T-Shirt. List them neatly like a restaurant menu, adding a price for each sexual favour (and the time allotted). The price structure could reveal your hang-ups or be humourous, and some might think it's fun to charge extra for acts of affection!

Spying

Use a telescope or binoculars to focus in on all the sexual capers around you: in other buildings, on roof-top parking lots and fire escape staircases. It's not illegal: as Zach Simms, the maestro, says: "it's titillating, it's kinky, it's hilariously bizarre and… well, it's free!".

Untouchables

Pretend that everyone you meet is an untouchable from another planet, deprived of sex and you, your God/Goddess of Sex is sympathetic but still cannot break the code. You may, however, make up for things by offering praise and verbal seduction, although you cannot touch.

Underwear Secrets

Wearing completely different underclothes has a profound effect on your relationship with Those Out There. Try it and see. Wear the opposite to normal: nappies, rubber, silk, or hair cloth. Men could try bras and panties; girls boxer shorts or a white liberty bodice and navy blue school knickers. Perhaps best on days you're not going to get run over!

Candid Camera

Carrying a Camcorder will draw exhibitionists and you can encourage them to flirt with the camera. Video series such as Bend Over, Ugly George and Buttman have proved this works, so over to you!

Stimulation Anonymous

This is Master Keith's slave girl game but it can also be played alone. Find some of those rubber tubes they put over petrol station forecourts to announce the arrival of a vehicle. Put your lead over the road outside your house or somewhere outside your home where there's occasional passing trade. The lead is linked to a gadget which gives gives you a tiny electric shock or your vibrator a buzz. The fun is imagining who it was that caused you all the pleasure.

Wrong Hand

A Billy Connolly invention: if you wank with the wrong hand it feels like someone else. Funny but true!

if you wank with the wrong hand it feels like someone else

Pocket String

This game was sent in by a reader who wants to share his thrills. Tie a piece of string around your dick or, if you haven't got one, the hair in front of your clit. Thread the string through into your pocket and pull it when you feel like playing with yourself.

Both of you with *someone new*

TS Treat

Hire a pre op transsexual prostitute. S/he will be accustomed to husbands and wives squabbling over their tits and prong. Don't lower yourself to

this however: take turns politely, and be kind: ask what he/she would like. If you give him/her a nice enough time, any possible craving for 'the operation' might be temporarily or permanently forgotten! This little caper requires meticulous Safer Sex attention.

husbands and wives squabbling over their tits and prong

Treasure Hunt
Send your lover on a sexual treasure hunt that you've planned with great care. The voyage will include visits to friends' houses where little sexy scenarios await them, with clues for the next treat. Hide presents under bushes. Leave paid-for gifts in shops and pubs where the person behind the counter will hand over packages with a nod and a wink. Stay by the phone, in case anything goes wrong. The last treasure might be someone to bring home to share with you.

Doctors and Nurses
Ask a lusty friend to come round to help you with your sex 'problems '. Suggest they come in uniform and carry a doctor' s bag. Allow them to conduct full physical examinations to determine whether you are compatible for each other, first unaroused and then fully aroused.

Knickers in a Twister
Invite a favourite person round to play Twister. Twister is a family game you can buy in the toy shop: you have a large mat you place on the floor which is divided into squares. Play all at the same time to get your legs tangled up.

Prowlers
You and your partner go out on the prowl to find someone new. Invent a code so that you can communicate with each other without your subject being aware of your plans. Here are some ideas for codes:

▶ Holding your head high:
  You want to watch the others
▶ Linking arms behind back:
  Let's both link arms with them
▶ Left hand on hip:
  Let's both go after them
▶ Scratch your head:
  No way!
▶ Both hands on hips:
  You'll wander off for 30 minutes

Have the codes written on pieces of paper which you both keep in your pocket in case you can't remember them. Sort out what you both want to happen (and what you wouldn't want to happen) before you set out.

Warm-up Party Games

Locked Inside
You need to warn everyone to arrive by a certain time, after which nobody will be allowed in or out for x number of hours. When people know they can't leave, they behave differently and much more wildly. It works much better when they really cannot leave: for example, when you're all in a boat off-shore, in a plane over the clouds or aboard a coach with no scheduled stops.

Rubber Night
Everybody comes to your party dressed in rubber garments: have some spare items of rubber for those arriving improperly dressed. Watch how the power of rubber will overcome even the most inhibited and bring out feelings long forgotten.

Who Dares Wins
Divide into two teams. Each team makes a line of clothing the people

in the team have taken off. The team
with the longest line is the winner.

Sex-Show
Everyone sits in a circle and draws a
card from a pack. The two with the
most similar cards go into the centre.
They pose as if they are having
intercourse in a bizarre position and
move in a sensuous manner to
impress the crowd. Polaroids may be
taken. Everyone in the party should
have a turn.

Gender-Swap
This is a party where people come
dressed in drag. Women: be sure to
have dildos strapped on and men,

men, choose your
ideal bra size

choose your ideal bra size. Stick to
the conventional role-plays,
especially in seduction techniques.

Nellie the Elephant
One person is in charge of the music
and the rest stand in a boy-girl-boy-
girl circle, preferably with tall people
next to short. Everyone puts their
right hand through the legs of the
person in front of them, and then
holds the emerging hand with their
left. Dance round in a circle to the
music. When it stops, turn round and
reverse hands. Slow music works
faster.

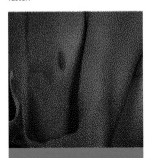

Purdah
Women go out with their bodies,
heads and mouths all veiled in black,
but their eyes beautifully made up.
They should flirt dangerously with
the natives before coming back to
the house at a previously arranged
time. In every room (or corner) each
man awaits the return of his harem.
The women divide up and act out
roles to pamper each man, listen to
his demands, and flirt unmercifully.

Longest Kiss
Play some smoochy music and start a
kissing contest. The couple who look
as if they'll kiss for the longest time
gets the most encouragement.

Tingle-Tangle
Everybody goes into the middle of
the room and the lights are put out.
Stretch out your hands in different
directions and wave them till you
find two other hands to hold.
Put the lights up a little and try to
untangle yourselves to make as
straight a line as possible without
letting go of hands. For a more
provocative game, people brushing
past each other should kiss, rub
chests or crotches.

Charisma Chair
All of you stand up, in various states
of dress and undress, in a circle of
man-woman-man-woman, very close
together, facing the person ahead of
you. Slowly sit down on the knees of
the person behind you. A self-
supporting circle will be formed. A
leader starts off fondling the person
in front of them, and this is
mimicked by everyone until it gets
back to the leader. Then the person
behind them starts a new style.

a self-supporting
circle will be formed

playing

Condom Relay Race

Divide into two teams. Each team has a dildo and each person has a condom. The teams stand in opposite corners of the room or garden. When someone says "Go", one member runs to the opposite corner carrying their dildo and the next person puts the condom on it, running to the first corner. The next person removes that condom and puts on a fresh one. The winning team is presented with a full set of un-torn condoms.

Soft Sex Swing Party *Games*

Soft Swinging is where couples only have sex with their own partners in a group setting

Hokey Pokey

Everyone congregates at one end of the room but one elected person goes to the other end, facing away. The person who fancies them most goes and stands behind them until everyone is in a line. The first person can bring the line round into a circle and stand behind the last. It's best if you have no idea who's behind you as they play with your parts.

Californian Tag

This is a favourite game of some readers in California. Start the game like strip poker. The first two players of the opposite sex to get completely stripped off and go into the

everyone is usually pretty much out of control

bedroom to lie on the bed together. The rest follow and surround the bed: women on one side, men on the other. The couple perform Safer Sex in front of everyone, but the voyeurs must not touch. After ten minutes, just one person from the audience joins them. Thereafter, every ten minutes, someone else joins in until everybody's on the bed. Then, the first couple who were on the bed get up and stand beside it. This continues until there are more people standing beside the bed than are on it. By this time, apparently, everyone is usually pretty much out of control.

Head Contest

Each woman is blind-folded and must guess the owner of every phallus presented to her. A women who fails to recognise her own lover/husband's shall be offered a line-up of all of them, so she can learn to distinguish by comparison.

Polaroid Party

Each couple brings along a Polaroid camera and stays with their partners to make love, everyone in the same room. Whenever one couple is doing something sensational, the others reach over for their cameras to take a photo. The couple who gets the most pictures taken of them is presented with an album with all the Polaroids stuck in it.

Spurting Contest

Each kneeling gentleman is played with by a lady and, on the floor, beneath each erection is a length of kitchen roll. The lady is in charge of pointing the tip in the direction of the roll. The shooting distances are compared. Ladies are not allowed to assist by taking it in the mouth then spitting it out.

playing

playing

Rubber Ball

Everyone comes to the party in PVC cat suits. Once you've all arrived, cover yourselves in baby oil and enter a room where there's a large plastic mat on the floor. The lights are put out so the room is pitch black and wild music is played. A huge mound of writhing bodies play with each other anonymously and anything goes except penetration.

Enemarathon

Based on the video of the same name. The start of the game is announced and it's a contest to see who can retain and maintain the most. Messy but fun.

Solitary Games

Knapp's Melon

Men: cut a hole in the top of a water melon, pour in a little hot water and enter it.

Guess the Dildo

Give all your dildos names. Put them in a hat and wear gloves so you won't be able to feel which one you've picked up. Place the hat behind you and pick out a dildo. Delight in its capacity to fill your eager orifice and see if you can name it. If you don't guess right, no pudding!

Whacking Off To Mahler

This is an original game plan which has received no real competition since Robin Ray wrote it in 1980. Any offers? The music used here is Mahler's Symphony No 5. You need a length of fine elastic which you thread through nipple rings, around genitalia and anywhere vibrations and strumming could delight you. The end could be beaded and go up your bum. Real enthusiasts might sew into their chest skin (use the Sandmutopia Kit sold by Desmodus,

listed in the Shopping section). As the music begins, make dignified, solemn vibrations to the Funeral March, accelerating vehemently to the second movement, plucking lightly to the *Scherzo* and using gentle, sensuous movements to accompany the *Adagio*, conserving energy for the *Finale* as your tumultuous orgasm occurs in the last bar.

Self Bondage

Unlock a padlock and put the key on a piece of string. Place the key in a container full of water, with the string hanging out of the side and place the container in the freezer. When the water is completely frozen you can begin. With the container on the floor nearby, decide where you want to bind yourself up and tie the end of the string to the base of your finger. The final bondage action will be closing the padlock with the keyhole facing your fingers. Then wait for the ice to melt.

Mr Vidor's Water Wings Wank

Lubricate a child's water wings and enjoy. For ultimate effect, according to one Mr Victor, place the wings between the mattress and the bed and probe in between. Women might like a vibrator behind the wings.

> ## your tumultuous orgasm occurs in the last bar

playing

Blue Movie

It's amazing what a video camera will do for your sex life! To make a home movie indoors, use a tidy space, with white walls. These are best because they reflect the light. Orange light hides blemishes. Make love to the camera, getting long-shots, mid-shots and close-ups and chat away to produce a highly erotic sound track. Many couples swap videos but remember *selling* hard core in Britain is illegal. Never film illegal acts, especially S/M since, as the men learned to their cost in the Spanner trial, they can be used as evidence in court.

Phantom Lover

A game based around one of Larry Tritten's stories. Each of you describes other lovers (fantasy or real) — their approach, techniques, skills, habits, and the thrills they offer. Give each 'lover' a name. Then, whenever you start to make love, you could say: 'I fancy a Bernard tonight', or: 'I need a Lucinda' and your partner will know what you mean.

Sex in the Past

One of you does Past Life Regression on the other, taking them back to one of their past lives. First you put them into a light trance by asking them to close their eyes and you count back from ten to one. Then tell them they are going back in time, to when they were really happy, centuries ago. Ask them to look down at their feet and describe their shoes, then the rest of their appearance. Ask them where they are and what is happening. Then make love as you would have, all that time ago.

make love as you would have, all that time ago

Revenge

Think of the people who tried to crush your developing sexual interest in the past and get your own back. You can do it in fantasy or reality. For example, you may remember your parents saying "when the children are quiet, we know they're up to no good". Mimic them, while you both grind away happily behind the sofa! Or have sex in the hall where Sunday School made you celibate. Each partner has their turn.

Stretching

Each of you writes down on a piece of paper those sex acts that you're afraid to do but yet arouse your curiosity. Cut your paper up so that each activity is on a separate piece; fold the pieces and put them all in a hat. One is drawn out. Discuss trying this activity out and if you feel courageous, go ahead. Otherwise select another. Save the rest for a braver day. Every time you play this game the sex acts will become more subtle and interesting as you both expand your horizons.

playing

Zen Sex

Make love spending infinite periods of time motionless, without thrusting. The lady may stroke the gentleman's organ with her vaginal walls by using pompoir (condom on) but keeping her hips still. Breathe together and feel the energy move between you both.

Ben's Sherbert

A reader, Ben, recommends putting sherbert on the clitoris or any sensitive area, wetting it with your tongue for delightful, long burning sensations.

Cling Film Figure

You can alter the figure of your partner by wrapping cling film around their body. Wrapped round twice, it is securely fixed. Render them helpless by binding arms and feet together or bind yourselves together, or just specific parts. Whatever you do, avoid the mouth and nostrils.

Sex Stereo

Each of you announces today's ten favourite places of the body to be touched. Take it in turns to treat each other, doing two things at a time. Blend the sensations of the G-Spot with the ear lobe, the back of the neck with the frenulum, etc. Aim at a stereo effect with a delightful combined sensation. You can intensify things by using blind-folds and ear plugs: sensory deprivation can even make you feel you're 'coming out of your body' or experience special euphoria.

stereo effect with a delightful combined sensation

NO!

One often forgets this simple ploy which is so alien to the likes of you and me. It requires incredible self denial. Just for once, deny your partner sex. Watch the amazing results. They'll probably be so confused that they'll think they're with someone else, until eventually, after much resistance on your part, you let them have it. Phew!!

Caution

Playing games which involve electric currents. bondage, suspension, cutting or other S/M activity can be dangerous without thorough knowledge. We recommend you read the excellent guidelines in the **Lesbian S/M Manual** *by Pat Califia available from Lace Productions PO Box 10037 Denver, Colorado 80210-0037, price $7.95 or* **The Leather Man's Handbook II** *by Larry Townsend, published by Carlyle Communications, 462 Broadway, New York NY 10013.* **SM 101** *is a good introduction to the subject of SM, written by Jay Wiseman and very safety minded, from PO Box 1261, Berkeley CA 94701.*

▶ *The precious book* **Handballing** *is recommended in the* **Reaching** *section under* **Handballing** ◀

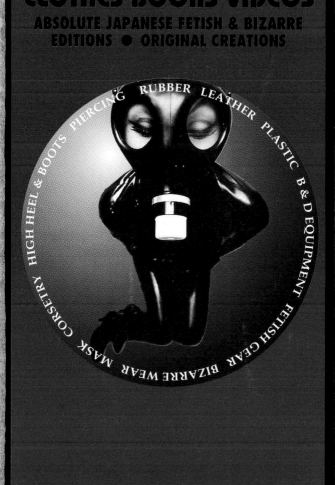

3 TRAVELLING

< I'm away to the frozen North

Where pricks are big and strong

Back to the land on the frozen stand

When the nights are six months long >

your entré to sexual fun wherever you go

▶ The current explosion of sexual entertainment and clubs around the world is so tremendous that this guide highlights only the most exotic specialities, and cannot cater to all tastes, wallets and needs in every city.

Remember that many clubs are only held on certain nights, and they come and go, getting closed down, changing venue and name. I can never quite decide whether to list the fashionable new spot or the established place which may be less exciting but more likely to last. Even if my listing becomes out-of-date, just having the name of a pre-existing club will help you find what has replaced it, when you ask for it in a taxi, hotel lobby, fetish or sex shop. Taxi drivers can be very knowledge-able but in large cities like Bangkok and New York, they may be taking back-handers from inferior clubs, so beware. When I travel alone, I find some taxi drivers get protective towards me as a woman and practically refuse to take me to my proposed destination, and I've always regretted it when I've given in and let them drive me to somewhere "nicer". Be firm. It's usually easy for a woman to pick up a local to escort you around the sleaze, and this book should tell you the best place to find someone who shares your tastes.

I am well aware that my readers include everyone from politicians and industrialists to anarchos and students, who have very different budgets. I warn against rip-off joints and recommend places of value. In my view, sexual adventures are so memorable they are worth the odd hole in the pocket.

Privately-run clubs require a letter or phone call from you first, so they can check you out before giving you the address. Many of the owners run their clubs for fun but have the tiresome task of weeding out all the time-wasters (known as *dweebs* in Scotland). As many as 90% of their calls come from these people, usually men, who have no intention of joining, but nevertheless try it on, as a joke or a turn-on. They may have a fantasy of orgying but would never dare to in reality. So please be patient if club organisers are initially defensive. Couples-only swing clubs may insist on talking to you both, to ensure you each really want to swing. Single men may get included if you seem like fun; single women are usually very welcome but are barred from some swing clubs because they are afraid of whores getting in. Never enclose an explicit photo unless requested. Should you fail to receive a reply, it could be that the club is full or they are just too busy having a good time to write back. Don't assume that my listing is wrong.

If you do find errors, however, things out-of-date or new and exciting, real treats omitted, please write and tell me — you could join my merry band of correspondents which would, in turn, expand your own voyages of discovery.

happy travelling!

COUNTRIES

argentina

buenos aires

Buenos Aires is a delight. The people are very good looking and crazy about sex. Events and agencies and brothels are listed in the English speaking *Where*. There are more sex motels than straight motels, some cheap and some glamourous and fully equipped with sex aids and furniture, also providing little amenity packs with personal necessities like condoms. They are called *hotel alojamiento*. Action centres around Avenida Corrientes where the **Paradise** and **Pussycat** clubs offer strip and ladies. Around the corner on Viamonte Street, **Scandal** offers you the chance

the people are very good looking and crazy about sex

to wrestle with topless women. **Karim** and **Nueve de Julio** are hot cabarets and **Acussuso Street** is the place for cool dudes and chicks on a Saturday night. **Bár Baro** is a funky place to find sexy friends.

▶ **Argentina Addresses**
   Country Code: 54

Bár Baro
Tres Sargentos 415, Buenos Aires

australia

sydney

Mistress Amanda holds B&D parties in Sydney for her clients. She runs the most gorgeous S/M parlours in the world, called Mistress Amanda's and Salon Kitty's. The **Hellfire Club** is the fetish event for those with a black sense of humour, celebrating life and worshipping pain, under the Blackmarket Café, on Thursday nights. **Sydney Bondage Club** hosts a camping tent-out in the bush every January.

most gorgeous s/m parlours

The **Sleaze Ball** as been taking place every October since 1982, as the fund raiser for the **Mardi Gras** Parade. It's a night to let yourself go and dig into the realms of your own personal fantasy. Although these are gay celebrations, everybody goes. Those who find it too mainstream frequent the **Subculture Sex Parties**, with 'radical performance art and theatre which confronts and disturbs, tugging at you in deep compassion'.

Quality brothels have always thrived here, and are considered to be of the best in the world, **A Touch of Class** being the classic. *Naughty Sydney* has the ads and listings. Easy-going, good value and upfront professional women can be found easily in Sydney, under *Home Situations* in the papers. This is where several girls work together and treat you like a real mate. They are safe and saucy. **Raptures** is an orgy brothel, open in the late afternoons in the week and later at weekends with nympho

female consultants flash their BOMs (books of men)

whores, rampant men & adventurous couples. Entrance costs Au$100 for men, $40 for couples, women free and this entitles you to free drinks & supper, in a suburb of Sydney. A similar club called **No 10** is more commercial. Now there are services for ladies, the most successful being **Adam's for Ladies Only**. Catering to female executives and tourists, and offering men for hire per half evening, whole evening or all night. Female consultants flash their BOMs (Books of Men) around offices and hen nights, showing off the gigolos for hire in their different styles. Most women are reluctant to pay much, apart from women working in the sex industry who are happy to pay properly for a night of being pampered. **Alexanders** runs a male escort service for women too. The striptease tradition is for lunch and dinner shows, where the girls perform on the tables and flirt with the diners. **The Governor's Pleasure**

in Wooloomooloo near Kings Cross, **Sydney**, and another near Wynyard Station, has waitresses in lingerie, striptease and double acts. A wild little Japanese bar called **Nonki's** attracts a strange mixture of singles, travellers, gays, harlots and Japanese, with Karaoke.The **Oxford Cinema** has live shows but is off the beaten track compared with the theatres around King's Cross where live sex sometimes takes place with members of the audience. **Pink Panther**, **Pink Pussycat**, **Stripperama**, **Porky's** and **Love Machine** are the best. 20 minutes upstairs costs Au$80-100. Table dancing is big here at **Dancers**.

Swing Clubs in Sydney are usually couples-only affairs held in the organisers' homes on a Saturday night; all the fun starts in the jacuzzis. They include the oldest club, **Adult Connections**, now under new management, **Club Artemis Spa** which bars hookers, **The Couples Club** which has a tropical spa and themed air conditioned rooms and **Couples Kingdom**, perhaps the best club in Sydney, run by Peter, on Fridays & Saturdayss. The hilarious Australian rag, *Picture* featured **Nookie Nights** promising boonting beanos — bring a franger! **Raptures**, mentioned above, has couples-only nights on Wednesdays. *Searchlight* is the long-lasting contact tabloid with adverts.

The Tool Shed is a fab sex shop

a fistful of confidence and an easy cool not seen since brando

claiming to put the "she" back into hedonism! The local sex shop for women is called **The Pleasure Spot**, an Annie Sprinkle inspired organisation run by Jo-Anne. *Australian Women's Forum* is a good source of ads for women who want to hire a man, as well as being a fascinating read. *Miss Wicked*, the glossy fetish dyke magazine, holds its annual contests, the last one won by Anna "Sex' Kissas who swept onto the stage with a fistful of confidence and an easy cool not seen since Brando. **Fu Fu Room** is a club for lovers of fishnet stockings, feathers and trashy romance with Mistress Pedro welcoming sluts of all persuasions, particularly transsexuals and butches who appreciate the subtleties of femme distraction. The **Sydney Bisexual Support Network**, *Wicked Women* and The **Transgendered Liberation Coalition**, **Tranny Anti-Violence Project**, **Seahorses**, **Boys will be Boys** and the **Dolphin Motorcycle Club** group together once a year to hold the **Black Sheep Ball** mid November in Sydney. A new monthly night for lesbians has opened at **King George's Tavern** in Islington, up near Newcastle.

Lady Jane Beach is Sydney's rudest beach on Watson's Bay. The two naturist/hippy festivals in the area are the **Homelands Cultural Revival Festival** in a commune 300 miles north of Sydney and the New Year's gathering at **The Grove** where there's lots of swimming and fun, and workshops on subjects such as non-monogamous relationships.

the men enjoying country barn dances

canberra

Canberra is extremely pretty and has a sexual whizz about it. The whorehouses are less classy than those in Sydney, the best being **Goldfingers** and **Club 77** in Fyshwick. There's a big gay community, the men enjoying country barn dances and there's a lesbian club called **The Meridian**.

brisbane

Brisbane's **Hellfire Club** has closed down and **O's Place**, the fetish club at Diamond's Night Club, Elizabeth Street, dwindled away. Local law recently shut down the blue movie swapping clubs, so people are starved of porn, so easily available in Sydney and Canberra.

table dancing gets crotches close to eyelashes

The **Cabaret Club** offers non-stop stripping. Queensland whores have been forced back onto the streets since a recent change in the law. Considering prostitution is illegal here, the ads in local papers like the *Sunday Sun* are extremely explicit and include swingers and body piercing enthusiasts. **Exclusively for Marrieds** runs swinging phone introductions, as does **Swingers Agency**. At Broadbeach on the Yarra, table dancing gets crotches close to eyelashes at **Club 20**.

melbourne

Top brothels in Melbourne double up as sex theatres and swing clubs. **The Playpen** has live sex acts at lunchtime and 11pm, sex services for men, women and couples, and on Saturday nights it swings in

54

luxury whorehouse style. The **Crystal Tee** does hen nights. Other top houses are **Daily Planet, Southside X, Top of the Town, Pickwood Lodge, Cromwell Heights,** and **Spoilers. Aussie Girls** has lovely girls not hardened to the lifestyle. Gigolo services include **Cromwell Heights.** St Kilda is the red light district although savage killings there have stopped many of the girls from using the area. **The Naughty Barber** has a spa and barbers chairs where hand jobs are performed. Hundreds of strip pubs compete and there's table dancing at **Santa Fé**

sitting in front of the guests and putting one foot one each ear

adelaide

Australian counter-cultural gatherings which is normally held at Easter time, in varying locations.

Adelaide's **Crazy Horse** holds Miss Nude events. **Club Femme** is a new erotica store for hetero and lesbian women and couples. They say they are "sensitive and informed".

Adelaide is the home of **Dirty Dicks**, the chain of bawdy old-time music hall dinner theatres and lingerie lunches, where nude waitresses serve. Full strip is unusual but happens at the **Reepham Hotel** every Wednesday in Prospect.

darwin

Darwin is more Australian than the rest of the country, defiant and unpretentious. **The Casino** is the centre of the nightlife, and many hotels have striptease, performers and hookers bought here by an

Gold where explicit shows include sitting in front of the guests and putting one foot on each ear! **Men's Gallery** is the new table dancing club, with lovely girls prancing in men's faces. **ACM** is the fortnightly contact magazine of long standing. The **Hellfire Club**, the main fetish club, run in the same way as its sister club in Sydney, is on Sundays at **Dream** in Carlton. **Jackaroos** is no-nonsense, leather, rubber, denim dress & play. **Saints and Sinners** parties are put on every three months or so. **Confest** is a loving, clothing-optional, back-to-nature event, the largest and oldest of the

entrepreneur called **The Rock Doctor**. Just before Christmas, the **Hooker's Ball** is put on in the Big County Saloon. *Flesh* is a little colour magazine which has ads fro..1 all over Australia . It reviews porn movies and is produced here in Darwin together with a blue movie mail order catalogue, *Axis*.

Perth is fresh and enchanting, an antipodean bohemia. It is the home of risque restaurants of which **Slic Chix** is the best. The **Site**, at the far old of Northbridge, is a huge barn with waitresses in bathing suits and the show has audience participation.

perth

The **Kit Cat Club** in Fremantle is another such joint. **Swanbourne Beach** is the site of miles of frolics. They have strong censorship here and, thanks to busts, the wonderful brothel scene has lost its edge, although **January's** still thrives and the **Sunday Times** has pages of ads for them. The **Support Information Education Referral Association**, whose director is Penny Lyall, includes members of the sex industry and **Workers in Sex Employment** attempt to convince the Government that decriminalisation and licencing would eliminate the scum from the industry. **Heavenly Bodies** is a swing parlour and **The Dungeon Room** speaks for itself. The whorehouses inland in Kalgoorlie are all around Hay Street but they are suffering with the recession and **Irene's** plans to turn into a sex museum. Australia has passed a law whereby Australians can be prosecuted for having sex with underage girls

a huge barn with waitresses in bathing suits

anywhere in the world. This is to clamp down on Australians who might be travelling around Thailand and having sex with a girl who is under 16. It must be the first time any country has introduced a law which can be inflicted on their subjects in a foreign country.

Raptures
(Susan &Pat)143 Stephen Street, Blacktown
☎834 2411

River Island Naturist Resort
POB 456, Mittagong, NSW 2575.
☎(048)889236

Salon Kitty's
Surry Hills ☎(0055) 33486 and Petersham
☎(0055) 33534

Searchlight
33 Francis Street, East Sydney 2010
(Au$89 per year)

The Sleaze Ball
PO Box 1064, Darlinghurst, NSW 2010
☎ 332 4088

Sydney Bondage Club
SBC Box 293 Broadway, NSW 2007

The Tool Shed
Riley St & Arnold Place, Darlinghurst
☎(02) 332 2792 and 198 King Street,
Newtown ☎(02) 565 1599

A Touch of Class
377 Riley Street, Surry Hills
☎212 2646/212 5962

Transformations
(transsexual agency) ☎360 9518

Wicked Women
POBox 1349 Strawberry Hills, NSW 2012.

Canberra (code 6)

Canberra Videos
PO Box 2579 Canberra ACT 2601
☎573 1664

The Meridian Club
34 Mort Street, Braddon, Canberra ACT
2601

Melbourne (code 3)

ACM
POBox 189 St Kilda Vic 3182 ☎5211796

Confest
c/o Down To Earth, PO Box 123, N.
Richmond, Vic 3121

Cromwell Heights
66 Cromwell Street,Collingwood
☎(03) 419 0144

Crystal Tee
672 Sidney Rd, Brunswick ☎383 2944

Daily Planet
9 Horne Street, Elsternwick ☎328 1922)

Hellfire Club
Dream 229 Queensbury St, Carlton, N.
Melbourne. ☎(03)3491924 c/o POBox 452
Rosanna, Vic 3084 ☎(018)104223

Jackaroos
Box 5064Y, Melbourne, 3001

Lace Escorts
☎521 3344

Naughty Barber/Club 77
77 Racecourse Road, North Melbourne
☎326 5933

Pickwood Lodge
120 Lygon Street, Brunswick

The Playpen Spa & Sauna
32 Victoria St, Richmond ☎429 1866

Saints & Sinners
☎521 1796

Santa Fé Gold
115 Russell Street, Melbourne ☎654 7034

Southside X
1 Joel Crecent, Moorabbin, Melbourne

Spoilers
14 Stevens Crescent, Springwood

Top of The Town
516-518 Flanders Street, Melbourne
☎614 1414

Darwin (Code 18)

Flesh
GPO Box 3000, Darwin NT 0900

Rock Doctor
☎89 34 21

Brisbane (code 7)

Anastasia's Hostesses
☎391 3242

Best of Both Worlds
(trannies for hire) ☎(018) 882 965

Diamonds Night Club,
Elizabeth St

Exclusively for Marrieds
Brisbane ☎393 1259

Lesbian Confest
c/o Dykewise PO Box 285 Alderley Q 5051

Swingers Agency
☎882 4545 & on the Gold Coast
☎(075) 711 000

Women Master Men
☎391 1421

57

Adelaide (code 8)

Crazy Horse
141 Hindley Street

Club Femme
73 Hindley Street ☎ 410 0636

Perth (code 9)

The Dungeon Room
395 William Street, Northbridge
☎ 328 6850

Heavenly Bodies
Perth ☎ 470 5850

January's
178 James Street, Perth

Kit Cat Club
Fremantle

The Site
432 William Street, Perth

Swanbourne Beach
NSBUA POB 35, Clairemont, WA 6010

austria

vienna

Swingers enjoy **Traumland**, a club in the centre of Vienna, which is kitsch and all-action. S/M and gay sex are both unlawful in Austria but that doesn't stop them. **Libertine** is the new Viennese fetish club on Fridays 4-10pm. **Priapos** put on parties and **Renate Ungar** still holds fetish nights at the **Monte Video** disco. Near the city of Klagenfurt a tiny S/M Bed and Breakfast run by a **Mr. Tuppen** has an S/M cellar and dungeon. Vienna is a city of whores, with three distinct districts: all along the Lerchenfelder Gürtel where you'll find the **Intime Sauna Treff 13** down to Mariahilfer Gürtell; around the Praterstern; and downtown around the Rotenturmstrasse. The only lively sex show is the **Orchidee**, way out in the SW of town, and right over the other side is the **Sex Museum** which also

tiny s/m bed and breakfast run by a mr. tuppen

has a sex cinema and striptease. **Nina** is a brothel full of girls in bunny dress where there's a whirlpool and lots of Champagne. **Butterfly** and **Clair** are both good hooker's bars. **Danube Island** in the centre of Vienna is almost entirely naturist so everybody is nude there in the summer.

▶ **austria addresses - country code (43)**

Butterfly
Marc-Aurel-Str 8, Vienna 1 ☎ (1)359931

Clair
Naglergasse 23, Vienna 1

Libertine
Postfach 63, A-1011 Vienna ☎ (5)689167

Orchidee
Schönbrunner Str 137, Vienna 5

Priapos
PO Box 143 A-1165 Vienna ☎ (663)01 85 11

Renate Ungar
A-1080 Vienna, Skodagasse 28/26 ☎ (1) 403 30 92

Sex Museum
Strasse des 1 Mai 51 Vienna 2 (Prater)

Traumland
Schlöslgasse 11, Vienna 1080
☎ (222) 427904/(992) 426694 evenings

Mr. A Tuppen
Wielen 10, A-9062 Moosburg
☎ (4272) 83496

brussels

Belgium lifted all censorship on sex and porno although there are still restrictions on S/M activity. It has always been a bit of a hotspot, although Brussels is quite straight-laced. Lots of hot swing clubs are hidden in country villages throughout Belgium, although few survive in Brussels. For example, the impossible-to-find **Hoeve Rietof** continues to hold raucous Saturday nights in its beautiful old contraption-filled house in Kapelien. **Mediterranée** has action-packed nights in a well-designed club: a red-light room, loft, & enticing holes in walls. **Rose's Garden** is a little paradise of water treats, porno and bedrooms. **De Ronde Tafel** is a sweet little non-smoking restaurant in Antwerp with only three tables, inviting sex play. Near the French border, an old farmhouse with a pool and dancefloor opens as **Vajrayana**, a weekend swinghouse. You get dinner and can stay over if you've come from afar. They put on the occasional S/M night.

The Belgian fetish scene is well catered to by *Secret*, a glossy magazine which lists the clubs and parties. They also hold their own events: like **Secret Mission**, a big fetish night at the Peppermill Castle

kapelien

antwerp

in Holland. Their Boutique Minuit sells all the top fetish gear in the centre of Brussels. *The Delice Garden* caters to fetish, piercing and bondage people in Charleroi. **Foire Internationale de l'Erotique** is an annual celebration in Brussels in early June with a fetish night called Nuit de Désir and their **La Nuit de la Belgique Interdit** is for scanty and

afternoon tea dances where housewives let loose for a kiss and a cuddle

tranny dressing. It's organized by the people who put out *Rendezvous* and *Maniax* magazines, which aren't the best guides in the world but have hard core photos with whores' and dominas' personal ads.
Europhantasm is a large S/M club with playrooms in Liège. **Fantasmic & Fetish Club** holds fetish nights in Namur.

Live sex shows are now legal in Belgium and the **Erotic Peep Show** at the bottom of Rue de Brabant in Brussels shows double acts for £5 a ticket. Country areas of Belgium still have afternoon tea dances where housewives let loose for a kiss and a cuddle.

59

▶ **belgium addresses - country code (32)**

Europhantasm
Av de la Croix Rouge 156, 4020 Liège
☎(41)438707

Delice Garden
Postbox 336, 600 Charleroi

L'Erotism Festival
Les Pyramides, Place Roger, 1210 Brussels
☎(077) 346050

Fantasmic &Fetish Club
POBox 184 5000 Namur

Foire Internationale de l'Erotique
Ville Neuve 89, Avenue Emile de Béco,
Brussels

Hoeve Rietof
Kalmthoutsteenweg 71, Kapelien 2080
☎(3)6051881

Mediterranée
Kruishoutemsesteenweg 178, 9760
Zingem-Huise ☎(91)845035

Boutique Minuit
60 gallerie du Centre, 1000 Brussels

Rendezvous
7 rue de L'Eglise, 1060 Brussels

De Ronde Tafel
Boterstraat je. 2040 Zandvliet, Antwerp
☎(323) 568 1650

Rose's Garden
241 Kortriksesteen, St Martins Latem

Secret Magazine
PO Box 1400, 1000 Brussels 1

Vajrayana
Chemin de Chaumont, 59132 Eppe-
Sauvage ☎(27) 618132

bolivia

la paz

Brothels here are like discos with back rooms. They are not particularly cosy and the rooms in **La Paz** tend to be unheated. Take a woolly! The people are extremely conventional but it is expected that husbands take lovers.

brothels here are like discos

brazil

rio de janeiro

Brazil is the one of the most erotic countries in the world. You can smell it as soon as you arrive. They know how to flirt and making love is a revered pastime. In Rio, you're immediately struck by the smallest bikinis you've ever seen and the most aggressive thieves you've ever encountered. Exciting bars like **Mabs** in Rio's Copacabana throb with luscious ladies eager to open up sexual liaisons for cash and stay with you for as long as you wish. **Rios** is its most exclusive sex club with expensive girls and wild live fucking shows until the early hours of the morning, as well as samba and strip. **Help** is the big disco on the Copacabana, where sexy hookers approach male tourists. Hundreds of other hooker bars and discos include **Barbarela**, **Franks**, **Scotch** and **La Cicciolina**, all in Avenida Princes *Rio This Month* lists escorts. The Rua Duvivier has a row of sex clubs where the best sex clubs are **Don Juan**, **Boite Baccara** and **New Munich**. The standard of the sex shows is incredible, the control and panache of the fuckers superb. It's worth going to Rio just for this. Don Juan is the best and only $10 to enter, which includes two drinks and the actors can be hired out. **Club Hi-Fi** at the Cabiria American Bar is the most professionally choreographed fuck show of all. **Oasis 123** is a sexy sauna with stripshow, **Centaurus** is open all night, and **Solarium** has action in the

control and panache of the fuckers superb

week and swinging on Saturdays. There's a sauna, pool, disco and massage.

Locals go off to **BARRA** and **BUZIOS** at the weekend. A highly romantic hotel in Buzios is the **Pousada Martin Pescador,** where you can lie in bed and look out over the sea. German tourists go to the Boa Viagem beach

salvador

in Recife which is swarming with beautiful young Brazilian girls, many of them naked. Salvador, in Bahia, has an African feel and the best place to go for Carnival where the streets are explosive day and night. Towns inland still have classic whorehouses where only the music and the girls have changed in the past hundred years and foreigners are rarely seen. The 'Island of Love',

sao paolo

Sao Luis, is known for its horny women and lusty cathouses, **Casa de Nelson** being right on the Olho d'Aqua beach.

Sao Paulo's brothels, erotic shows, swingers clubs, sadomaso bars, boites, singles bars porno cinemas, saunas and motels, are all neatly listed in the *Só Para Maiores* paper. Prostitution is legal in Brazil and the church-backed Institute of Religious Studies runs a Prostitutes and Civil Rights group and publishes *Streetkiss*, a magazine for prostitutes. There's a disturbing increase in child prostitution and drug involvement. Some brothels only cater to oriental customers. AIDS is rife. Porno is legal: it may be imported but not exported.

61

▶ **Brazil addresses - country code (55)**

Bon Vivant
(swing) Caixa Postal 51.695, CEP 01499, Sao Paulo

Centaurus Sauna
Rua Canning 44, Ipenema, Rio
☎(21)267 5941

Escort Motel
Estrada de Gavea 674, Rio

Hawaii Motel
Estrada da Barra da Tijuca 3186, Rio

Mirante Motel
Estrada dos Baneirantes 1280, Rio

Rios
Avenida Prado, Rio

Clube "O"
Sao Paulo ☎(11) 820 1829

Pousada Martin Pescador
Buzios ☎(0246) 231449

Solarium
Rua JJ, Seabra 21, Jardim Botanico, Rio
☎(21)294 6599

VIP's Motel
Avenida Niemeyer, Rio

bulgaria

sophia

Sophia's most south-eastern quarter is the lively part of the city, day and night. It's safe but totally without any sleaze. To find the alternative scene, you might spot adverts on posters or go to the **Union Jack Pub**

where raucous Brits will fill you in. It's open till 2am.

▶ **Bulgaria Addresses country code (359)**

Union Jack Pub
Sveta Sophia 5

raucous brits will fill you in

cambodia

The authorities keep cracking down on prostitution but basically, it's simple to find and cheap. In Phnom Penh, close to the dyke in the midst of other rickety houses in Vietnam Road, many brothels employ keen women who are unaware of AIDS but use condoms for birth control.

Tuol Kork (pronounced "Do a cock") is the name of this area, and **Martinis** the most happening bar.

> ## tuol kork (pronounced "do a cock")

canada

montreal

There's a very rude sex club in Montréal run by **Simon and Denise** and you can reach them through, **Paul and Boop**, who also throw their own parties every summer in their hill-top garden, and welcome swingers from out of town. **Shangri-La** is an adult social club near Montreal and *Coeur à Corps* the successful Montreal swing contact magazine. The Village in Rue St Catherine East is where most of the street action is but Rue St Dennis sees plenty of outdoor activity in the summer. The *Montreal Mirror* has interesting ads for sex.

toronto

Toronto's well established and loved **Club Eros**, run by a good ol' Nottingham gal Wendy and her husband Ron, still puts on swing dances in motels. As Eros gets more way-out, Ruthy and David Miller's **Club Privé** provides straighter swinging parties in downtown Toronto and at **Blondie's Bar** in nearby Brantford, run by Mike & Heather Milton. Swingers from out-of-town get in free to these monthly themed dances and motorcycle rallies. The newest adult club in town is **Exit II Eden** and

Society Couples is a more downmarket club near the Airport. **Ramblewood** is still a terrific nudist resort holding themed sex parties outside the city. Singles live in Yonge and Eglinton (nicknamed Young & Singleton) and hang out in **Berlin's** or **Yuk Yuk's** where there's a raunchy cabaret. **The Single**

> ## wildside is a fantasy transvestite hotel

Gourmet is a singles club with plenty of action. Artists, rockers and skinheads hang out at **City TV Station**. The Gay and Lesbian community centres around Charles Street and Wellesly and plastic

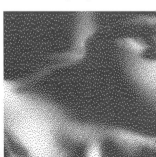

fantastic singles frequent Center Town's Bloor & Avenue Road at **The Bellair Café** and **Hemingways**. The hottest strip clubs are out of town: the **The Landing Street**, near the airport at Mississauga, where there's lap dancing and more. Downtown, **Zanzibar** puts on a good show. **Wildside** is a fantasy transvestite hotel with a boutique, transformation service and girls to chat with. Hookers stroll on Jarvis and Church, from Carleton to Wellesly, looking most outrageous between 9pm and 3am. *Now* is the free weekly entertainment paper which has a steaming hot classified section.

The Affiliate is a group of people who hold events such as Art at Heart, Concepts and Nature's Way in The Nude. **Aren't We Naughty** is the local chain of adult toy & fetish shops around Toronto where you can ask about what's going on in the club scene. **The Betty Page Social Club** is fortnightly at the **Boots Bar** in the **Selby Hotel**, and there's more fetish action at the **Lizard Lounge**. **X-Corriga** is an exclusive group who offer exchange of S/M ideas and put on interesting events.

calgary

In Calgary, **Social Forum** is a sweet, long-lasting club with its own newsletter and summer camp-outs, hot-tub parties, and visits to clubs in other parts of the country.

There are plenty of strip clubs in Calgary, including two **Peepers**, **The French Maid** and **Porky's**.

vancouver

Vancouver is proud of its strip traditions and the clubs are equipped so that a big screen descends across the stage at intervals, giving you the latest football and sports scores and highlights. Body rub parlours are for you-know-what and the best of the bunch are **The Swedish Touch** and **Garden of Eden**. There are gay bathhouses such as **Club Vancouver**, and **The Lotus** is a lesbian bar. **Vancouver Activists in S/M** provide

vancouver is proud of its strip tracditions

happy parties and pressure groups, and **New Friends–New Faces** holds dances, picnics and publishes a newsletter for swingers. *Redemption* is a Canadian fanzine for the alternative & adventurous *Boudoir Noir* is their bi-monthly mag serving the leather-fetish community, *Tab International* the tabloid for commercial sex, with swing and singles ads, *Canada Naturally* their book of nude beaches and resorts, *Tatmag* a sweet handmade magazine on tattoos, and *Pornorama* their stroke zine for sexual dissidents.

The Affiliate
c/o Peter Riden, 777 Barb Road, Vanleek Hill, Ont. Trial issues of their mag cost $5.

Aren't We Naughty
130 Main St, M Brampton, 5203 Yonge Street, 1959 Weston Road, Weston and 1300 Finch Ave, West Downsview, Ont ☎(905) 564 3063

Ashley's Fetish Boutique
2737 Dundas St, W Toronto Ont M6P 1Y1 ☎(416) 767 0379

B&B Leatherworks
6802 Ogden Rd SE Calgary T2C 1 ☎(403) 236 7072

Bellair Café
corner of Cumberland Street & Bellair, Toronto

Betty Page Social Club
Box 66 Stn F, Toronto, M4Y 2L4 ☎(416) 972 1037

Boudoir Noir
Box 5, Sta F, Toronto Ont M4Y 2L4 $5 6-issue sub, and £18 overseas

Bumpers Club
(strip) 1740 Elice Way, Winnipeg ☎(204) 775 7131

Cabaret Showgirl
1196 St Catherines Montréal ☎(514) 861 5193

Canada Naturally
$30 from Richard West, 404 Barb Road, RR#1, Vankleek Hill, Ont K0B 1R0

Cecil
(strip) 1336 Granville, near Austin, Vancouver

City TV Station
betw Bay and Spadina, Toronto

Coeur à Corps
10181 Pie IX, North Montréal H1H 3Z4, Québec ☎(514) 325 5282

Club Eros/Caresse
Box 561, Stn Q Toronto, Ont M4T 2N4 ☎(416) 690 5910 fax 691 5390

Exit II Eden
312 Adelaide Street West, Toronto ☎(416) 351 EDEN

Drake
(strip) 606 Powell, on Vancouver's waterfront

Flash One Pub
(strip) Austin Motor, 1221 Granville Street, Vancouver ☎(604) 685 7277

The French Maid
302 2nd Street, Calgary ☎(403) 269 7544

Garden of Eden
846 Denman, Vancouver ☎(604) 520 0836

Gay group HQ
1170 Bute Street Vancouver

Jason's
25 Chatham Street E, Windsor ☎(519) 253 7992

Hemingways
Yorkville Avenue, Toronto

House of Lancaster
1 689 The Queensway Toronto ☎(416) 259 6155

Little Sisters Art Emporium
feminine boutique in Vancouver

Lizard Lounge
Yonge Street, Toronto

Madame X
fetish fantasy parlour Toronto ☎(416) 762 9925

Mints
(strip) 5951 Main Street, Niagara Falls ☎(416) 357 0471

Margold Group
(fetish) PO Box 7326 Station E, Calgary Alberta T3C OP9

New Friends - New Faces
POB 27212 Collingwood PO, Vancouver BC V5R 6A8. ☎(604) 4361161

No 5 Orange St
(strip) 203 Main Street, near Chinatown, Vancouver ☎(604) 682 0985

Northbound Leather
19 St Nicolas Street, Toronto Ont M4Y 1W5

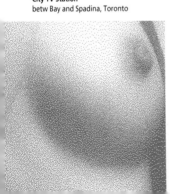

Paul &Boop
PO Box 801 Sta A, Montréal H3C 2VS

Peepers
1621 Center St N Calgary ☎ (403) 277 7531
and 4510 Macleod Trail, Calgary
☎ (403) 243 5511

Porky's
(strip)1825 50 SE Calgary ☎ (403) 272 9881

Club Privé
30 Park Road, Rosedale, Toronto Ont M4W
2N4 ☎ (416) 944 9005, fax 944 9268 or in
Brantford ☎ (519) 752 2660

Pornorama
c/o L Lava, C.P. 59109 rue St Hubert,
Montréal Quebec H2S 3P5

Redemption
$2.50 per issue (checks to Alex Corstens) at
91 Rideau Crescent, Peterborough, Ontario
KPJ 1G7

The Rumpus Room
(strip) 15540 Stony Plain Road, Edmonton
☎ (403) 484 3331

Selby Hotel
592 Sherbourne St Toronto

Shangri-La
PO Box 7172 Victoria, BC, V9B 4Z3
☎ (604) 727 0837

Silver Fox Pub
(strip) York Hotel 265 13th Street N,
Lethbridge, Alberta ☎ (403) 328 4406

Social Forum
Suite 199, 110, 2675-36 St - NE, Calgary
Alberta TIY 6H6 ☎ (403)735 7114

Society Couples
c/o 50 Graydon Hall Drive, # 801, Don Mills,
Ont M3A 3A4 ☎ (416) 761 7690

Swedish Touch
581 Hornby ☎ (604) 681 0823

Tab International
Mailshoppe Inc, 1 Yonge Street, Suite 1801
Toronto Ont M5E 1E5

Teasers
Welland House, 30 Ontario Street, St
Catherines, Toronto ☎ (416) 685 7371

Wildside
161 Gerrard Street East, Toronto, Ont M5A
2E4, ☎ (416)921 6112 (24hrs)

Vancouver Activists in SM
☎ (201)746 4200 or 746 5466

Club Vancouver
339 West Pender ☎ (604) 681 5719

X-Corriga
POBox 277, Postal Station "A",
Toronto, Ontario M5W 1B2

65

chile

santiago

Santiago's live entertainment is a mix of vaudeville and 50's style, and there's plenty of dancing at the **La Cucaracha** and fun at **Bellavista**. The wonderful **Hotel Valdivia** survives as one of the world's most elegant, bawdy, old-time brothels. Divorce is illegal here, so there's lots of bigamy and, with 40% of all births outside marriage, one wonders why they marry at all!

world's most elegant, bawdy, old-time brothels

> **Chile Addresses**
>   **country code (56)**

La Cucaracha
Bombero Nunez 159

Hotel Valdivia
Calle Garcia, Valenzuela 45 Santiago
☎ (2) 222 6644

beijing

Beijing's favourite haunts for foreigners are **Charlie's Bar** and **Brauhaus**. Most of the discos have a ladies' night once a week and these are good pickup joints, often attracting more and more hookers until they get closed down. There is no red light district but barmen know where to point you. Even rock bands face licencing problems with venues so good-time places rarely get advertised. You will have to ask. Prostitution is becoming popular but, with corruption, there are unpleasant associations and sex slavery is escalating. The modern sex shop called **Adam and Eve** is state-run. Shanghai is now known as "the second Hong Kong" — it is swinging into seedy sleazeville. There are little bars with high screens behind which are booths and couples go inside to masturbate, often men with professionals.

shangai

Brothels are well known: the **Ming Ren** is for high-ranking officials only. **Casablanca**, **Dedo**, **Top Ten** and the **Shangai Venue Recreation Club** are all decorated with Berlinesque decadence, courtesy the Public Security Bureau and People's Liberation Army. Everybody is out for a good time! The Rainbow Hotel's **Casablanca** is a high society

prostitutes, who may even charge you to dance with them!

meat market with hundreds of pretty women dancing by themselves waiting to be picked up. The **JJ Disco Square Entertainment Centre** is infamous and the brashest club in China. In the discos and nightclubs, prostitutes may even charge you to dance with them! Some hotels are fussy about bringing people back. Foreign visitors are all welcome at the TGIF at the Australian Consulate between 7-9pm, where you can learn where to go next. Women can have fun here too in bars, although, as yet, there are no male escorts for hire. In Ulanbator, Mongolia, the **Ulanbator Hotel**'s disco is seething every night except Mondays,and great for pick-ups.

ulanbator

▶ **China Addresses country code (86)**

Ming Ren
240 Beijung Road Shanghai

Shanghai Venus Recreation Club
Shanghai ☎(21)248 8888

colombia

cartagena

The **Americana** is an excellent bordello in Cartagena. Blatant porno is stacked at the bottom of the magazine shelves while kids comics are

at the top. Huge posters on hoardings inform you that masturbation leads to psychological problems and impotence and that drugs lead you to homosexuality

Aphrodite Award

Presented to:

Look for the Union labia.

P. O. N. Y.

PROSTITUTES OF NEW YORK

Have you been a sex worker? Have you been a sexual freedom fighter?
Have you been sexually promiscuous? Have you been a sex healer?
Have you given your sexual service to your community?
If you can answer yes to any of these questions,
…CONGRATULATIONS!!!
You have earned the **PONY** Aphrodite Awards.
Simply photocopy it and fill in your name.
Give some to friends who deserve them.
We feel it's about time that people who give pleasure
should be honoured and awarded
(not just people who suffer - like war heroes and martyrs).
So, take pride. You're wonderful. Keep up the great work!

The Aphrodite Awards: Conceived by Annie Sprinkle, designed by Les Barany,
illustrated by Andras Halasz and named by Emilio Cubeiro

which is illegal. Gays coming here get upset by having to look at the young police officers, often aged 18 or 19, in crotch-enhancing uniforms. While the police campaign to close the brothels down, nuns are helping prostitutes with their fight for survival.

crotch-enhancing uniforms

cuba

havana

Cubans are incurably flirtatious and excited by foreigners. Havana's seaside area, the Malacon (known as "the couch") is where many end up, making love in the soft Caribbean waves. Some of the most beautiful hostesses are at the **Tropicana**, **Habana Libre**, **Hotel National**, **Hotel Commodore** and **Marina Hemingway**, and you can take them into the cottages in the grounds, in the most romantic of settings. Even if you're paying, it's incredible, cheap and lovely. Foreign currency is welcomed as is your company.

making love in the soft caribbean waves

czech republic

prague

Filled with night clubs, bars and galleries, Prague echoes the soul of Paris in the 20's. The area of Václavské námésti has dancespots called *pivnice* or *vinárna*. The alternative crowd meet at **Bunkr**, a converted air raid shelter painted black and the new club **Radost** (which means Joy) is a hot club, café, gallery, music and video shop all in one. There are least fifty porn mag titles to choose from. Czech brothels, especially in Prague, are extremely good: well organised and a delight to visit because the females are fresh and eager . The biggest two massage salon/bar brothels are the **Lotus Club** and **Club 2000** Both have dozens of girls to choose from. **U Petra Voka** and the **T-club** are hostess bars. SKM is Prague's only swing club and it also runs a contact magazine by the same name.The *NEI Report,* put out by the

a delight to visit because the females are fresh and eager

Orgán Nezávislé Erotické Inactivy, has articles on swinging with ads and photos. The **Erotic Party** does campaigning for sexual freedom.

▶ **czech addresses - country code (42)**

Club 2000
Braunerova 20, Prague 4 ☎ (2) 66310017

Bunkr
Lodecká 2, Prague

Erotic Party — Nezávisla Erotická Iniciativa
Mikojanova 379, 109 00 Prague

Eve Club & Sauna
Prague ☎ (2) 57622

Prince Club
Prague (strip) ☎ (2) 864329

Lotus Club
Kupeckeho 832, Prague 4 ☎ (2) 7917825

Radost
Belehraddská 120, Prague

Sex Shop
Rial Wilsonova il Milady Horakove 84

SKM
Jablonova 60 Prague 10. ☎ (2)756122

T-Club
Jungmannovo nám. 17, Prague 1
☎ 2369877

U-Petra Voka
Add.- Na Beldle 40, Prague 5 ☎ (2) 537531

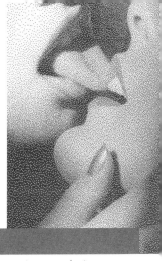

denmark

Rosetten runs a summercamp with horses, cages and pillories where people, brandishing birches and stinging nettles, torment and tie each other to trees. Accommodation is basic. Back in Copenhagen, the new fetish boutique **Conflicto** is designed tomb-style to show off

brandishing birches and stinging nettles

their futuristic rubber and leather clothing. The **Black Society** is an expensive S/M club for experienced players and **SMil** is a long-standing, pleasant licenced club-house for discussions and play. It has groups in Copenhagen, Odense, Alborg and Arhus. **Club 20** is a hostess group-sex-bar where couples can join in noon-1am midweek, or for couples only on Saturdays. There isn't much wild abandon there but it's pleasant. The porn shops are near the railway station and

copenhagen

amazing to most foreigners, as nothing is banned. It's also quite normal for women to brouse and buy or sit in the little booths to watch the hardcore videos. The **Intim Topless** in Copenhagen has a sexy show where girls eat popcorn off their nipples and inserts balls up their cunts whilst outstretched on the counter. Despite its name, **The Spunk Bar** is rather straight and the sexy bar **Maxim's** is a bit of a rip-off. **Bar Bue** is experimental and hip. Whores can be found sitting in hotel bars. The town is really boring for shows but there's an **Erotic Museum** on four floors, filled with erotica, historic porn, wax dolls and intriguing sexmomorabilia. The **Hellas** solarium pool and sauna at Skibby is a naturists' delight in winter months. **Club Amigo** is a huge gay sauna with cinema. Copenhagen has an HIV info line for people with hearing difficulties on Wednesdays 5-7 on ☎ 3391 2319. Odense's sexy club is called **Prince** where topless dancers play with candles and men's flies.

skibby

Club 20
Godsbanegade 20, kld, DK-1722,
Copenhagen V ☎31 23 31 61

Club Amigo
Studiostraede 31A, Copenhagen

Conflicto 1
Johnstrup Alle, DK 1923 FRB C,
Copenhagen ☎3135 0380

Black Society
PO Box 2018 Kobmagersades 1012,
Copenhagen K ☎35 36 37 55
7-8pm, 8-9pm for women only 1st & 3rd
Tuesday in month

Erotic Museum
Vesterbrogade 31, Copenhagen

Club Rosetten
POBox 131 DK 8500, Granaa ☎86-33-47-71

Prince
Vindegade 67-69, 5000 Odense C
☎6612 98 88

SMil
Sorgenfrigade 8A DK 2200 Copenhagen N
☎31 81 05 50

dominican republic

The Dominican Republic is notorious for its sexual generosity, especially on Costa Caribe (**Casa Bon Sua**), Santo Domingo (try **Le Petit Chateau** at Autopista 30 de Mayo) and the **Casa de Campo** resort at La Romana. Away from the tourist areas, girls appreciating foreign boyfriends, forget the cash, especially if they are treated well.

notorious for its sexual favours

dubai

Everything is behind closed doors but, with all that money and not much to do, hot sex parties and illicit affairs are top priority. Picking-up is often done in cars. You write your phone number on a tape cassette box and hand it over to the driver you are trying to pull, saying you think they might like the music. Affairs are conducted over mobile phones but even these are bugged so that bored horny strangers can listen in. Women do not have to cover themselves as much these days and, anyway, underneath the robes are shimmering chemises, provocative lingerie and shaved pussies.

hot sex parties and illicit affairs are top priority

Unmarried and high class married women usually have lots of lesbian fun and most men live bisexual lives, although homosexual acts are looked down on if you're over of 35. Men are allowed three wives. Bordellos exist but addresses are kept secret. Pimps bring in women from the Lebanon, Britain and India — all foreign women are regarded as sluts and men often travel to Thailand to go whoring. Servants are expected to screw the man of the house and also his guests

egypt

Cairo's **Semiramis Intercontinental** nightclub is the big pick-up place in town. Much of the nightlife centres around hotels, which usually have belly dancing shows, as do all the night clubs and sporting clubs.

Today's belly dancing is rock-influenced, more frenzied and perhaps less flirtatious than the slower, graceful dances of the past which instilled meaningful moments of sexual electricity. The government issued instructions that men should no longer walk arm in arm as it gave tourists the wrong idea.

cairo

belly dancing shows

el salvador

The **Il Leopardos** in San Salvador is an exciting club where the male performers wave their dicks at the audience. It's a great tradition and everybody comes to see it.

england
London and the South East

london

Try to come in March when we hold the **Planet Sex Ball**. On the London club scene, the most erotic, if getting a little tired, are the fetish clubs: **Whiplash** (2nd Wed of month) for action — although they got busted the week before we went to press, **Fantastic!** for exuberance, **Submission** for sleaze & cute outfits, **Torture Garden** for piercing, tattooing and alternative networking, the **Rubber Ball** for fashion trendies. **Sadie Maisie's**, **The Fist**, and the **Anvil** are for gays, and the **Clit Club** is for lesbians. **S/M Pride** marches through London every

doors
left ajar
with red-lit
staircases

October followed by afternoon of workshops and a party in the evening. **Skin Two** runs a fetish hotline telling you what's coming up and *Fetish Times* reviews the action. You can find flyers for clubs in the numerous fetish shops, particularly **Libido**. **Whiplash** runs a successful **Sunday Market** on the 2nd Sunday of the month, which is very sociable. **Cobblers** sell cheap antique fetish and glamourwear. If you want to sample one of our famous spanking clubs, try **Janus**, **Kane** or **Prosperity Parties**. **School Dinners** have "school girl" and "dream boy" staff who cane and force-feed guests with whipped cream puddings. Swing clubs are forbidden to allow sex on the premises and swinging is not at all exciting in London. The **Paradise Club** has become the main stable for adventurous couples, a nice little weekly event in Victoria run by Hussein and his lady. **Toucan** is similar. The **Forum Society** lists several swing groups in and around the area, particularly the **One Step at a Time Club** for first timers. They also run trips to swing clubs in Holland, as do the **Wicked Bus Company**. The **Chain Gang** run mystery nights called **Café Ensemble**. **Honeycomb** holds parties in members's homes from their base in Berkshire. **Exposure** is for exhibitionists and voyeurs. Dogging takes place within limits in the East Heath Road car park of Hampstead Heath but more frantically in certain car parks along the A3. You can enjoy it also within the saftey of the grounds of **Eureka** which is a liberal naturist club with

travelling

parties every Saturday night. On the tranny scene, Caroline Egerton who publishes the *Transvestites' Guide to London* puts on several events a week which are extremely friendly and never dull. **Girls Like Us** offers a styling and photographic studio of exceptional quality for trannies. Drop into the groovy shop **Boy** at 13 Moor Street, Soho to pick up the flyers for London's trendy and gay club nights. **More than Vegas** is a saucy 50's club on Fridays at the **St Moritz** in Wardour Street. The **Café de Paris** in Leicester Square on Saturday night is a proper pick-up night for mature glams. Most of Soho has gone extremely gay. Young girls hang around Kings Cross for trade and there are doors left ajar with red-lit staircases in Gt Windmill Street and Shepherds Market but the standard is often pretty dismal. There's subtle street action along the SW end of Oxford Street. West End phone boxes are plastered with fascinating prostitutes' business cards. **Lovejoys**

phone boxes are plastered with fascinating prostitutes' business cards

in Charing Cross Road has a basement with a good selection of magazines including the latest contact mags. Try *Rascals* and *Provider*. *Rascals* also put on swing parties. **Sh!** is the women's sex store and **Zipper** is well stocked with mags featuring men's hard-ons. You can buy hardcore in Soho but a new ruling may stamp this out. **Connoisseur Collection** is a new vintage porn shop in Turnmill Street, Farringdon.

The best escort service in the South is **Annabelle's** and you can find ads for female escorts in **Men Only** and **The Sport**. The gigolo service which British TV and press featured some time ago was a hoax and when you answer any of the ads for male escorts in **For Women** magazine, the men sound absolutely desperate for a customer! Peter Stringfellow has opened the first "gentlemen's club" in London, bringing lap and table

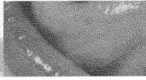

dancing over from America. His glamorous subterranean club, called **Cabaret of the Angels**, is at the lower end of Shaftesbury Avenue. These strip clubs in Soho are OK: **Sunset Strip** is conventional, **Carnival** better value and more spice. **Raymond's Review Bar** is more of a choreographed show, horny in parts, and **La Capannina** is open later. Outside Soho, striptease is giving way to the antiseptic road-show and wet T shirt competitions at places such as **The Zone** in Tottenham. However, there are pubs where you can see a really high quality of striptease. Most of these strippers are supplied by **Rainbow** who put on a Strippothon in July at the **White Horse** in Shoreditch High Street. The strip pubs are nearly all in **Shoreditch**, **Enfield** and near **Heathrow**. Some, like the **Penny Farthing** (2 Kingsland Road E2) and the **Queen Anne** (Vauxhall Walk SE11) have continuous shows all day and evening, but the shorter shows in other pubs tend to be more exciting. A real sleaze-spotter's paradise is **The Flying Scotsman**, at the bottom of the Caledonian Road, King's Cross. Hanging out in these pubs, you will inevitably get wind of their forthcoming 'stag nights' which are hotter shows that take place

real sleaze-spotter's paradise

behind closed doors after hours. They cost about £10 and are well worth it. There's the occasional raucous hen night too, for the ladies. London has a few good cinema clubs showing hard-core films. Some discourage hanky panky although couples enjoy going there to play. The **Albatross** and the **Willow** are the respectable hard core cinema clubs with strict rules. Others, where people queue up to sit in the back row(!), won't let you in unless you are brought along by a member. *Time Out* doesn't have a sex section, but lists the gigs, clubs and events of the week, but it's best to call first to check. *What's On* lists the expensive hostess bars such as **Churchill's**.

a guy in a wheelchair got fined £50 for curb crawling

Beware of hostess bars in Soho (and street girls) as they are there to fleece you. **ZM** workshops in ancient & modern intimacy & sexual energy (but no sexual activity) are held at weekends by Zek & Misha Halu. **The Utopia Sauna** out in Romford has girls of all ethnic backgrounds. Aldershot has a strip pub with topless barmaids called **Rhythm Station.**

Down in Southampton, the new **Club Sophia** "So good it hurts" is a great hit, a fetish club in a gym where nudity is also allowed. Derby Road is where ladies sit in windows, but cameras now survey both here and in Niverton Road. A guy in a wheelchair got fined £50 for curb crawling. **Cerebus** is a good sex shop in Bournemouth where they know about local clubs and action. Brighton's a very gay town with the **Zap** for clubbing, **Bristol Gardens** for sauna activity, **Wildcat** for piercing & alternative connections and lots of prostitutes advertising in the evening paper. The local *Evening Echo* papers have the best ad in the south.

southampton

bournemouth

brighton

travelling

▶ **London & South East England addresses**

ACE Sauna
508 Kings Road, Loondon SW10
☎(0171) 352 1370

Albatross Cinema Club
52 Plashet Grove, Upton Park London E6
1AE ☎(0181) 471 6570

Angie's Massage
Colchester ☎(01255) 240712

Annabelle's
☎(01273)693697

Bristol Gardens
24 Bristol Gardens, Brighton
☎(01272)698904

Carnival
Old Compton Street, Soho, London W1

Centrefold International Escorts
☎(0171) 225 3244

Cerebus
25 The Triangle, Bournemouth, Dorset
BH2 5SE ☎(01202)290529

travelling

Chain Gang
BCM 4542 London WC1N 3XX
☎(0171) 284 2180

Cobblers
49 Stratford Lane, Stratford, London E15
☎(0181) 519 8327

Eureka
Manor Lane, Fawkham, Longfield, Kent
☎(014747)704418 / 564207

Exposure
BM Exposure, London WC1N 3XX

Fantastic!
Pagan Metal, basement, 29 Brewer St,
London W1 ☎(0171) 287 3830

Fetish Times
£32.25 annual sub BCM Box 9253
London WC1N 3XX

Forum
c/o PO Box 418 Cardiff CF2 4UX

Girls Like Us
POBox 62, Whitstable, Kent
☎(0171)3592289

Honeycomb Club
PO Box 6 Hungerford RG17 OUE ☎(01488)
681 350

London Lesbian and Gay Switchboard
☎(0171) 837 7324

Lovejoys
99a Charing Cross Road, London W1
☎(0171) 437 1988

Madame Jo Jo's
8 Brewer Street, London W1
☎(0171) 734 2473

Pagan Metal
basement, 29 Brewer St, Soho, London W1
☎(0171) 287 3830

Paradise Club
PO Box 493 London SE26 5DY
☎(0181) 663 6522

Rascals
c/o Lisa's PO Box 161 Reading, Berks
RG2 0UQ ☎(0831) 377 680

Rhythm Station
266 High Street, Aldershot

Rio's Unisex Sauna
241 Kentish Town Road, London NW6
(0171) 485 0607

Rude Food Dining Club
PO Box 3626 London N7 OLX
☎(0956) 33304

Saidie Maisie's
BM Box 414 London WC1N 3XX

School Dinners
1 Robert Adams St, London W1
☎(0171) 486 2724

Severin's Kiss
first Tue of month in Broadwalk, Green St,
Soho, BCM Box 2578 London WC1N 3XX
☎(0181) 342 9136

Sh!
22 Coronet St, London N1
☎(0171) 359 6533

Skin Two
23 Grand Union Centre, London W10
☎(0181) 968 0234 Fetish Nightlife Line:
☎(0891) 445911

S/M Pride and Spanner Campaign
c/o Central Station, 37 Wharfdale Road,
London N1

Club Sophia
AC Box 16 Bishops Waltham, Southampton,
Hants SO32 1WA

Submission
c/o Libido Boutique 83 Parkway,
London NW1 ☎(0171) 284 2180

Sunset Strip
30 Dean Street, Soho, London W1

Toucan Club
Suite 401, 29 Margaret Street, London
W1N 7LB ☎(0181) 758 0231

TransEssex
(TV) PO Box 3 Basildon, Essex SS14 1PT
☎(0268) 583761

Transvestites Guide to London
POBox 941 London SW5 9UT.
Tranny Line ☎(0181) 363 0948

Utopia Sauna
825 Romford Road, E15 ☎(0181) 514 5355

Venus Health Studio
2 Brunswick Road, Hove, Brighton

Whiplash
c/o Suite 10, 2 Old Brompton Road,
London SW3 ☎(0171) 603 9654

Wildcat International
16 Preston St, Brighton ☎(01273) 323758

Willow Cinema Club
87 Great Eastern Street, London EC2
☎(0171) 739 4279

Zap Club
Old Ship Beach, Brighton ☎(01273) 821588

Zipper
281 Camden High Street, London NW1
☎(0171)284 0537

ZM
POBox 1002 Forest Hill, London SE23 3QJ.
☎(0181)699 2333

england
the midlands and east anglia

birmingham

More down-to-earth than the southerners, there is much fun to be had in the cities and country villages. Britain's most successful swing club is near Birmingham, although they had a nasty raid in 1993 which set them back and lost them theiroriginal venue. They now call themselves **X-Stasia**, after the swing clubs at Cap d'Agde. Run by real enthusiasts, they accept everybody who joins and give them value for money at their Saturday night events which are always held in a club within a hotel, so you can stay overnight if you like. Every hour, on the hour, they dim the lights, have "ladies' choice" and enjoy ten minutes of exquisite smooching, with delightful-to-watch lady-lady contact. Dogging is extremely popular: the Beacon carpark overlooking Birmingham is a really popular site for putting on

run by real enthusiasts

tremendous sense of freedom

performances in cars. **The Massage Circle** taking place near J10-11 of the M1 offers naturist gatherings on the last Sunday of odd-numbered months. On the fetish scene, **The Events** are still thriving. Their

derby

Birmingham venue is a huge night club in the middle of nowhere and you feel a tremendous sense of freedom as soon as you walk through the door. They also have a club in Derby and have started doing fetish

fetish nights get more and more exciting

travelling

nottingham

markets in Birmingham. In Warwick, **Domino Designs** provide weekend B&B in a show dungeon. In Nottingham the **Marquis Masquerade** fetish nights get more and more exciting, with a suspension harness and lots of stalls and events either held in **Rock City** or a smaller venue. Other fetish events include the **Bulldog Bash** for bikers, tattooists & piercing people near Stratford on Avon.
Birmingham Council now offers

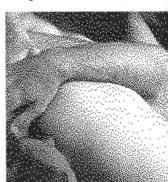

licences to the massage parlours, meaning they must be registered with the fire and planning departments. The parlours, I hear, are not as good as they were. The best strip pubs are the **Review Bar** in Soho Road and the **Hot Spot** in Exeter Street. The red light district of Balsall Heath is spoilt by local men standing on just about every street corner, intimidating the prostitutes and any potential clients who dare

leicester

nights, and this is advertised in the local papers. There's a country house which advertises as **Total Relaxation and Fun** near Milton Keynes. Saunas and massage parlours are plentiful in Leicester, advertised in the *Leicester Mercury*.

kettering

lincoln

Kettering's red light district is in St Andrew's Lane in Kingsthorpe. The **Chaplin's Arms** has

norwich

travelling

to pitch up. The rest of the population is not quite clear whether this is done on moral grounds or to improve house prices on the Heath. The houses in Cheddar Road have half their windows smashed in and residents warn any stranger that their car number will be reported to the police. Police vans and expensive Cop Granadas cruise past. There's still plenty of action from women in the area, all documented in the local *Phoenix* magazine. Northampton police have taken some of the pressure off and there are nice Thai massage and other parlours to visit. Nottingham police are still trying to hound the girls off their streets. For wild nightlife, **Rock City** still attracts goths, punks and rockers from miles around on Saturday nights. Striptease for men and women sometimes gets put on at the **Golden Flamingo** in Milton Keynes on Friday

northampton

milton keynes

striptease in Lincoln. Norwich's red light district behind the railway station has police women dressed up to entrap customers whose

great yarmouth

names end up in the local paper. Great Yarmouth has strip at the **Gallon Can** and a massage parlour called **Body and Soul** in Gorleston. **The East Anglia Forum Group** is a private and independent group, not associated with any other British swing club, holding really happy sex parties every month in different homes. It has a sister club in Los Angeles called **The Generic Club**. There's a tiny little sex shop in the middle of the fens in March called **Wendy Jane**, run by herself, stocking an exceptionally nice range of underwear and fetish gear for TVs and sexpots.

march

exceptionally nice range of underwear

Body & Soul
Sussex Road Business Centre, Sussex Road,
Gorleston, Norfolk

Bulldog Bash
Avon Park Raceway, Long Marston Airfield,
Near Stratford on Avon

CCP For Marital Harmony
33 Summer Row, Birmingham

Martin Cole
40 School Road, Mosely, Birmingham

Domino Designs
PO Box 159, Warwick CV35 8JG

East Anglia Forum Group
GPO Box 15, Thetford IP24 1BW
☎(01922) 27935

Erotica Book Shop
4 St Peters Road Great Yarmouth, Norfolk

The Events
PO Box 2292, Acocks Green, Birmingham
B27 2UD

Gallon Can
30 South Quay, Great Yarmouth

Golden Flamingo
Leisure Plaza, Milton Keynes

Lisa's Jacuzzi
Birmingham
☎(0121)33 7837

Marquis' Masquerade
25 Monk's Way, Silverdale Nottingham
NG11 7FG ☎(0115) 9 81 91 13

The Massage Circle
☎(01582) 455955

Northampton Books Unlimited
84 Wellington Road, Northampton

Phoenix
(£6) 23 Little Broom Street, Camp Hill,
Birmingham B12 OEU

Promises Promises
fetish & sex store 56 Dale End, Birmingham
B4 7LS

Soho Sex Shop
147 Radford Road, Hyson Green,
Nottingham

Taboo Cinema
43 Summer Road, B'hm ☎(0121) 236 1106

Thai Massage
Northampton (01604) 721022

Total Relaxation and Fun
Leicester ☎(01525) 261280

Touch of Class Escorts
Birmingham
☎(0121) 624 6439

Wendy Jane
62a Station Road, March, Cambs
☎(0352) 661467

X-Stasia
near Birmingham ☎(01922) 279035

79

travelling

england

the west country, wales and the channel islands

plymouth

There is a dearth of sexy clubs in the
South West. The mentality of the
prudes here is to squash any
anything that begins. It's not
until you reach Plymouth that
you'll find a strip clubs and
these are small and seedy.
Avis is the best nightclub in
Plymouth for strippers and
horny singles. Exeter has two
sex shops in Fore Street, a

exeter

Private shop and a nicer one
which doubles up as a fancy
dress store. An Exeter naturist
group, **Shanklin** run by Peter
and Lillian Newman has a gym
and sunbathing facilities.
Westward Bound is a private
bondage guesthouse for couples
only, equipped with dungeon
furnishings, dog kennels in
bedrooms and slave chariots. It is a

fantasy hideaway on the Devon/Cornwall border.

The Bristol fetish shop **Religion** puts

dog kennels in bedrooms and slave chariots

bristol on a fetish club, **Spank**, on certain nights at Vadim's and their **Inner Circle** is more private, for bondage, piercing and spanking, with special slave and masked nights. **De Sade** continues to hold its exciting fetish club nights on the last Saturday of every month in Weston Super Mare.

weston

Bristol has plenty of massage parlours: **The City Centre Sauna**, **Goldie's The Penthouse** and **Topaz**. On the City Road in St Paul's, the red light district is hairy and even taxi drivers might refuse to take you. Swingers, TVs & nudists are welcome to camp or stay at the **Garden of Eden** in West Wales. It's run by some liberal-minded people and provides a hydrotherapy pool, lovely Jacuzzi, 10-seater sauna and relaxation area all under glass. Fine Welsh girls wait for business in Cardiff's Crichton Street and locals assure me of good times. Up in Rhyl, holiday

travelling

cardiff

makers and day trippers can usually find a saucy show at the **Queen's Hotel**.

jersey

Jersey is the liveliest of the Channel Islands and, although it's tiny, many of its inhabitants commute to London and elsewhere so tend to be worldly and into sexual mischief. **Lido's** in St Helier caters to millionaire lawyers and glamourous women at lunch and during the afternoons, **Friday's** is full of bankers and secretaries, the **Lillie Langtry** full of swingers, and **The Office** horny ladies. **Café de Paris** is rather cliquey. The **Old Court House** is a lovely little naughty hideaway inn. The biggest and best nightclub is the **Inn on the Park** and, after this everybody goes to **Ryders**, **Thackereys** or **Yesterdays**.

'extras' who are flown over from paris or amsterdam

Raffles is low-life and **Les Arches** full of yokels. One of the restaurants in Berisford Street is known to arrange "extras" who are flown over from Paris or Amsterdam for their regulars or special visitors.

▶ **West country, Wales & Channel Isles addresses**

Bristol & Weston (01179)

The Broadway Health Studio
13a Broadway, Roath, Wales

De Sade
PO Box 4 Weston Super Mare BS24 9BB

Garden of Eden
Nevern Nurseries, nr Newport, Pembroke SA42 0NQ ☎ (01239) 820330

Goldie's
3 Victoria Road, St Philips's, Bristol

The Mayfair Parlour
112 Woodville Road, Cardiff ☎ 390772

Mint Adult Supplies
105 & 106 Fore Street, Exeter, Devon EX4 3HY

Oasis Health Centre
39 Lochaber Street Road, Cardiff ☎ 493311

The Penthouse
54 Old Market Street, Bristol

Plymouth's No 1 escorts
☎ (01752) 768961

Shanklin
120 Wardrew Road, St Thomas, Exeter
Devon EX4 1EZ

Religion
50 Park Row, Bristol BS1 5LH
☎(0117)929 3754

Topaz
354 Stapleton Road, Bristol

Westward Bound
c/o 27 Old Gloucester St, London WC1N
3XX ☎(01566)776907

Jersey (0534)

Les Arches
St Catherines

Café de Paris
Halket Street, St Helier ☎24065

Friday's
Halkett Place, St Helier 32769

Inn on the Park
West Park, Esplanade, St Helier

Lido's
Market Street, St Helier ☎22358

The Lillie Langtry
La Motte Street, St Helier ☎26046

The Office
Wharf Street, St Helier ☎23685

The Old Court House
St Aubin ☎46433

england
the north

The uninhibited and sexually excitable Northerners love fucking in the Ainsdale Dunes between Ainsdale & Southport, one of the best dogging sites in Europe.

uninhibited and sexually excitable northerners

They have, however, been slow to catch on to the fetish craze and the first club, **Intrigue** has only just opened up in Liverpool. It's on the first Tuesday in the month, insisting on a strict fetish dress code. **Babylon** is at the **Pink Parrott** with strict dress code fetish fun on the first Thursday of the Month. **Garlands** has a regular club every Saturday, its guests arriving in eccentric and fetish clothing. Liverpool's red light district is in the Granby Street / Lime Street area, where you might enjoy the **Montrose Pub** and **Pickwick's Singles Club**. Liverpool 's new cruise bar, **Time Out**, is at the junction of Cockspur Street and Pownal Square. The flamboyant tranny club is called **Loose**. Crackdowns on cock and hen nights in pubs up north have almost killed striptease altogether, except in the working men's clubs. "Interactive strip" makes the **Time Gap Bar** in Blackpool the raunchiest show in the North of England. Open till 2am, it's opposite the Central Pier. **The Merseyside School of Massage** is running Massage for Couples weekends in Liverpool. **Norwegian Wood** is a naturist centre where you can get a massage.

Manchester's **New Boardroom** has mixed swing nights on Wednesdays and couples only on Fridays and Saturdays, and the **Adam & Eve** sauna's sexy parties are on Saturdays. The **VIP Cinema Club** has been knocked down and **Jackie's** closed although there's still

liverpool

blackpool

manchester

travelling

strip along the Ashton Old Road and on Sundays at the **Blue Parrott** down in Macclesfield. Whally Range and Sackville Street are Manchester's red light districts but you're better off in Chorlton Street, near Piccadilly, which provides lots of choice. Three saunas thrive: **Blade's**, **Samantha's** and **Curves**. **Unlimited** fetish events at The

floors of gay and straight youngsters with wild trannies every Saturday night. **Flesh** at the **Hacienda** on the last Wednesday of every month welcomes drag queens, S&M dykes, trendy students and sweaty gay ravers. **Too Kinky** is another outrageous tranny night on the first Thursday of the month at **Home**. **Northern Concord** publishes *Crosstalk* and has big transvestite costume balls as well as regular pub

> the flying
> teapot has all
> the flyers

Victoria are timed to celebrate each issue of their mag *Unleashed*. To find out what's going on on the club scene, visit **The Corn Exchange** where **The Flying Teapot** has all the flyers and is in the know. The exchange also has good body piercing by **Anna Kai** and **Irene** (pronounced Irena) doing body art at **Secrets**, also selling by mail order. There are sex mag shops outside the Exchange. The **Corner House** has started to have exhibitions and film screenings with S/M themes.The area around the coach station is trendy and has sex shops, **Club Cry 101**, an extremely fashionable and wild club on Mondays, and **Strangeways**, a mostly gay club starting at 2am on Sunday mornings. S/M nights are starting at **The Hacienda**, and **The Paradise Factory** has three throbbing

nights at **The Rembrandt Hotel** , a small friendly hotel which welcomes trannies and non-straights. Behind the Rembrandt are the sleaziest of rent boy bars. **Ethos** holds a "TVs and Maids Night" every Friday. **Central Park** is for trannies and fashion students. The hip gay place to meet up early in the evening is the **Athenaeum**. In Broom Street, you might enjoy the **New York** pub and **Clone Zone**, the trendy gay sex shop. Princes Street is Manchester's gay village. The local **Lesbian and Gay Switchboard** gives out club info. The **Leeds/Manchester Forum Group** runs parties in Manchester run by a dishy Leeds couple, who also play with couples and singles in Leeds whenever they get the chance. Yorkshire has plenty of action. **Stimulation** is "an orgy of sexy feel-good sounds" at **Tower Nightclub**, Anlaby Road, Hull, on the last Tuesday in the month. The dress code is

rubber, leather, PVC, fantasy, no furs etc. Upstairs in the fetish bar you can get sensual in the dark red velvet

> **get sensual
> in the dark red
> velvet corners**

corners. **The Beat** is a saucy place to visit. Hull's hookers stand in Waterhouse Lane and Myton Street. The **Earl de Grey** pub is exotic, and male and female strip shows are shown at the **Vauxhall Tavern**. The **Relax Health Studio** is busy. **Cheeky Chops** is a late night massage *cleethorpes* parlour — the town is full of them. Cleethorpes has plenty of strip joints, the best being **Tokyo Joe's**. Grimsby's red light zones are in *grimsby* Alexandra Docks and Corporation Road. Leeds has **Glamourpussy** every month at **The Warehouse** in Somers Street and **Vague** at the Warehouse drawing all the fetish-clad, glam trannies and even real women go wild. Leeds' Chapeltown frightens the local white community but go *leeds* and enjoy the amazing stripclubs (taking only a couple of quid in your pocket, pick-pockets will go for you!). Try the **Lamport** on Sunday afternoons and the **Straeger** on midweek nights, with fun and

dancing at **Delaney's**, also known as **The Olympia** in Roundhay, on Sunday afternoons. **Coast & Country**, *sheffield* a club of thinking naturists, meets every other month in a Sheffield sauna. Sheffield has always been good for saunas — scattered all over the less salubrious areas of the city. On any night you can turn up with a party and *scarborough* use the facilities. **Ambassador** has been tarted up and has a pool. **Rose's** is also in Sheffield, a transformation house for fun trannies. She holds her **Harmony Weekends** in Scarborough at the end of October and publishes *Repartee*. **Added Zest** has naturist/non-pressure swing parties with themes and games in a private health club in South Yorks. **The Buck** in Rufforth *york* near York has strippers several nights a week. **Echoes** sells period clothing and victorian underwear in Todmorden. On top of the *todmorden* **Cockpit Pub** in Derby is the **St Trinian's Health Centre and Leisure Spa** *derby* which offers saunas, massage, and it's open every day from 11am to late. Rosehill Street is

period clothing and victorian underwear

the red light street, and the **Windmill** runs a Sunday lunch strip. Newcastle, South Shields and Sunderland have *newcastle* some hot striptease on certain nights of the week. Newcastle at **Rockshots**, **Zoots**, the **Gallery Cine** *south shields*

Club, **Ship in the Hole** and **Central Park**; South Shields at **Images, Jax** and **Lacey's**; in Sunderland at **Idols**, the **Brunswick** and **Dolphin**. Middlesbrough's girls are renowned for being nice and good value and can be found around Florence Street in the suburb of St Hilda's. The **Three Rivers Club**

sunderland

middlesbrough

has naturist swimming weekly in the Jesmond Baths, a monthly sauna in Cramlington New Town, and visits free beaches on the coast in the summer.

Middlesbrough girls are nice and good value

travelling

North West

Adam & Eve
206 Liverpool Road, Eccles
☎(0161) 689 8500

Blade's
Tib Street, Manchester ☎(0161) 832 6752

Clone Zone
Sackville Street, Manchester

Corner House
Oxford Street, Manchester

Curves
Fennal Street, Manchester
☎(0161) 832 7375

Ethos
1102 Stockport Road, Manchester

Flying Tea Pot
Unit 50, Manchester Corn Exchange

Garlands
off Dale Street, Liverpool

The Georgian Massage
Manchester ☎(0161)678 7916

The Hacienda
Whitworth Street, Manchester
Info line ☎(0161) 236 5051

Harmony Centre
sex shop Cross Street, Manchester

Home
Ducie Street, Manchester

Intrigue
The Batcave, 62 Duke Street, Liverpool

Lesbian & Gay Switchboard
Manchester ☎(0161) 274 399

The Merseyside School of Massage
☎(0161) 709 9701

Northern Concord
PO Box 258 Manchester M60 1LN
☎(0161) 236 1311

Norwegian Wood Naturist Leisure Club
The Row, Market Street, Hoylake, Wirral
☎(0151) 632 2479

Number One "The Boardroom"
1 Cheltenham Street, Salford
☎(0161) 736 5849

Paradise Factory
Upper Brook Street, Manchester

Pink Parrott
Duke Street, Liverpool

The Rembrandt Hotel
Sackville Street, Manchester
☎(0161) 236 1311

Samantha's
Oldham Road ☎(0161) 682 1206

Secrets
94c Old Church Street, Newton Heath,
Manchester M40 2JS ☎(0161) 681 7255

Sex Shop & Dungeon
11 Springfield Road, Blackpool FY1 1QW
☎(01253) 752087

Time Out
30 Highfield Street, Liverpool 3

Unlimited
PO Box HP50 Leeds LS6 1TR

Yorkshire

Ambassador Sauna
Sheffield ☎ (01142) 272 4461

Added Zest
(Doncaster) c/o Forum Society,
PO Box 418 Cardiff CF24XU

Cheeky Chops
43b Otley Road, Headingly

Coast & Country
3 Mayfield Ave, Scarborough
☎ (01723) 370691

Echoes
Hebden Bridge Road, Todmorden, W Yorks

Empire Cinema Club
Huddersfield ☎ (01484) 540978

Goldthorpe Hotel
Doncaster Road, Goldthorpe

Leeds/Manchester Forum Group
c/o Forum Society,
PO Box 418 Cardiff CF24XU

Relax Health Studio
Division Road, Hull ☎ (01482) 20770

Rose's Repartee
Roundel Street, Sheffield S9 3LE

Rotherham Trades Club
Greasbrough Road, Rotherham

Stimulation
Flying Fuck Productions, The Grosvenor
Hill, Wincolmlee, Hull HU2 8AH
☎ (01482) 218068

Tokyo Joe's
Old Custom House, Cleethorpes

Derbyshire

St Trinians Health Centre and Leisure Spa
76-82 Osmaston Road, Derby
☎ (01332) 372095

Windmill Pub
Dairyhouse Road, Derby

North East

Brunswick Hotel
Brunswick Street, Sunderland

Central Park
New Bridge Street, Newcastle

Dolphin Hotel
Ashdown Road, Sunderland

Gallery Cine Club
Westgate Street, Newcastle
☎ (0190) 232 3759

Idols
Highstreet West, Sunderland

Images
John Williamson Street, South Shields

Jax
Victoria Road, South Shields

Lacey's
Hudson Street, South Shields

Prestige
massage for men and ladies
☎ (0831) 538283

Rockshots
Waterloo Street, Newcastle

Ship in the Hole
Wallsend

Three Rivers
c/o 67 Woodburn Square, Whitley Bay,
Tyne & Wear NE26 3JD

Zoots
Waterloo Street, Newcastle

travelling

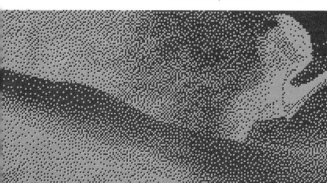

estonia

tallinn

There's rumour of a sex club starting in Tallinn, with striptease and live sex taking place. In the **Palace Hotel**, you can mingle with some very pleasant professionals in the **Sky Bar** where, twice a week, they have a saucy dance show. Similarly, the Hotels **Olympia** and **Viiru** attract hookers, expecially on the nights they have striptease.

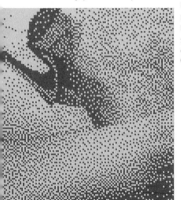

finland

travelling

helsinki

Helsinki goes all night and most people are very friendly and speak English. The only strip club is **Pikku Pietari**. Ladies of the night are mostly Russian or from Eastern Europe. **Club King Caarle XII** is a pub disco which gets packed on Thursday nights at **Club Jam**. Young people go to the **Kaivohuone**, and older ravers to the **Hesperia Hotel**, **President Hotel**, **Mikado** or **Fidzi**. The opulent **Cafe Adlon** is a good pickup joint. **Gambrini** is gay/mixed. **Kinky Club** claim to be the largest fetish club in Finland but there's also the **SM Group**.

The northern Scandinavians are rather innocent. Although they are open about sex, they are somewhat conformist and married couples often sleep in single beds or on two separate mattresses.

▶ **Finland Addresses**
    country code (358)

Cafe Aldon
Fabianinkatu 14 ☎(90) 664611

Gambrini
Iso Roobertinkatu 3 ☎(90) 644 391

Kinky Club
PL 9, SF-00521 Helsinki

S/M Group
c/o Setary, Toinen linja 10,
00550 Helsinki 55

**open
about sex**

paris

In October 1994, **La Messaline**, the divine swing club south of Paris, celebrated ten years of swinging. The club provides what might be the most sensational Saturday nights of group sex in a lovely house in a rural setting with good food and wines, all laid on by the cheerful Chantal and Michel. It's well worth the journey down the N20 towards Orléans, but if you prefer to swing in the city, here's the vast choice of clubs to choose from. **The Cléopatra**, a unique classy swing club, expensive

long-standing orgy and peep/sex show house

and a bit formal, with well-planned theme nights & erotic adventures contrasts **Le X Bis**, the long-standing orgy & peep/sex-show house catering to single men in the afternoon. **Les Chandelles** is a lovely new club near the Louvre, singles in afternoons, open daily. **La Cheminée** is for no-nonsense sex. They improved its décor and the two rooms upstairs and downstairs have showers and are joined by a bar between. A maid walks round picking up used condoms, putting them in a box on the wall. In the dim lights, everyone can just about see what's going on. Women take on queues and groups wax and wane. **Chris et Manu 1** also provides multiple safer sex opportunities in the evenings. It's better towards the end of the week but a bit of a dive. Mostly horny husbands showing off and wives wearing tights and

trousers! **Chris et Manu 2** has nicer people and is a very pleasant afternoon gangbang club open seven days a week till 9pm. **Adam's Club** is open again, is slightly S/M oriented and employs semi-pros. **Le Prélude** and **Dany's** are new, and people say Dany's is great. **Club 46** is the best swing sauna in Paris open to couples on Mondays & Tuesdays, but a long way out of the centre and hard to find, and **Sauna Relax** has

dinner and afternoon *dansants coquins*

87

adult babies and all kinds of pervery! Another good sauna is in rue de Courcelle. **Le Clos** is a small club with afternoon gangbangs & swapping later, and **Le Connivence**'s elegant clientele enjoy adventurous and

travelling

tender fingering. **Deux + Deux** has dinner and afternoon *dansants coquins* for couples only, every day of year including Xmas, midday till dawn. **Feelings** is a classy club forbidding singles. **Péplos** caters to the smart set and holds fascinating sexy dinners in a huge suburban house every other Friday. People dress in togas. **Au Roi René** is often good for single men in the afternoons and they are now putting on swinging dinners on the Fridays alternate to Péplos. **Au Pluriel Club** has lots of crannies for action and an inspiring décor. **Le Triangle** is a relaxed downtown club, allowing singles in afternoons. *Couples* mag lists and reviews French swing clubs, differentiating between HARD clubs where you strip & get on with it, and SOFT where action is slow but sure. Many Paris swing clubs are open for single men in the afternoons and couples only in the evening, or singles by appointment only. Many of them are closed in August.

If you're not a swinger and want some raucous fun, try **Nos Ancêtres Les Gallois**, an outrageously saucy restaurant. Most restaurants here are friendly places where you can make friends. The fetish scene in France is completely different to elsewhere. Despite, or perhaps because of the Marquis de Sade, S/M is not allowed in clubs and even mention of it in publications can cause problems. To fight such censorship, a new organisation called **Reseau Voltaire** has been set up. Even so, the magazine *Dèmonia* has the largest circulation of any fetish magazine in the world: 40,000 copies sold in supermarkets throughout the country. Their shop

most fabulous underwear shop in the entire world

La Boutique Dèmonia is in the heart of old Paris with books, toys, jewellery for pierced and non-pierced people, and fetish clothing. Big Dèmonia fetish events are also arranged. **Phylea**, perhaps the most fabulous underwear shop in the entire world, also organises fetish events. *Offrande*, the affectionate S/M magazine holds parties too, but

most of Paris S/M nights are private affairs. You will meet up with all kinds of little groups if you use Minitel (the Dèmonia code is 3615 SouM) — interesting little groups like **AVI** which is for exhibitionists into pissing. **Lili la Tigresse** is an S/M bar with fetish trollops go-go dancing & trapezing, and the **Chochotte club** has S/M shows. Paris has a museum called **The Martyrs of Paris** which shows the history of

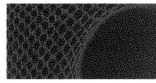

European torture, including a "garotting chair", a sophisticated form of punishment which, when performed in a ritualistic form was much enjoyed as a spectacle".

The Queen, at the top end of Paris' Champs Elysées is an exciting club which fills up with bubbles for **The Bain Mousse** on the first Tuesday of every month. It's gay/mixed. Be sure to go in old shoes, swimwear and take a snorkle, if you have one. If you wear contact lenses, take goggles. The most amazing sex scenes take place in the bubbles. The door staff are beautiful and a good time is had by all. **Aldo** has been enlarged and still attracts the most unbeleivably beautiful trannies, and no real women are allowed. Post-operative transsexuals are now legally recognised in their new gender by French law.

Pariscope lists the **Paris**' hardcore sex theatres, swing clubs, high class erotic dinner shows and lesbian performances. **The Club** is the latest hit and has striptease for women. **The Loving Chair** and **French Lovers**, at the same address in rue Pigalle, both put on full sex shows with limited audience participation for 300 francs. Rue St Denis has the highest density of the most scantily dressed of all the pros who stand on Paris streets. It also has peep shows with glass partitions which slide back for bodily contact if you pay more. Pigalle is the main sex area for tourists, and rue Budapest a less intense alternative. The Latin

highest density of the most scantily dressed of all the pros

Quarter on the Left Bank is also sexy, with **Théatre Orotique** providing a divine show. Parisian women find the **Chippendale** dancers a source of amusement rather than erotic attraction. The French **Erotica 94** takes place twice a year — mid March and at the end of October — and is the most successful sex fair in the world. Paris can also boast the best erotic art gallery: **Les Larmes d'Eros** which has continuous shows of compemporary artists from around the world. **Le Scarabée d'Or** is a huge erotic book shop and **Curiosa** the most intriguing and fun to browse. The American book *Everywoman's Guide to Paris*, published by Avery might help with your shopping.
Local give-away papers in France list whores. The authorities, worried by

the sharp rise in HIV infection, now provides for French hotels to stock condoms in every room and supplies campsites with machines that dispense condoms at no charge. 40km South of Paris, there's a relaxed naturist club called **Heliomonde** which can get quite naughty.

lyons

People often say what a wonderful time they have at **Eden Patio,** a swinging hotel in the Ardeche, SW of Lyons, which only opens in the summer (and its future is in question). Plan to spend a while to get accustomed to its pace and customs. Le Quai Claude Bernard at Lyons is where couples meet up for sex in cars on Sundays and locals go to **Le Dialogue** for its sexy ambiance. It's mixed, then couples-only after 10pm (Sun &Mon 4-9pm). Another swing club whose name I don't know is listed beneath under **Lyon**. **Mira Lyon** is a local heavy gay S/M club sharing an address with and **Cuir LAtex Club** holds fetish nights called **Serials.**
The French prefer to swing where they aren't likely to be known, doing it in Paris or else on holiday. There's a wonderful holiday magazine called *Loisirs 2000* which, along with cycling and other outdoor activities, features the saunas, dominants, personal ads, nudists beaches and swing clubs in central and south of France. It comes out five times a year, and costs 250F for a subscription. Everyone piles down to the vast **Cap d'Agde** every summer, the sexiest naturist resort in the universe. Beach activity is rampant and it has its own swing clubs and specialist clubs.Try to find **Le Boeuf** which is essentially a

travelling

cap d'agde

gay & lesbian S/M club in Cap d'Adge but it has lots of wild sex going on. It doesn't open till 2am. There are other summer swing clubs nearby: **L'Exstasia 2** is sometimes run by the outrageous Alexio and Sonio from the **Athena Club** in Milan, and there's sex in the pool. **L'Extasia 1** has really outrageous things happening in the woods behind it. **Le Club Azur**, near Cannes, is now under new management and is picking up again — it's a lovely little swing club offering good food. I've listed many of the South of France swing clubs in the directory. Even if you're not a swinging couple, give them a call to see what their schedule is. On the nights they're not catering to couples only, they are usually open for anybody to come

and meet sexy people and find out what else is going on; whores may be in attendance. In St Tropez, La Plage de Pampelonne is where couples misbehave in front of club **Le Bouch**. More serious exibitionism

takes place along the coast on the Layet beach, Cavalière. Marseilles is a hard-core city with an interesting street scene, mostly in Place Opèra. At the crossroads of Boulevard D'Athena and La Conebière, women of 70 and 80 await their special clients and transvestites wait in rue Breuteuil.

women of 70 and 80 await their special clients

▶ **France addresses - country code (33)**

Paris & Environs

Club 41
41 rue Quincampoix, central Paris
☎40 27 07 90

Club 46
46 rue de la Marjolaine, 95100 Argenteuil, Paris

Le X Bis
10bis rue de l'Embarcadère,
near Port Maillot, Paris. ☎45 74 12 32

Adam's Club
3 rue Brey, near Arch du Triomph, Paris
☎42 67 72 18

Ancêtres Les Gallois
39 rue Saint-Louis en L'Ile, Paris
☎46 33 66 07

L'AVI
7 rue M.Berthelot, 92700 Colombes

Les Chandelles
1 Rue Thérèse, Paris ☎42 60 43 31

La Cheminée
11 rue des Fossés, St Marcel, Paris 5e
☎07 07 66 66

Chochotte
34 rue Saint-André-des-Arts, Paris
☎43 54 97 82

Chris et Manu 1
5 rue St Bon, Paris 4e ☎42 72 52 18

Chris et Manu 2
43 rue de la Rochefoucauld, Paris 9e
☎42 81 00 17

Cléopatra
19 avenue d'Italie, 75013 Paris
☎45 89 55 69

Le Clos
5 rue Bernard Palissy, Paris 6e
☎45 49 087

La Connivence
62 rue de Charonne, 75011 Paris
☎49 29 05 86

Couples
NSP 38 rue Servan, 75544 Paris Cedex 11

La Boutique Dèmonia
15 Cité Joly, Paris 11e (Métro Père Lachaise)
☎43 57 09 90

Curiosa
Passage Jouffrey Paris 12e (closed on sats)

Dany's Club
9 rue Truffaut 17e Paris (42) 93 04 45

Deux + Deux
70 rue de Lhomond, Paris 5e ☎47 07 25 81

Erotica 94 Salon Erotica
4 Impasse Abel Varet, 92110 Clichy,
☎47 39 70 10, fax 47393017

Feelings
24 rue Vavin, Paris 6e ☎43 54 06 04

French Lovers
62 rue Pigale, Paris 9e

Heliomonde
La Petite Beauce, 91530 Saint Cheron
☎64 56 61 37

Lilila Tigresse
98 rue Blanche 75009 Paris ☎48 74 08 25

La Messaline
Oinville St Liphard, 28310 ☎37 90 08 23

Les Larmes d'Eros
58 rue Amelot 75001 Paris ☎43 38 33 43

Loving Chair
62 rue Pigale Paris 9e

Offrande
APMC, PBP No 6, 75462 Paris cdx 10

Théatre Orotique
Rue St Andres Des Arts, Paris

Péplos1
Grande rue, 78850 Thiveral
(on N198 beyond Verseilles).
☎30 54 35 66

Phylea
61 rue Quincampoix, 75004 Paris
☎42 76 01 80

Au Pluriel Club
13 rue Francois Miron Paris 4e
☎40 29 07 52

Le Prélude 1
rue Richelieu, near Comédie Francaise,
Paris

Reseau Voltaire
Annabelle Faust 8 rue August Blancqui,
93200 St Denis ☎48 09 22 10

Au Roi René
184 rue de Versailles, Ville d'Avray, France
92410, near Paris ☎47 50 25 30

Sauna
177 rue de Courcelle, near Place Péreire
☎47 64 11 76

Le Scarabée d'Or
61 rue Monsieur le Prince, 75006 Paris
☎46 34 63 61

La Scene
fetish mag AF75, 102 Avenue Champs
Elysées F-75008 Paris

Sortilege
witchcraft fetish mag CP91, 189 rue
d'Aubervilliers, F-75886 Paris, cedex 18.
☎46 07 60 36

Triangle
13 rue d'Argenteuil, Paris 1e ☎42 61 68 28

Lyons and South of France

Club 54
(swing) 54 rue des Ponchettes Nice
☎93 62 10 22 / 93 29 18 82

Le Club 95
(swing) 95 rue St Jacques, 13006 Marseilles
☎91 81 47 30

Arles Sauna Club
(swing) 6 rue Marc Sangnier 13200 Arles
☎90 93 15 73

Bora Bora
(swing)18 rue de la Croze, 30150
Roqumaure ☎66 90 20 87

Cleopatre
Cap d'Agde 67 26 93 96

Le Club
(swing) 39 rue de las Chaussé, Toulouse
☎62 26 77 77

Le Club Azur
(swing) L'Oustaou du Moulin, 11 rue du
Moulin, Vieux Cannet 06110 Cannet
☎93 69 16 20

Cap d'Agde
action in dunes & in sex clubs BP 545, 34305
Cap d'Agde ☎67 26 32 89

Cuir LAtex Club
BP 3010/69394 Lyons ced 03 ☎78 00 63 08

Le Dialogue
9 rue St-Paul 69005 Lyons ☎78 30 00 19

L'Extasia
(swing) Rte de Meze, 4km from Marseillan-
Ville in l'Hérault, between Montpellier and
Cap d'Agde ☎67 77 96 46

L'Exstasia II
Rte de Palavas, 34970 Lattes, nr Agde
☎67 68 95 01

Le Feeling
(swing) Quai du Chapitre, 34300 Adge
Town ☎67 94 88 62

Le Lady Club 2
(swing) 10 rue Dominique Paez, Nice
☎93 83 30 32

Loisirs 2000
B.P. 3032 - 30002 Nimes Cedex

Lyon
(swing) ☎78 64 08 61

Sauna Les Thermes
22 rue Mazagran, 13001 Marseilles
☎91 47 77 05

travelling

the gambia

banjul

Older British women fly over to **The Gambia** to find gigolos and lovers. Young men await them on the beaches of the Banjul peninsula. However, the new young president is a strict Moslem and is not happy with this and is doing his best to discourage the women from

92

> **rape is practically non-existent**

coming. Sex for hire is cheap, cheerful and readily available here. Sex between men and women, married or not, is an open activity, and rape is practically non-existant. Lesbianism is common. The Gambia has topless sunbathing around the pool but no naturism, and watch out for pickpockets! Abidjan has a sophisticated ever-changing nightlife offering many possibilities. The closest thing you're likely to find to porn is an old copy of *Penthouse*, if you're lucky.

abidjan

travelling

germany
the north

hamburg

In German saunas everyone is completely naked: nudity is a tradition. Prostitution is legal, as is bestiality and swinging. Germany's sex is highly commercial but but very flamboyant. Hamburg is the commercial sex capital of Europe. Newcomers might like to take a Hamburg-by-Night bus tour which leaves the main railway station every night at 8pm, enabling you to see the incredible sex scene without effort. It goes through the main nightlife area, St Pauli, along the Reeperbahn and Grosse Freiheit where the streets are crammed with sex establishments. One street, Herbertstrasse, prohibits women who don't work there and has specialist whores in windows. It's so overwhelmingly hardcore it makes Bangkok's Pat Pong seem tame. Over

2,500 women work here selling sex. It's relatively safe but naive punters may get ripped off. **Salambo** offers vulgar live sex shows where the girls' dances include lowering themselves onto candles, bananas and live dongs. Usually there's audience participation and you can fuck the girl of your choice on the premises. Amazing brothels such as **Lausen** on the Reeperbahn treat men to the most amazing nights of fun and loving. **Hotel Rasputin** houses French transvestites. **Amphore** offers group sex and you can just sit and watch or

> **lowering themselves onto candles, bananas and live dongs**

join in. The *Hamburg Stadtplan für Manner* will help you see all these places at a glance. All the clubs here are glitzy and hot but St Georg, particularly Hansaplatz, is a safer and nicer sex area in the evenings. Another area near the station, Hauptbahnhof, is where you find **Crazy Boys**, with striptease and more for women. Fischmarkt is an area for male and female prostitutes and Querstrasse is another "window" street. More elegant houses include **Club Aphrodite** and **Maxim's**. Germans say that the fetish scene is much friendlier in the north. *Schlag Zeilen*, the Hamburg fetish mag with stunning black & white photography, lists forthcoming events all around including their

diners in full fetish finery

own **Les Fleurs du Mal** at the Molotow, and **Domination 7** at COX. **Latex Lack & Leder** hold dinner & torment every Saturday night at 8pm, diners in full fetish finery. The friendly **Lampe** fetish clothing showroom is in Hamburg, for gorgeous rubber and plastic designs. You can also get fetish gear at **Puls Drugstore**, **Boutique de Sade** and **The Leather Cage**. The **Revolt Shop** does piercing and body jewellery, as does **Endless Pain**. **Club De Sade** and next door's **Justine** are rip-offs but do have some quite good action. **Paradies-Vogel** is a highly recommended swing club run by Petra and Klaus, allowing single men in for 120DM. **Dschungel** is an alternative dance club. The **Erotic Art Museum** is exquisite and extremely interesting, with special art exhibitions on show. **Anders-Artig** in Hannover is the best

hannover

semi-public German S/M group for parties where the action is hardcore.

bremen

The S/M partyhouse in Bremen is a soirée hard. Now that it has been nominated to become the new capital of Germany, Berlin is having trouble maintaining its own

berlin

particular brand of whore-life, which is very street and kino oriented, rather than using showbars and brothels.

Prostitutes are giving sex tours of the sex district as a campaign to save their tradition. While all this is going on, the Minister for Youth and Family plastered the city with promotional posters of himself naked, to attract votes, claiming that he's an "honest politician with nothing to hide!" To find a hooker, *BZ* is full of ads. **Mona** is in the thick of the sex area of Stuttgarter Platz

sit on the plush seats and get a blow job

which has hearts in the window plus photos of the girls who are working. Also on the Platz, on Stuttgartenstr, is **Starlight**, one of the many kinos where you can either sit on the plush seats and get a blow job while watching the blue movie on the screen or else go inside a little cubicle for more interesting hanky panky and a vast choice of films to watch.

An exciting new Berlin bar called the

travelling

93

Kloster has sadomasochistic decor, attracting hardcore punks and goths with regular S/M events. *Twilight Berlin* is Germany's new S/M magazine listing events and happenings. Manfred Oschatz runs his fetish **Ex-Kreuz** every Saturday. **Qualgeist Dildo-Night** says, "everybody brings a dildo, otherwise no entrance", a non-commercial group of SMers, fetishists and other strange-taste people for men only in Berlin.

Eva Krüger runs a sex shop for women called **Erotik-Shop** where men are *verboten*. Swinging in Berlin is somewhat dead. Grunge and punk survivors frequent the **Ex'n'Pop** but Berlin has gone techo at clubs like **E-Werk**. Clubbing is all night and some clubs don't start till 4am. The **Love Parade**, officially a demo for peace, joy and pancakes is a flamboyant jubilant gay parade in mid June. The **Antinous Institut** provides erotic massage, shiva dance & Tantric group sessions. **Blub** is the name of an air and bath paradise in West Berlin where you can play in the water nude.

germany
central and western germany

Neue Liebe is a brothel for women in the centre of the industrial part of Germany, in Habinghorst. The lively and enthusiastic gigolos are prepared to travel. The choices are from tender to dominant. Bedrooms are upstairs and in flats nearby. The deal of the house is: an orgasm or you get your money back! The men

the lively and enthusiastic gigolos are prepared to travel

are good looking, well mannered and take pride in knowing how to treat a lady, in bed and out. *Happy Weekend* is a good source for brothels in Germany and most houses offer extreme fantasy and prostate fulfilment.

Cologne's **Erotica '94** launched Peter Czernich's new magazine, *Marquis* in 1994 and this will become an annual event in November. **Madame Cornelitas** opens her S/M studio once a month for parties and they are exciting nights, if only for the amazing S/M equipment her boyfriend makes in leather and metal. On the swinging scene, the best club here is **Club Gerlinde** which is situated near Cologne Airport and is elegant and well-equipped. There's also **Marselles Club** for group sex which always has three times more men

all street clothes are left in lockers

than women and is specially for women who want to be gang banged or take on lots of fellas. Over

cologne

and over again, I hear praises sung about the **Maihof Club** in Germany. So, if you want a really wonderful swing experience, get over there while it's still working so well. It's right out in the country and you can go for the weekend. Dusseldorf's **Aldstadt** is the "longest bar in Europe" with outdoor drinking and **Relax** is a good pickup joint on a Saturday night. Just outside Dusseldorf (and not easy to find by car) is **Die Eule** a large swing club with fab facilities including a pool, mat rooms, huge bar and restaurant. Husbands tend to lead the way and wives look saucy in their undies. All street clothes are left in lockers.

Nearer Bonn, **Traumland** is another large swing club which has raucous nights. **RMN Dreams** is a newer club with both off-premises and on-premises parties and no membership is required.

There are three types of fetish club here: fashion nights such as Cindy and Heinz's **GLL Parties** in Aachen and **Pourquoi Pas** erotic rubber, chain and fetish dress happenings in Saarbrücken, all of them listed in *Marquis* magazine; non-commercial clubs which are run for self-help and fun; and the hard S/M

clubs, these being listed in *Arbeits Gemeinschaft S/M & Offentlichkeit* which also publishes *S/M Depesche*. A **Bizarre Boarding Dungeon** in central Düsseldorf run by Miss Jayne who loves British guests. She provides a playhouse with kennels, medical rooms, and overnight facilities. Germany has some pretty strong S/M mags but animal sex porn is banned.

Frankfurt's classy sex sauna is called **Tucholskystrasse 16**, with stunning girls and an "English Club" atmosphere. Over the river, Sachsenhausen is a fun place to hang out, and good clubs

düsseldorf

bonn

aachen

frankfurt

travelling

düsseldorf

playhouse with kennels, medical rooms, and overnight facilities

are **Central Park** for rocksters and hippies or **Cooky's** for trendies. **Madame** is lesbian and **Schweig** gay. **Hexenhaus** is the best swing club in the area, "a dream for couples" welcoming new ones on Fridays.

Jail's is one of the most popular fetish clubs in Germany, meeting at the Kellerbar at the **M&S Connexion**

in Mannheim

In Saarbrücken there is a latex lovers' shop called **Porquois Pas** which puts on great events and on the A3 to Amsterdam from Frankfurt is a nice swing house called **Haus Romantica**.

germany
bavaria and stuttgart

Munich is fast becoming one of Europe's most progressive towns, with an interesting combination of fetish, tranny and sexy nights. Armin Rahn still puts on two **Schabernacht Balls** during Fasching (just before Lent) when everyone goes wild. The fetish scene is far from dead: Randy Mikels of **Cutglass Piercing** puts on annual events such as **Exzentric Fashion**, a **Tattoo Convention** and **Sex-o-Mania**. Wolfgang Kreuzer has an **Erotic Night**. **Boutique Highlights** is a shop selling fetish clothes where Thomas and Ute Scheider can tell you about fetish clubs, including their own parties and pub nights.

FreleSMünchen is a local S/M group. A fetish night, **Tempel** makes up part of the hardcore dance festivals that take place in Munich. **Fetish Revolution** is put on by **Club Sin** every Saturday. Transvestites perform at **Cabaret Broadway** on Schiller Street. **Charly M** is the snazzy nightclub where professional and other girls groove hoping to attract rich and successful men. **Sudfass** girls are especially delicious (and even

match the women in their ads!) — the Munich house is outstanding. Munich's most extravagant whorehouse is **Club Babylon**. Tourists party in the Schwabing district, others mellow down in its Southwest area, and **Oly** is a bohemian bar. The **Englisher Garten** is full of naked people on sunny days. Munich has Germany's first women-only sex shop. Called **Ladies First**, it's quite pretty, selling dildos, books and a bit of rubber & leather.

germany's
first
women-only
sex shop

Stuttgart has no central nightlift area. **The Casino** is where the young alternatives hang out, **Röhre** is fashionable, and **Café Stella** gay. Professional girls stand on the streets around the Stuttgart Messe hoping for good trade. **Club Caprice** holds conventional fetish gatherings twice a year.

The North

Amphore
Hafenstr 140, Hamburg ☎31 52 09

Aphrodite
Rahlstederstr 110, 2000 Hamburg 73
☎677 09 56

Anders-Artiq
Hannover ☎(511) 232527

Boutique de Sade
Erichstr, Hamburg ☎29 319 41 62

Bremen Hard Club
☎421 616 8539

COX
Conventstr 8-10 Hamburg

Endless Pain
Eichholz 56, Hamburg ☎31 35 40

Fleur du Mal &Schlag Zeillen
Postfach 306 352 D-2000 Hamburg 35.
☎(40)432299

Hamburg Erotic Art Museum
Bernhardt Nochtstr 69, 2000 Hamburg 36
fax ☎(40) 317 4758

Peter Lampe
Goethestr 37 ☎38 76 64

Latex Lack & Leder
Intrigenkeller, Branstwiete 32,
20457 Hamburg 11

Lausen
Reeperbahn 59

Maxim
Lockstedter Stadium 86, 2000 Hamburg 54
☎56 31 37

Molotow
Spielbudenplatz 5

Paradies-Vogel
Wohlwillstr 18, 2000 Hamburg 90 Altona
☎040 31 77 2853

Puls Drugstore
Bahnhof 3 ☎319 060

Club de Sade
Erichstr 41 ☎319 38 71

Salambo Erotik Theater
Grosse Freiheit 11

Sauna Venus
Vahrenswalderstr 321 Hannover
☎511 63 71 59

Berlin

Antinous Institut
Mansteinstr 14, D-10783 Berlin
☎(30)2166654 fax 215 7850

Blub
Buschkrugallee 64, 1000 Berlin 47
☎(30) 606 6060

Erotik-Shop
Wilmersdorf, Brandenburgisch Str 28, near
Ku'damm, Berlin

E-Werk
Wilhelmstr,betweenLeipziger & Zimmerstr

Ex-Kreuz Club
Berlin ☎(30)87 40 97

Ex'n'Pop
Mansteinstr 14, Berlin

The Kloster
Friedrichstr 114a 101117 Berlin
☎(172) 306 83 68

Qualgeist Dildo-Night
c/o Mann-O-Meter, Motzestrasse 5, D-
10777 Berlin ☎030 694 7829

Sex Clusivitaten
erotic boutique ☎(30) 302 2253

Twilight Berlin
Katzbachstr 17, 10965 Berlin

Central and Western Germany

Arbeits Gemeinschaft S/M & Offentlichkeit
Holstenstrasse 5, 24534 Neumünster
☎(0431)732443

Bizarre Boarding Dungeon
Reichsgasse 17, 40217 Düsseldorf
☎(0211)37 56 91

The Castle S/M parties
Dortmund ☎ 201 76 21 42 or 234 43 27 14

Central Park
Holzgraben 9, Frankfurt

Madame Cornelitas
Cologne ☎(221)5463367

Erotica '94
c/o Plastique GmbH, Königstr 8, 47798
Krefeld ☎(2131) 8803071-2-3

Erotik Museum
Helenenstrasse 18 Cologne

97

travelling

Erotischen Landhaus Party
Coblenz ☎(02654) 1414

Die Eule
4030 Ratingen-Hösel, Ernst-Stinshoffstr 68,
near Dusseldorf ☎(2102)96880

Club Gerlinde
near Cologne airport ☎(2203) 32313

GLL Parties
PLK 039814 D, D-500668 Cologne 1
☎(2645)4642 (weds 6-8pm)

Hexenhaus
Brunnenstr 15, 5431 Gorgeshausen, nr
Frankfurt ☎(06485)4414

Jail's
Kellerbar in M&S Connexion, Angelstr 5-9
68199 Mannheim ☎(0621) 85 9626

Madame
Alle Heiligen Str, Frankfurt

Maihof Freizeit für Paare
D-6719 Maihof, near Frankfurt 1020
☎(06356)8016 / 8015 (English) / 356
(reservations), fax (06356)

Marquis
c/o Peter Czernich, Flensburgerstr 5, 42655
Solingen fax ☎(212) 58656

Marselles Club
Cologne ☎(221)63 22 172

Neue Liebe
Langestr 109, Castrop Brauxel, in the
Habinghorst suburb ☎(02305) 75876

Pourquoi Pas
Ludwigstraase 29, 66115 Sarbrücken
☎681 417 0418

Private Party for Couples
Heidelburg ☎302646

Relax
Jahnstrasse, Dusseldorf

RMN Dreams
Hauptstr 5, Sulzbachtal 67734
☎(06308)1765

Haus Romantica
Hauptstr 5, 4236 Ringenberg ☎02852 2478

Scweig
Schäfergasse, Frankfurt

Show Center
(live sex show) Rottstrasse 16, 4630
Bochum, near Dusseldorf

Traumland
Schmelztalstr 51, 5340 Bad Honnef 1, near
Bonn ☎(02224)2144/3058/2505

Treffpunkt
(for couples) Essen ☎27 26 13

Tucholskystrasse 16
Frankfurt ☎(069 62 58 21)

Bavaria & Stuttgart

Casino
Mörikestr 69 Stuttgart

Club Caprice
POB 700331, 7000 Stuttgart 70

Club Babylon
Munich ☎(89) 359 9111)

Charly M
Maximiliansplatz 5 Munich

Cutglass
Piercing Holzstr 21, 80469 Munich
☎(89) 263508

Boutique Highlights
Gabelsbergerstr 68, 80333 Munich
☎(89) 527475

Exzentric Fashion
c/o Postfach 440125, 8000 Munich 40
☎(89)26 35 08

Highlights
Gabelsbergerstr 68, 8000 Munich 2
☎(89)52 74 75

Röhre
Wagenburgtunnel, Neckarstr 34,
Stuttgart

Club Sin
Munich, information line ☎(911) 709 017

Sudfass Oase
Peter-Andersstr 4, 8000 Munich 60
☎(089) 884520

Wolfgang Kreuzer's Erotic Nights
Landsbergerstr 152, 80339 Munich.

Ladies First
Kurfurstenstr 23, 80801 Munich
☎(89)2718806

Oly
Helene-Mayer-Ring, Munich

Schnabenackt Balls
c/o Herr Rahn, Nymphenburgerstr 2,
Munich 2 ☎(89)775044

Café Stella
Haptstätterstr 57, Stuttgart

Tempel
Munich ☎(89) 325029

greece

eos

Eos is the island where the horny young people go for holidays in the Cyclades archipelego. Mykanos is the nudist, swinging and gay resort with freedom and hot night life. The Skyros Centre runs holistic holidays where you can be nude and free. Athens' Omonoia Square is the centre of fun and deviance.

mykanos

Hardcore porn is available in all the kiosks. Red and Yellow lights are the sign of a brothel and the best are found in Odos Euripdou, Odos Menandrou and Odos Phyles. The "all day clubs" are all whore bars in Nikis, off Syntagma, Omonia, and in the port of Piraeus where cabarets of the wildest nature are put on to entice customers. Transvestite whores are very popular. There's striptease at **Maxim** and **Copacabana**, and amazing nightlife to choose from:

athens

boites, discos and bouzoukia. Many of the trendy clubs move to the coast in the summer months. Open Forum

cabarets of the wildest nature are put on to entice customers

is a very liberal magazine coming out of Greece aimed at an international market.

▶ **Greece Addresses country code (30)**

Copacabana
Kallirois 4 ☎ 923 2648

Maxim
Othonis 6, Syntagma ☎ 3234831

Open Forum
£5 from Lianos, PO Box 8343 Athens (Omonia) GR 10010

Skyros Centre
c/o 92 Prince of Wales Road, London NW5 3NE ☎ (071)267 4424

travelling

holland

The **Paradise Club** has become the talk of Amsterdam amongst swingers. It's a local club — 20 minutes walk from Central Station after you've taken the ferry north of the station. After a few steps at the entrance, it's on one level so it's wheelchair accessible. Singles are not

the record number of men fucking one woman in a gangbang is 32

allowed on Saturday nights and pay 50 guilders on other nights (Thur-Mon 8-2, Satúrdays till 2am). There's a swimming pool and three big saunas, blue movies and couples performing on a big round bed. The record number of men fucking one woman in a gangbang is 32 but that seems to be creating competition. The old **Candy Club**, which has been happily swinging for at least 20 years is still in a class of its own. Single men are allowed on Friday nights for watch &

amsterdam

wank but not to touch. Phone after 10pm. Lots of foreigners go to **Kasteel Waterloo** in the South of Holland where there are many rooms designed for sexual intrigue, holes in the wall for feeling through, and S/M nights on 2nd & 3rd Friday of month. More relaxed, however, is **Landgoed Zundertseweg 84** which is in a large house with a pool, bar and lavishly decorated rooms in the same area, Southwest of Breda. They open

south of holland

Monday-Friday 2pm onwards, have stripshows and videos, allowing

entrance to couples only on Saturday nights. **Club de Zaar**, also in the south, is a cosy house with a reputation for enthusiastic sex. The club **Revo** just outside Amsterdam has gone downhill: there are too many hookers and the sex tends to be unimaginative. *Chick,* the sex magazine, held their marathon fucking contest there. Look in the *Telegraf* on a Saturday for swing ads under *Paren.*

occasional party where everyone gets looked after

Demask, the fetish shop run by Steve English, runs a regular weekend club, **Kinky**, and twice yearly **Europerv** extravaganzas at the Artis at the Amsterdam Zoo. **Club Maitress** gathers at **Café Karim** or **Café Perry** on a regular basis — very good for developing your S/M skills. **G-Force** is a new S/M venue which is in the red light district and doesn't require a dress code or an entrance

fee. You just watch S/M videos or read the magazines, drink and talk. They have a cellar with a cross, bondage table, sling, stocks and cage which you can rent. **Mistress Shiva** runs a sweet little S/M parlour, **SBIC**, providing fabulous equipment and has the occasional party when all the guests' fantasies are looked after. She also holds transvestite evenings. A new fetish store called **Wrapped** sells magnificent techno clothing is a delight to visit. **Ellen Schippers** is still selling her stunning fetish clothes through **Studio Kat. The RoB Gallery** has a wonderful display of S/M things, as well as being a good shop for gay S/Mers. There are several really good gay guides to Amsterdam, some of which you can buy at the airport or any gay bar or store.

Although everything is available in Amsterdam you can still get ripped off. You have to remember the Dutch sell sex because they will sell anything! *The Eros Guide* is a sales tool for Erex and won't guide you anywhere much. The **Federation of Operators of Relax Businesses** have a plaque awarded to brothels with proper hygiene and conduct standards, so look for these plaques when in search of fun. Most of the Thai massage parlours in Amsterdam are a rip-off but one has been recommended by someone who always enjoys himself there. Unfortunately he can't remember its name but it's in a tiny street off the Oude Achterbourgwal called Bardesteeg. You get told there is no fucking but you can get lucky!

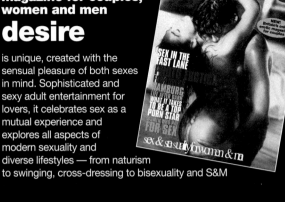

CUPIDO

DET EROTISKE MAGASIN

Hverdag A/S Pb. 9121 Grønland N-0133 Oslo Norway

worth knowing if you're into watersports

Columbian girls can be found in the Geldersekade, worth knowing if you're into watersports. Amsterdam taxis carry cards for top brothels, **Yab Yum** being the most extravagant but they say you can get the same girls cheaper elsewhere. Unique to Amsterdam is **Jan Bik** who has catalogues of housewives who will take you upstairs while hubby is in the sitting room watching telly. The girls sitting in the big shop windows of Oude Zjids Achterburgwal are usually quite lovely and when you go in, they draw the curtain and get on with it. Holland has a service specially for disabled people called **SAR** which provides trained whores.

You can see live sex shows with couples making love on stage in a comfortable theatre called the **Casa Rosso**, and nearby is the **Banana Bar** where all the acts on the bar are banana-oriented. At the **Moulin Rouge** there's even more audience participation — don't go if you're afraid of being lured up on stage to screw or play with the performers. Of the two **sex museums**, the best is on the Damrak, just below the Central Station. It's better and cheaper than the one on Achterburgwal. There's nothing new or exciting about the porn shops. The bestiality mags are now seal-wrapped so you can't browse them. People staying at the **Centrum Venwoude (School of Body & Soul)** gain experience in new mind/body enlightenment and you can have advanced sex lessons at the **New Ancient Sex Academy**. De Kosmos, the hippy complex, sometimes puts on Tantric events.

Club Doma in The Hague is the hardest show & club in Europe, or maybe the world. Friday night means party night and people come from all over the globe to be strung up by the nipples or whipped in public. The rest of the week it's a high-tech domination

you'll be lured up on stage to screw or play with the performers

parlour with clientele who like extremes. The Hague's red light district was purpose built, with modern windows displaying girls for hire. It lacks a certain character but functions as a model for foreign

strung up by the nipples or whipped hard

governments considering setting up red light areas in their cities.
In Haarlem, three swinging couples bought brothel so that, at weekends, they can use it as a sexy party house. This is called **Passion**. On the first weekend of the month, it's for S/M and on every third Saturday the female guests act as whores, charge the men 10 guilders for twenty minutes and must not go over time. Other decadent nights take place. Also in Haarlem is a three-story club called **Wildside** which is commercial except once a month when they provide food for a party which is refreshingly

haarlem

stimulating reaching top gear. For more information on this, enquire at Amsterdam's **Maitress**. Rotterdam's **Studio Amanda** is a new small, but well-equipped commercial club which throws intimate but lively fetish parties on the third Saturday of the month. It is the trend in Holland for clubs to operate like this and in Utrecht, **Hot Shot** employs whores during the week but at weekends it becomes a swingers' club. **Erolife 94** is the Dutch sex trade fair which takes place every November in Utrecht. It has a mix of stalls, fashion shows and attractions and part of its charm is that it's a local show.

rotterdam

utrecht

**refreshingly
stimulating
and top quality**

▶ **holland addresses - country code (31)**

Studio Amanda
Henegouwelaan 63c, 3021 CS Rotterdam
☎(10) 425 7923
Candy Club Eikenweg 29, Oesterpark, Amsterdam ☎(20) 6947379

Casa Rosso
OZ Achterburgwal 106, Amsterdam
☎(20) 6278954

Centrum Venwoude (School of Body & Soul)
Postbus 59, 3740 AB Baarn ☎(02156) 8447

Chic Magazine
☎(075) 280 979

Erolife 94
Sluithek 6, PB Leusen, Postbus 333, 3831 Leusen ☎ (33) 944 700

DeMask Boutique
Zeedijk 64, 1012 BA Amsterdam
☎(20)620 5603

Doma
Asterstraat 107, 2509 The Hague
☎(70)360 1823, fax 365 4180

Expectations
male fetish storeWarmoerstraat 32, 1011 JE Amsterdam

Hot Shot
Utrecht ☎(30) 960049

Jan Bik
3 Buiten Weininger, off Haarlemmerstraat
☎(20) 623 1584

Kasteel Waterloo
Postbus 394. 6040 AJ Roermond (LB)
Reuver-Beesel ☎(04704)3030

De Kosmos
Prins Hendrikkade 142, 1011 AT
Amsterdam ☎(20) 6267477/6237102

Landgoed Zundertseweg 84
Zundertseweg 84, 4715 SC Rucphen.
☎(01654) 3280

Mail and Female
erotic boutique for women ☎(20) 693 6074

Maitress
Postbus 15448, 1001 MKAmsterdam
☎(20) 638 0521

Massad
Postbus 3061 3003 AB Rotterdam

New Ancient Sex Academy
Alexanderboersstraat 30, 1071 KZ
Amsterdam ☎(20) 6644670

Paradise
Schaafstraat 26, 1021 KE Amsterdam
☎(20) 6373416

Passion
Haarlem ☎(23) 251715

RoB
Gallery Weteringschans 253
1017 XJ Amsterdam

SAR
Postbus 875, 3700 AW Zeist
☎(03404) 60390

SBIC / Shiva's
Mamixstraat 48, A'dam ☎(20) 624 2988

Studio Kat
Erst Jan Steenstraat 112, 3rd Floor, 1072 NR
Amsterdam ☎(20)66 23 883

Topmodels Escort Fest
c/o Boei PO Box 9887 1006 AW Amsterdam
☎(20) 6731069

VSSM
(Dutch Society for Sexual Reform) Postbus
3570 1001 AJ Amsterdam

Wrapped
Singel 434, 1017 AV Amsterdam

Yab Yum
Singel 295 ☎(20) 62 49 503

Club de Zaar
5971 NJ Grubbenvorst, Zaar 2
☎(077) 821235

hong kong

Tsimshatsui and **Wanchai's Lockhart Road** are the glitsy tourist areas with just a few gems, like the **Diamond Palace**, a smart sauna/massage place where you can ask for a special. Lockart Road as far as Fleming has blatant sex. **Someplace Else** in the

the best looking men are found at jj's

everyone
swoons around
in the mud
misbehaving

Sheraton's basement is like an American singles bar with hordes of stunning and expensively dressed Chinese girls looking for partners. **The Neptune** is another good singles pick-up bar. The Upstairs bar at the **Mariner's Club** is a fashionable haunt for the young. Out of the area is **Joe Bananas**, full of British Airways crews who swear by it! The smarter bars are on Lan Kwai Fong. Women say the best looking men are found at **JJ's** in the Grand Hyatt in North Wanchai. Lan Kwai Fong is the nightclub area of town. On the Island of Lanto every autumn, an extremely kinky ceremony takes place call the **Mudympics**. Organised by the **Frog and Toad** pub, everyone swoons around in the mud misbehaving themselves.

travelling

island of lanto

▶ **Hong Kong Addresses**
   country code (852)

Joe Bananas
Luard Road, Wanchai

Mariner's Club
11 Middle Road, Tsimshatsui ☎368 8261

Someplace Else
Sheraton Hong Kong Hotel & Towers, 20
Nathan Road, Tsimshatsui ☎369 1111 ext 5

hungary

budapest

There is no censorship in Hungary and their magazine *Extra Bizarr*, a compillation of foreign porn which comes out every three months, features photos of women screwing with animals and is on sale quite openly. Most of the fun places in Budapest are on the east side of

you can simply order a partner from the cashier

the Danube at Pest and the red light district is Josef Körüt (beware of pickpockets). Everything is easy: in many nightclubs, such as **Caligula**, you can simply order a partner from the cashier or bar staff. There's a lovely erotic live show in the topless **Tiamo** and **La Dolce Vita** has a sex show with ladies for hire every night 10pm-6am. **Intim** is a peep show palace and there's even a barber's that does topless haircuts. **Fortuna** and **Moulin Rouge** are proper strip clubs, as is the **Pink Pussycats** which is frequented by both men and

lesbians. Hungary's most famous drag queen, Istvan "Csepi" Balazs, known as the Hungarian Madonna can often be seen at the best gay bar, **Angyal**. An alternative crowd appreciate the great beer at **Tilos AZ A**. The Engish language magazine *Budapest* has interesting addresses in the classifieds including escort bureaus. **Hotel Gellert**, the triumph of *Belle Epoch*, has the most fabulous chandelier lighting its romantic swimming pool. The thermal baths **Szechenyii** in the city park Verosliget can be a sensuous place to make friends. Sex is quite open in Hungary.

lake balaton

topless sensuality and sexuality

Around Lake Balaton, for example, you see topless sensuality and sexuality. When having sex with a Hungarian, you need to be able to distinguish between *még* (more), *meleg* (hot) and *elég* (enough)!

travelling

▶ **hungary addresses - country code (36)**

Caligula
Szilagyi erzsebet fasor 37-39, Budapest
☎1352723

Angyal Club
sulla via Rackoczi, Budapest

Dolce Vita
Oktober 6 utca 5, Budapest ☎2670214

Extra Bizarr
Levélpressz, Budapest VII, Dobutca 17

Hotel Gellert
Geller ter 1, Budapest ☎460700

Moulin Rouge
Nagymezo utca 17, Budapest

Pink Pussy Cats
Wesseleny 28, Budapest

Tiamo Hölgyek
Cim: IX., Ferenckrt 19-21, Budapest
☎114 2290

Tilos AZ A
Kalman Miksssszath ter 2, Budapest
☎1180684

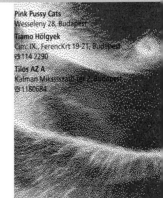

iceland

reykjavic

Nightlife in Reykjavic is very much a weekend scene and the discos *(listed below)* are expensive but, after a couple of drinks, everyone goes completely orgiastic: women throw themselves at men and foreigners often wonder what has hit them. As well as the night clubs, you could visit the more conventional **Hótel Island** which is a huge dancehall. **Tungeid** is a bisexual disco. In summer, topless sunbathing goes on into the late evening on the beaches. The

women throw themselves at men

leyline running through Iceland attracts pagans.

▶ **Iceland Addresses country code (354)**

Casablanca
Skúlagata 30, Reykjavic

Cuba
Borgartún 32, Reykjavic

Hótel Island
Armúli 9, Reykjavic ☎ (1) 687111

MSC
gay S/M PO Box 5521 125 Reykjavic ☎ (91) 62 12 80

Tunglio
Laekjargata 2, Reykjavic

Utopia
Suourlandsbraut 26, Reykjavic

india and sri lanka

travelling

bombay

In Bombay, **The Blue Nile** on Colaba Causeway has floorshows, including lesbian performances. Nearby is **Leopolds Bar** where foreign singles hang out, and **Trishana**, near the Museum, is crowded with young people at weekends. Gays frequent the **A/C room** of the **Gokuls Bar**, behind the Taj Mahal Hotel, where you can pick up a copy of the contact mag, *Bombay Post*. There are the classy call girls of Malabar Hill, the AIDS-ridden areas of Forres Road where the hookers are mostly trannies, Suklaji Street and Colaba. Then there is Falkland Road. This has a new Indian name now but taxi drivers will know where you mean. Many of its houses are sex slave camps, with children sharing beds with punters and women controlled by brothel keepers. **711 Falkland Road** is the only place to be recommended.

There is some swinging, partners meeting up through ads in magazines but Indian wives tend to be rather are reticent.

delhi

Delhi's GB Road is where the prostitutes are and the evening papers sometimes run ads for cabaret nights which are mild strip shows, occasionally at the **Lido** or **Kamal**.

colombo

Colombo has brothels where you can pay either for short or long time. In massage parlours, such as the **Green Jade Health Centre** of the Hotel Lanka Orchard, you can fondle the girls but not screw them: they make you come with their hands. The locals enjoy meeting foreigners, and most of the hotels have nightclubs and the beaches beach bars. Swingers and singles meet through *Club Lanka*.

morena

The island of Morena in the south west is home to the Bhediya tribe who, without any stigma live entirely off prostitution. As soon as a female reaches puberty, her nose is pierced with a decorative pin symbolising her initiation; the pin is then removed at a celebration when she has her first client. **The All Kerala Penfriends and Philatelic Association** campaigns for sexual freedom.

▶ **India Addresses**
   country code (91)

The All Kerala Penfriends and Philatelic Association
XIII/600 Pallippadam-Polpakara, PO 679 576 Kerala

Club Lanka
PFCC Salaka Apo Code ☎1, 466 Union Place, Colombo 2, Sri Lanka

indonesia

djakarta

Some people love Djakarta but for others it's still cockroach city. The Tanamur disco is like a toilet with music but packed with hookers. Take a bus to the new harbour and then hire a motorbike to a prostitute compound. Block 'M' is a place for action. At night, take a taxi to the picnic tables of Ancol Park. There's a red zone in the north end of town called Kramat Nunggak. Most cities have sex compounds. Surabhaya has a fancy area called "Doley" where girls in alleys are frightened by sex but the older ones sell it. The oil town of Nagoya is known for its country girls looking for boyfriends, many of whom get free board in a place like the **Golden Star** because they attract customers. Men say they have to pay the women to leave them alone, but don't have to pay for sex. Thieving is common. Porn is absolutely illegal.

nagoya

men pay the women to leave them alone

ireland

steamy, repressed

sexuality

Steamy, repressed sexuality expresses itself in unexpected outbursts. One of the most remarkable things is the tradition for well-organised prostitution, particularly in Dublin. *The Irish Times* sometimes publishes articles about which kind of women stand on which streets or work, in which particular massage parlours. The cheapest street girls, they say, are around the quays; more expensive in Fitzwilliam Square, Herbert Street, Waterloo Road and around the **Burlington Hotel**. *In*

dublin

Dublin, the respectable "what's on" weekly is a goldmine for club news and contact ads from kinky and swinging people, parlours and general fun. **Stars** hires male escorts to women and **Mais Oui** caters to couples as well as singles. Similarly,

The Cork Evening Echo lists personal massage and escort services, and escorts are also advertised in *Limerick Times*. The other liberal aspect of Eire

The girls in the Irish massage parlours are said to be some of the nicest in the world, doing massage with their breasts and other divine treats. Down in Limerick, O'Curry and Alphonsus Streets are where the whores hang out and **Private Temptations** is a great massage parlour. Singles go to **Brazenhead**, gays to the **White House** and couples looking for something else to

the girls in the irish massage parlours are said to be some of the nicest in the world

resulted from the Incitement to Hatred Act which made it illegal to utter public comments which abuse, insult or incite hatred against certain minority groups, including gays and lesbians. Now gays have equal rights, the age of consent being 17 and the gay scene in Dublin has now exploded with **Hooray Henry's** as the top club with the **Incognito Sauna** and **Frankie's Bed and Breakfast**. **Shaft** is no longer strictly gay and is the place to go after everywhere else shuts down. *Hot Press*, the rock paper, sometimes recommends gay venues. **Ladybirds Agency** looks after TVs and they enjoy themselves at **Parliament Inn**. Leeson Street in Dublin continues to attract the good-time ravers in their endlessly-changing string of nighteries. Baggot Street has lively pubs and **Risk** is a fun club off St Ann Street. **Bad Bob's** is a singles bar and the **Pink Elephant** is for young groovers. **Lillies Bordello** is a swapsies establishment and recommended massage parlours are the **New Imperial Studio** and the **Lotus Club**.

Newtown Pery and **Dirty Nellies**. In Cork, **Nite Owls** is still the happening club, with alternative types frequenting **Sir Henry's** and gays going to **Loafers** and **The Other Place**. The **Washington** and **The Hanover** are still the most popular massage parlours and Lapps Quay and the **Oliver Plenkett** in Lower Street are the place to find whores. Southern Ireland now has **Minitel** which, on the face of it, seems entirely straight, but it's linked to the French system and the sex contacts can be quite astonishing.

The Bachelor Festival at Ballybunion used to be wild, with the women screwing all the men they could lay their hands on, and plenty of gay sex in the toilets. Sadly, the contest has gone out of vogue, and is no longer so sexy.

Now that condoms are available in Eire, a Dublin-based company called **Futurecare** sells personalised condoms for rock bands to hand out to fans, reckoning they will be more

travelling

portrush

belfast

useful than T shirts. One of the most fascinating establishments is **Kincasslagh House**, an all-female Victorian/1920's household with maidservants and civilised ladies where fantasies can be realised.

Nobody could say that the Irish don't know how to enjoy themselves, which is also true in the North. Nightclubs in Portrush such as **Kelly's** throb till the last drop of spunk has oozed out and it's time to go home. Belfast buzzes with hyped up, if small-minded enthusiasm around Botanic Station where the **Manhattan** and the **Botanic Inn** spill over into the **Wellington Park Hotel**. Young men seeking older women go upstairs in the **Windsor Bar** on Wednesday nights and for younger girls to **The George** in Bangor. Hookers can be found in **The Limelight**, off Ormeau Road where students also hang out, but the whores work the streets behind too. More expensive hookers are in the

Europe Hotel. **Bob Cratchettes** on Lisburn Road buzzes all over the weekend and disabled people come here because it's so friendly. The sex shops in Gresham Street are rip-offs but you can buy hardcore videos in most of the straight video shops under the counter, but not in the big chain stores. Rugby clubs have strip nights but there are no strip clubs. Swingers advertise in the Surrey-based *New Directions* because they don't trust the local papers who might decide to expose them. Shaw's Bridge is where all the cars are parked for snogging and swapping. Gays do not fare so well in the north, although the student population is more open minded. Fetish wear is ordered by mail from Britain and there are, as yet, no fetish clubs.

you can buy hardcore videos in most of the straight video shops

▶ **ireland addresses - country code (353 for Eire)**

Body Positive
Dublin ☎(1)671 2363

Botanic Inn
Malone Road, Belfast

In Dublin
7 Camden Place, Dublin 2 ☎(1)4784322

The Hanover Sauna
Cork ☎(21) 276045

Frankie's Bed and Breakfast
8 Camden Place, Dublin 2 ☎(1)4783087

Hooray Henry's
26 Dame Street, Dublin 2

Incognito Sauna
Bow Lane East, Dublin ☎(1)4783504

Kincasslagh House
Burtonport, County Donegal ☎(75) 42030

Mais Oui
Dublin escorts ☎(088)53 7463

Pink Elephant
South Frederick Street, Dublin
☎(1)677 5876

Parliament Inn
Parliament Street, Dublin 2

Shaft
22 Ely Place, Dublin 2

Sir Henry's
South Main Street, Cork

Stars
Dublin ☎(088) 560543

World of Friends Pen Pals
30 Oakfield Park, Sligo

israel

tel aviv

Many of the whores' and swingers' ads in the papers are in Hebrew but most hotels have little magazines listing the phone numbers for escorts, massage and sauna clubs, with plenty to choose from. There are fewer girls in Tel Aviv's Hayarkon Street these days but the bagel bar on the corner at Kikkar Bet Be-November is a pick-up spot. Tel Baruch Beach by the Colony and Mandarin hotels is where men drive for a fuck in the car with a pro, the most glamourous of which are trannies. Russian women hang around scantilly clad, as it's much warmer than Moscow and they are known to accept less money than local girls. **Tel Aviv Today** has ads for escorts in the back. Sex shops such as **Dizengoff** sells hard core sex mags, videos and loads of blow-up dolls.

whores'and swingers' ads in the papers are in hebrew

italy

travelling

Italy is exploding with all different kinds of sexual entertainment and ideas, perhaps as a result of their highly successful sex fairs where innovations have been exhibited to the public and debates amongst the sex radicals have been lively. **Erotica** takes place in Bologna in the Spring and the new **MiSex** in the autumn of 1994 attracted over 60,000 people in Milan. Italy has an exciting new kind of sex club, combining disco, topless performance and swinging, springing up in small towns in Tuscany, Romagna and Lombardy, usually hosted by Italian porno stars.

new kind of sex club, combining disco, topless performance and swinging

Le Ore features up-to-date information on them with gossip and reports. **Harmony** is the leader, situated in the small town Montemerlo di Bondeno, between Bologna and Florence, closely followed by **Topazio** in Rossi, *rossi* **Nabilia** in Parma and **New Life** in Turin. *parma* Swinging in Italy is more frantic than elsewhere. *turin* Voyeurs go crazy and spice up the excitement even more. *milan* Clubs have been opening and closing like overactive sphincters because of the political upheavals, but **L'Europa** is still alive and kicking outside Milan in Binasco, *binasco* and so is **Athena** in Milan and Savanna continues under its new name **L'Escale**. Turin now has a swing club called **Happy Day**. **The Associazione Amici** in Florence and

travelling

rome

the **Noi Club** are small exclusive clubs for swingers. The **Adam and Eve** in Rome rarely has any parties any more but the **Lucky Club** has parties in different locations. Maurizio stopped his wonderful club although there's another similar one, called **Les Folies** opposite the Julio Caesar cinema in Santa Maria. Water drips from the ceiling but it's friendly and cheap. The couple who run it don't speak English. Car sex in Rome takes place in the Villa Borhese and near the Olympic Stadium and the couples get their fair share of peeping toms. **La Villa**, **Villa Gatsby**, **L'Incontro**, **Club Privato**, and **Selice** are new places where you might find swing activity. Swing magazines include *Fermoposta*, *Contattiamoca* , *La Coppia* and *Videotel* has swing ads on page 28345.

florence

It is easy to find prostitutes on the street: in Lungo Arno by the river, La Cascine Park, via Fiume and Piazza della Stazione in Florence (where there is also a very nice little brothel at 4 via Magenta); viale Tizano and viale Christophoro in Rome, the Caruggi area in Genoa, where the girls sit in doorways; and Viala Umbria, Viale Abruzzi and Viale Pirelli in Milan, with the TS's standing in via M Gioia, near the Pirelli skyscraper. Whores stand around fires in the winter near the motorways around Rome, and on Tor di Quinto. Naples' flea market, **Forcella** is full of whores and a Naples speciality is the *feminella*, a boy who has been brought up all his life as a girl by his parents for fun and profit. You can always find whores around convention centres and the transvestites are in the streets

genoa

naples

a naples speciality is the *feminella*

surrounding the railway stations and in parks at night. If you bring someone back to your hotel, regulations say they must also register: so it's no use trying to sneak them in. Professionals also advertise in *Il Corriera della Sera* under relations or massage. Centre **Relax** is known to be the best place for a massage and a hand job in Italy. Men play with themselves and each other in the sex cinemas. **Volturno** and **Blue Moon** are Rome's best blue movie and strip theatres.There is hardcore porn on every bookstore and video shop.

Nightlife is very high tech, with computer matching, pools with slides, and rooms full of bubbles. On the coast in Rimini, vast clubs like the **Baracuda** create strange happenings to amuse the holiday crowds. **Peter Pan**, famous for its trannies, is obviously not so liberal, as one couple got told to stop snogging on the sofa by a bouncer, and the **Coco Rico**, which doesn't like to be labelled, is full of transvestites. Florence has a hot club with lovely Brazilian girls called **Marcana**. **Frau Marlen** is a big transsexual, gay and swing club which goes pretty over the top in Livorno.

rimini

livorno

The Italian fetish magazine *The Club* became so elitist and secretive that a new organisation, **Legami** (Tie Me), has sprung into action, touring around the country, putting on exhibitions, shows and parties. There are good fetish and sex shops including **Eurostudium**, **Carpa Diem**, **Carón** and the **Eros Center**.

Il Buco beach has wild goings-on in Ostia, near Rome. It's 11 km from Lido going south towards Torvaianica, and you have to climb through a hole to get to it. La Bassona - Lido di Dante is also hot and nude, and the **Camping Pizzo Greco** is the most erotic naturist camp.

Sexpol is a small political group campaigning for sexual rights which has gone underground because it is considered illegal.

legami (tie me) has sprung into action

Adam & Eve
Box 6265, 00195 Rome ☎ (6) 310432

Associazione Amici
C.P. 12, 43036 Fidenza (PR)

Athena Club
Via Livigno 6, 20158 Milan ☎ (02) 6884236
fax (2) 29402127

Camping Pizzo Greco
PO Box 57 Loc. Fratte 88076 Isola Capo Rizzuto CZ ☎ (962) 792249 / 791771

Cáron
via Stradella 12, Milan ☎ (2) 2826356

Carpe Diem
via M. Polo 32 bis, Turin ☎ (11) 590735

Centro Relax
via Satolli 1, Rome

Eros Center
viale Dante 116, Riccione (FO)
☎ (541) 648686

Erotica
via Boldrini 22, Bologna (51) 243880

L'Escale
Milan ☎ (2) 891 27 090

L'Europa
via X Binasco No 94, Guido Cesare Casalne, Binasco ☎ (2) 905 4997

Eurostudio
Corso Raccenigi 49, Turin ☎ (11) 388512

Frau Marlen
Torre del Lago Puccini Lavarron
☎ (584) 342282

Villa Gasby
Misano Adriatico (Fc)
☎ (541) 613328 613005

Happy Day
Turin ☎ (11) 593007

Harmony
Montemerlo di Bondero, Ferrara (532) 890062

L'Incontro
Piazza Ischia 12, Portoverde, Misano Adriatico (Fo) ☎ (541) 612262

Legami
c/o Paolo in Rome on ☎ (6) 504335

Lucky Club
Rome ☎ (6) 844 0330 / 862614

Maracana
via Faenza 4, Florence ☎ (55) 210298

Misex
Milan (2) 38002901

Nabila
Parma ☎ (521) 46489

New Life
Turin ☎ (11) 535992

Noi Club
C.P. 29, 33084 Fondtanafredda (PN)

Club Privato
☎ (187) 627286

Restaurante Selice
Conselice (RA) ☎ (545) 89798

Topazzia
via Pellegrino, Rosa 21 ☎ (2) 6465990

La Villa
Rome ☎ (336) 787634

Volturno
via Volturno 37, Rome ☎ (6) 492 7537

travelling

jamaica

negril

Professionals here rub you down with Aloe Vera so beware of this getting in contact with your condoms and weakening them. Carry KY. Most tourists go to Negril, a town streching along beautiful beaches and cliffs. The finest hookers can be found there. Swingers will

superclass all-inclusive hedonistic beach resort

travelling kingston

enjoy **Tropical Connections** where anything goes, in Kingston, and **Vita Forbes'** little swinging resort in a quaint country town on the beach. The **Treasure Beach Hotel** Is an easy going, horny hotel, set in perfumed gardens with

young amenable staff and fun to be had along the beach, but the most fabulous establishment is **Hedonism II**, a superclass all-inclusive hedonistic beach resort. Phoning home and any kind of rushing is banned. When lust is seen to begin, rafts of fruit and drinks are floated out to the couple or group to keep them refreshed. Bliss! **Gran Lido** is a beautiful swinging resort on Negril Beach, with some rooms on the nudist beach.

▶ **Jamaica Addresses country code (809)**

Gran Lido
PO Box 88, Negril Beach ☎ 957 4010 fax 957 4138

Hedonism II
PO Box 25, Negril ☎ 957 4201 fax 957 4289

Treasure Beach Hotel
Treasure Beach ☎ 949 1183

Tropical Connections
PO Box 108, Kingston 15

Vita Forbes
PO Box 108 Kingston 15 ☎ 954 2476

japan

The big thing in Japan at present is the *Bulusela*, underwear stores which stock used schoolgirls' knickers and school uniforms. Visit **AD** in Osaka and Tokyo, the **Lemon Club** in Osaka and **Lope** in Tokyo. Sometimes the girls attend to present the panties and clothing to the customer with a signed photo. Panties worn longer are proportionally more expensive. Teenage prostitution is looked upon as a current problem, especially since the legal age of consent is twenty.

The **Tele Cula** (Telephone Club) which was once used by university students is now used by high school girls for selling their services. There are sex magazines for teenagers, with readers' letters and "how-to" articles. Also, some new magazines called *Oshili Club* (Bottom Club) and *Oshiko Club* (wee-wee club) appeal to the young. Young people are heavily into CD Rom interactive sex games.
Being a consumer society, you can imagine their sex products are highly

bulusela, **underwear stores which stock used schoolgirls' knickers and school uniforms**

gimmicky: pop and kitchen vibrators, a huge variety of *figuas*, sex doll kits and vibrator kits. Not content with this, the Japanese try all sorts of gadgets, and there's been a craze for using bicycle pumps up the bum. The Japanese don't have a complex about being small. They think women having a tight pussy is good and Japanese penises are very hard and hot. They enjoy long, lingering sex. Although it is the tradition for Japanese businessmen to stay out and use whores at night, wives are not above finding partners for themselves via the Tele Cula or even selling it themselves on the side. Nightclubs have had to make restrictions on women arriving dressed too skimpily, as many have arrived in G-Strings or naked. The women claim they are fed up with having to look so demure by day. Only very rich housewives and women who run night clubs (mamas) use male prostitutes but young women travel to the Bari Islands for the gigolos. Japanese condoms are beautifully wrapped, very thin and feel like real skin. The female condom has not arrived yet. Little brochures with colour photos of girls are left in phone boxes.

Fashion Health means massage, *No Pan Kissa* is the name for coffee shops where girls wear no knickers and the floors are mirrored. *Bideo Bokkus* is the name for tiny chambers to sit in comfort and watch porno, alone or with a partner. *Lolicon* means younger girls, *Soapland* means sexy turkish bath. At Soaplands men get devoted sexual attention, the best in Toyko being **Koshitsu-YU, Bell Commons** (the very best) and **Korista!**. The best Tokyo strip clubs are the **OS Gekijo**

and **Doutonbori Gekijo**. The Japanese take their sex shows very seriously. Once the labia are

live goldfish are inserted (called *shinkigyo*, or 'deep sea fish')

exposed, they clap and there's Tokudashi — where they pass a big magnifying glass round in order to look at their finer details. Live goldfish are inserted (called Shinkigyo, or "deep sea fish") and pink vibrators retrieved from cunts. However, live sex acts are rarely seen. Erotic performance is not in vogue. There is very little radical performance, and **Azzlo** are the only ones that import or invent it. Perhaps this is because the commercial stuff is so intensely inventive (if naff). They have incredible fantasy establishments, decorated like classrooms, rush-hour trains, hospital rooms, S/M parlours, where girls act out the theme and where men are allowed to misbehave with them. Clubs change their themes every two or three months.

The women's movement lags behind most cultures but there is a consciousness now. Young women read "Lady's Comics", which are erotic softcore love and sex magazines. They read them quite openly on trains and many of the pictures have pubic hair. This is normally banned, but the drawings are considered "art" not pornography. Japan had its first lesbian and gay march in 1994 which was a big step forward. It is considered distressing to one's

family to come out as gay so homosexuality is virtually invisible, even in large cities. Disabled people are rarely seen. Ancient Shinto fertility festivals survive, and humanism and sex education lag sorely behind.

Tokyo is not an easy city for an outsider to cope with so here's some simple guidelines. You can pick up a copy of *Roppongi and Akasaka Night Map* from telephone boxes to find the local sex services, or take a nightlife tour on the Hato Bus which will include an Oiran ("courtesan") show. To do it yourself, go to the Shinjuku train station then wander under the red arch into the red light district of Kabukicho, which has lately had new flood-lit government office complex constructed adjacent to it, making it seem even more garish. It isn't threatening, and women will feel safe on this journey as well as men. Strip shows, date bars, soaplands , gay bars, peep shows and massage parlours are plentiful and large phone booths are let by the hour for couples who can't afford a hotel! Love Hotels with names like **Hotel Me and You** are numerous. The Shitamachi area of Asakusa is sex centre where, at **Furansu-za** you can watch sexy shows and **Rock-za** is a nude theatre. Pink movie houses are also found here.Tokyo's Topongi is the main night club area where **Bauhaus** is the gutsy club. Young people live and hang out in Shimokitazawa. The

transvestite area in Tokyo is Shinjuku-3-chome. Piercing and tattooing is becoming popular, and the **Paradise** is where to find it. **Queen Bee** is a parlour for SM pleasure and the **Alpha Inn** is a bondage & discipline-kitted love motel, behind the Russian Embassy. S/M is usually men dominating women and the clubs are either for fashion or for finding a partner. The fetish fashion has extended to school uniform, nurses, kimono, fairy tale and air hostess gear. The S/M video Shop called **Hobby** has a private room where you can view videos at 10% of the price of buying them. The **Azzlo** store is the fashionable fetish shop with a gallery and they put on fetish nights in night clubs. **Dream** also sells fetish items. S/M play clubs are called **Cool, Room, E & Ca** (for scat and nappy attention), **Etsu, Adam and Eve** and, for soft S/M massage: **Miyashima**. **Club Nude** has midnight sub/dom performances every other Saturday.

Thai and other indochinese girls, many of them HIV positive, are flooding into Japan, to earn more money than they can whoring back home. They normally get a bit of a shock. Firstly, because Japanese men expect to be able to dictate the menu, offering the sex worker no choice (the girls are now trying to set up unions). Secondly, the women have to repay enormous sums to the "broker" who brought them over here before they can earn money for themselves. Prostitutes are also coming from Russia and South America.

Swingers in Tokyo can enjoy **Fellow** where singing, sake/whisky precede grouping together and driving off to a motel with nighties and condoms. There are about 35,000 sex hotels in

Japan, 4000 of which are in Tokyo. Some are high tech and minimal while others highly elaborate, with beds built in fantasy style and sunken baths. Chairs may have leg rests instead of arm rests. They are used by young single people who seldom live together before marriage, young couples who have to live with one of their parents, parents who want to get away from the children, and professionals with their clients. Rarely do foreigners find them but Pocket Books publish a *Love Hotel Guide* which is not in English but you can read the phone numbers and work out where they are from the dialing codes.

Kyoto is a friendlier but less dynamic city than Toyko. It's business area, Gion, is also the main entertainment area, with bars and geisha places just south of the river in Pontocho. The contrast is fascinating. Walking past the corner of Shinjo-dori and Hanami-koji you can see the red ochred walls of the most famous Geisha tea houses of the past then you slip up to the lively red light cabaret houses just to the north, which fulfil the sexual demands of today's Japanese businessmen. There's strip at the famous **DX Tohji de Luxe** which is full of the strippers' fans. The *Kyoto Visitor's Guide* is a monthly which lists what's going on.

In Osaka, there's a huge shop called **Elos no Yakata** for S/M toys and costumes and the play club here is called Kiya. **Mickey Mouse Club** is the Osaka swing club. In Sapporo and Kawasaki, sex establishments are less clandestine than elsewhere. The Susukino district of Sapporo, south of Opori Park is the centre of nightlife in the north, and the best disco to head for is **Exing**. Hiroshima has the **Japan Liberated Lifestylist League** off-premesis swing club. In Kagoshima, you can sit in a pool of steaming hot water, heated by the smouldering volcano Sakurajima.

The Japanese use blood groups like we use astrology to match

the japanese use blood groups like we use astrology

themselves up. A people are modest, straightfoward and often boring; O's are self confident and simple but some are calculating and wild; B people are dynamic, moody, funny, emotional and artistic, and the AB's are cool, objective but wired up.

▶ **japan addresses - country code (81)**

Tokyo

AD
901 Grotia 2-19-17 Shibuya, Shibuyaku
☎(03) 5485 8953

Adam and Eve
Nakano ☎(03) 3365 0150

AZZLO/Discipline Gym
21 Sakamachi,Shinjuku, Tokyo 160. ☎(3) 3356 9267 fax (3)3356 9810

The Alpha Inn
Tokyo ☎(03) 3200 3001

Bell Commons
☎(03) 3874 8567

Betty Page Social Club
(postal club only) 308 Metropolis, 22-24 Tomihisacho Shinjuku-ku

Cool
☎(03) 3589 0509 from 3pm

travelling

Dream
2-15 Sudamch, Kanda, Chiyoda-ku
☎(03) 3258 3592

Doutonbori Gekijo
2-28-7 Dougenzaka, Shinbuya-ju
☎(03) 3463 8006

E & Ca Kikaku
☎(03) 2205 6228 12-10pm

Ersu
☎(03) 3589 4801

Exing
South 4, Wst 3, Green Building 8/F
☎(03) 511 3434

Fellow
2-9-10 Nishi Azabu, Minato-ku, Tokyo 106.
☎(33) 4098008

Hobby
1F 1-13-3 Nishi Shinbashi Minato-ku

Image Pool Solana
(photographic brothel) 495-250 Shimohara
Subashiriasz, Shizuoka ken, 7410-14 Japan
☎(0550) 75 3999 / (03) 3714 9666

Japan Liberated Lifestylist League
K&G 1222-76 Mukaihigashi-Cho,
Onomichi-shi, 722

Korista!
2-17-2 Dogenzaka, Shibuya-ku
☎(03) 3476 4020

Koshitsu-YU
7-12-22 Nishi Shinjuku, Shinjuke-ku
☎(03) 3363 0044

Lope
9F 11F 2-19-7 Takadano-baba, Shinuku-ky
☎(03) 3208 8369

Miyashima
Kamedo-Kitaguchi ☎(03) 3684 1233

Club Nude
2 Floor, My Square Bild, 2-10
Azabujiyuban, Minato-ku, Tokyo

OS Gekijo
7-12-2 Nishishinjuku, Shinjuk-ku
☎(03) 3367 9494

The Paper Moon
Tokyo ☎(03) 3770 8281

Paradox
4-10-212 Udagawa-cho, Shibuya
☎(03) 3770 2026

Queen Bee
#1101 New Ikebukuro H, 1-33-4 Higashi
Ikebukuro,Toshima-ku Tokyo
☎(03) 3590 3775

Room
☎(03) 3354 4573

Osaka

AD
4-3-4 Nishinakajima, Yodogaya-ku
☎(06) 304 8078

Elos no Yakata
Osaka Nanba, Sennichi-Mae
☎(06) 648 0898

Kiyo Club
☎(06) 307 1213

Lemon Club
#408 Nishinakajima, Yodogaya-ku
☎(06) 304 8078

Mickey Mouse Club
Lions Mansion No 202, 1-29-2
Uchihonmachi, Higashi-ku, Osaka 544
☎(06) 5351185

kenya

Sex may, to the foreigner, seem a little wham bang thank you Ma'am: Africans copulate where Westerners kiss, it's so automatic that it seem unerotic to the average Westerner. Prostitutes approach male foreigners looking into their eyes and clasping their dicks. It's sometimes difficult for a foreigner to tell who's on the game and who isn't when you're out at night because many girls think that, if they're going to have sex with you, she may as well charge! AIDS is spreading rapidly and you should be extremely careful.

mombassa

The Castle Hotel in Mombasa is a wild joint and an unfailing source of pick-ups. Lesser know is the **Rainbow Hotel**, where many of the girls have rooms. The **Sunshine Day and Night** is a noisy place with a sexy floor show where both men and women can get what they are looking for very quickly. Lamu is an idealistic little Swahili resort without cars, where beach boys are on the prowl but nude sunbathing and whoring offends locals and it's not unheard of for a naughty tourist to be axed to death. In Nairobi, young trendies meet up

lamu

nairobi

early evening at the **Norfolk Terrace** and the fave rave is **Bubbles**, a tacky meat market for ex-pats. **The Green Bar** is never shut and always full of interesting characters. The main clubs, packed with whores, are the **Modern Green Day & Night**, the **Florida 2000** (both of which are open 24 hours and have rude shows) and **Buffalo Bill's**, the **Beat House** and **New Florida**. Successful film moguls are known to go out at night to these clubs in mini-bus, collect the hookers they like the look of, pack them up and take them home for an orgy. Women don't need to go to bars, men home-in on you if you're unaccompanied. East of Nairobi on the River Road, some local bars are also wild and seductive. Prostitution is rife but eroticism, as I said at the beginning, is lacking.

119

travelling

> collect the hookers they like the look of, pack them up and take them home for an orgy

---

▶ **Kenya addresses - country code (254)**

Beat House
Kimathi Street, Nairobi

Bubbles
International Casino, Museum Hill, Nairobi

Florida 2000
Moi Avenue, Nairobi

Green Bar
Tom Mboya Street, Nairobi

Modern Green Day and Night
Latema Road, Nairobi

New Florida
Koinange Street ☎ 334870

Norfolk Terrace
Harry Thuky Road, Nairobi ☎ (2) 335442

Penfriends Contact Club
PO Box 3092 Kampala, Uganda

Rainbow Hotel off Moi Avenue, Mombassa

Sunshine Day and Night
Moi Avenue, Mombassa

korea (south)

soeul

There's plenty of sex for sale in Soeul, and most massage parlours will do either sex, but professional girls here tend to ridicule Western men for taking such a long time to come. Apparently Korean girls there like it short and often rather than a few long sessions. **Itaewon** is the foreigner's ghetto frequented by homesick GIs. Better go for one of the "yang kong ju" girls, groupies who like Westerners, and hang out in **JJ Mahoneys** in the Hyatt Hotel. **Chongyangni** has local girls who sit in windows, ideal for newcomers. A cyclo, or pedal taxi driver will take you. It's better than the Chonho-dong area of Miari, which is a rabbit warren of shops showing doll-like faces vividly made up in exotic oriental costumes, where foreigners get really second-hand treatment. **Room salons** are over-priced hostess bars for business men, and the **Kisaeng** houses are like Japanese Geisha houses and are monstrously expensive. The girl will play the flute for you, or whatever, but is nowhere near as refined as the Geisha. If you want to enjoy the company of a Korean girl while you are there, all you have to do is advertise in a student rag offering English lessons. Over-paid Mama-sans and rich, bored women are apparently visiting *host bars* to spend their money on young *chebis* — male prostitutes. Blind masseuses are on call in hotels, and girls work in barber shops sucking you off as you get your haircut.

professional girls here tend to ridicule western men for taking such a long time to come

latvia

Hotel Latvia in Riga has sexy shows with lovely looking artistes, and plenty of whores to choose from. All the hotels have a lot of prostitutes sitting waiting for custom. This is only the second place in the world to legalise homosexual marriage.

the second country in the world to legalise homosexual marriage

macau

This is more of a gambling den than a sex capital but the Crazy Paris show at the **Hotel Lisboa** is cleverly staged and imaginative.

malaysia

kuala lumpur

The new Jalan Pinang nightlife centre in Kuala Lumpur is all very clean and straight. The **Tin Mine** at the Hilton is still the most civilised place to find women who want to trade sex for cash. Chow Kit Road, Hicks Mansions and Brickfields are renowned for their whores. In Georgetown, Penang, men can just sit in your rickshaw and wait for the question, "you want *gig-gig*?". In order of increasing price, you have three choices: local Malay girls in specific hotels; Chinese massage where you can pick your girl once you arrive at the parlour; or an Indian or Bangladesh girl. The censorship here is very repressive and even female/male kissing and hugging in public is banned.

you want *gig-gig*?

Ipoh's raunchy night life is no more, and the town is deserted by 10pm but there are still massage parlours. **Rainbow City** is a nightclub where anyone can go but it's full of businessmen being chatted up by hookers. **The Titiwangsa** has a younger crowd.

121

▶ **Malaysia Addresses country code (60)**

Rainbow City
Jalan Sultan Idris Shah, Ipoh ☎ 508 961

Titiwangsa
274 Jalan Sultan Iskandar, Ipoh ☎ 501 202

travelling

mexico

mexico city

In Mexico City, the **Bar Blue Beard (Barba Azul)**is the classic and most stylish of the whores' bars where the trendy people hang out for fun. It has a resident band of dwarfs and alternative people, crazy-lady wall hangings and a beautiful atmosphere. You can find it near the local working class red light district of the Garibaldi area of Mariachis, close to downtown. Here dwells the most excellent hardcore sleaze, with vaudeville burlesque, tranny shows and mud wrestling. More popular with the tourists and middle classes is the district called the pink zone, or Zona Rossa, between Reforma and Insurgentes Streets. The **Sambors La Americas** is *the* TV place on Insurgentes, the top cruising spot for gays and transvestites arriving later at night. Whorehouses are known by taxi drivers. *Tiempo Libre* only lists arty events but the *Lucha Libre* magazines list the erotic wrestling matches where the women go crazy because of their fetishistic appeal. There are no fetish clubs as such, but fetish wear is exhibited in the trendy night clubs and raves which have a Fellini style decadence about them. Acapulco is a resort used by Americans and the **Tabares Club** puts on

acapulco

the most excellent hardcore sleaze, with vaudeville burlesque, tranny shows and mud wrestling

santiago

famous strip artistes. **Cozumel Sun Socials** run on-premises swing parties and B&B on the Caribbean coast and **El Refugio de Pepe Telaranas** is a private nature reserve in Santiago, welcoming swingers with in their glamorous thatched cottages. There are no more donkey shows on the border towns but many of the San Diego kids venture down to Tijuana to slam dance in

Red Square, **Fierro's** and **Iguana's**.

▶ **Mexico Addresses**
country code (52)

Cozumel Sun Socials
Apatardo Postal 251 Cozumel, Quintana Roo, East Mexico

El Refugio de Pepe Telaranas
Santiago b/fax 333 30616
European fax ☎ 31-20 266 680

Tabares Club
Bellavista 131, Fracc. Farallon, Acapulco, Gro Mexico

tijuana

122

new guinea

travelling

At the Yam harvest, there's free-for-all sex. Sex is very much female-led here and often takes place in the day. Port Moresby is a tropical Harlem — you need to be equipped with a fast car and the skill of Nigel Mansel, otherwise they land on you.

new zealand

Buying a copy of **The Truth** will give you a good idea about what's happening, as it has an eight-page adults-only section, and offers surprisingly frank personal ads. It's sold in most dairies (grocery stores) and bookstores. New Zealand's first fetish club, **The Midnight Club**, has opened in Auckland and is on every Friday 10pm-late. S/M is very popular in the brothels and most of them offer

auckland

escort agencies offer group sex and a wide range of services

domination, golden showers, etc., the best to be found at **Rack & Cape**. **L'Amour**, the fetish sex shop, publish a magazine called **Fetish** which has personal contact ads. Escort agencies offer group sex and a wide range of services. **Laura's** has men, women and couples available as escorts and provide for all kinds of sex including fantasy and voyeur sessions. **The Establishment Lodge** is a sauna with fantasy suites on hire to couples and friends for swinging, and tasty women on hire too. The commercial area is in Fort Street. K Road (Karangahape Road) is now pretty dead for sex. The **Firehouse** is a strip review where one man is snatched from the audience and treated to all kinds of pleasures such as a nude shower on stage. It's open seven nights a week and packs them in with local and overseas performers such as the *Electric Blue* girls. The **Sunset Strip Review** in Fort Street also arranges for girls to come from all over the world to star in their shows. **Superstar a Go-Go Bar** shows Thai women doing pole dancing. The **Staircase** is the gay club and *Out!* the gay magazine with listings runs a healthclub/sauna and info shop for

international stars such as nina hartley performing

gays and bis. **Coverboys** offers male escorts. You can buy hardcore porn only from the sex shops but it's good quality and value for money. Beautifully painted dicks are on show to be admired on the wooden statues at the **Arataki Visitor Cenre**. It is illegal for streetwalkers to offer sex, so you have to ask. In Wellington, they stand at either end of Marion Street, off Vivian Street, real women one end and TV/TSs the other — see if you can work out which! More are on Cuba Street. Check out the entertainment classified ads in *Dominion* and the *Evening Post* for what you want. The most active swing club is the **New Zealand Swing Club** which holds parties on the last Saturday of the month here and occasionally in various cities around the country and, although they started out pretty tame, swingers have become more adventurous now, thanks to the encouragement of the proprietors, Koos and Denise. Their A5 glossy magazine *Eros* gives little

wellington

away about the parties but includes readers' letters, hard core photos and personal ads. The **Paradise Club** is newer, holding monthly events run by Francis & Phylis in various venues in Wellington. They have a policy to promote safer sex and welcome disabled people. *Private iii* is another national contact magazine published here. Wellington has a classy strip club called **Tiffany's**. Gay and TV haunts include the **Nutcracker**, nick named "The Hole in the Wall", and the late night cafe, **Evergreen**. A local weird magazine called *Killer Kung Fu Enema Nurses* lists some of the underground activity.

In Christchurch, **Route 66** is a night club and restaurant providing both male and female strippers, with international stars such as Nina Hartley performing on special nights. **Alley Cats** is a disco with theme nights. The largest spa offering sauna/massage sex is **Alamen** and the **Carlton Lounge** provides non-stop fun. **Select** hires both male and female escorts. Ghuznee Street, off Cuba Street mall downtown, has some seedy strip clubs. At the other end of the spectrum, up in the mountain range on the West of the Island, right at the bottom of a glacier lies a sumptuous hotel, ideal for sex, called **The Hermitage**. Quite out of this world.

In Dunedin, **Club 118** is a free admission disco on Wed-Sat. **Penthouse** is a nightclub with fun contests. **Taipei** has Kareoke and dancing. **Reflections** is a sumptuous brothel and **Golden Scenes** a friendly new dive.

christchurch

travelling

dunedin

Auckland (code 9)

L'Amour
St Kevin's Arcade, K Road, ☎790 497 and 270 Onewa Road, Birkenhead
☎480 140 (PO Box 34-554, Birkenhead)

Coverboys
☎623 1094

Don't Tell Mama
disco 340 Karangahape Road, Newton
☎79 0320

The Establishment Lodge
☎360 2832

The Firehouse
18 Fort Street ☎3580956 / 309 6560

Geisha Bath House
55 Customs Street ☎79 2394

Laura's
597 Sandringham Road, Sandringham
☎846 4598

Leather Headquarters
888 Karangahape Road at Howe

The Midnight Club
37 Albert Street

Mistress Kane & Mistress Zelda
☎846 2065

Out! bookshop
1st Floor, Dixon St ☎385 4400

The Rack and Cape
☎849 6400

Shop Six
adult mags 44 Queen Street ☎3733 771

The Staircase Superstar a Go-Go Bar
13 Gore St, off Fort Street ☎302 0748

Wellington (code 4)

Adult Bookstore
Corner of Cuba & Vivian Streets

Affairs Escorts
☎47 222 52

Carlton Lounge
☎65 0504

Exclusive Adult Store
119 Manners Street

Killer Kung Fu Enema Nurses
(£2/US$5 PO Box 27432 Upper Willis Street, Wellington

Liks Ladies Bar
(male strip, Thurs-Sat) 141 Vivian Street

New Zealand Swing Club
PO Box 27-350/1st Floor, 14 College Street
Wellington ☎(4)38 48 214/801 5909 / 801 5964

The Paradise Club
PO Box 656 Wellington

Private iii
PO Box 40-279, Upper Hutt

Tiffany's
143 Vivian Street, Wellington ☎384 7516

Christchurch (and Mount Cook) code (3)

Adam & Eve
sex boutique 539 Colombo Street
☎379 4916

Alamen Escorts
☎66 7698

Alley Cats
152 Manchester Street ☎77 2703

Firehouse
293 Colombo Street, Sydenham ☎332 9208

Hermitage Hotel
Mount Cook ☎435 1809

Route 66
103 Armajh Street ☎77 2832

Select Outcall
Service ☎66 7667

Dunedin code (3)

Club 118
118 High Street ☎477 0752

Golden Scenes
☎442 6812

Penthouse
The Mall, Queenstown ☎442 7575

Reflections
☎474 1367

Taipei Cabaret
163 Rattray Street ☎477 7403

travelling

norway

oslo

In summer, Oslo becomes Scandinavia's nightlife capital. People boogy night and day on Karl Johan where clubs stay open till 4-5am. It is the home of one of the most advanced sex magazines in the world, *Cupido* which, despite its PC devotion not to be sexist or ageist etc, still gets attacked by local anti-sex feminists. Oslo's **erotic fleamarket** sells antiquarian books and postcards and old Swedish porn every Saturday morning 7am onwards, in Neuberggata. The **Oslo Piercing Studio** is open Monday, Wednesday, Friday 17.00-20,00, Saturday 13.00-18.00, where you can ask about the sexy happenings of the moment. Their club, **Colorful People** has irregular events and but their contact magazine lists ads from devotees of genital depilation, erotic tattooing, piercing and fun with body play. All this is run by a sweet guy called Havard Frisell. Norway has its own branch of **SMil**. It also has its very own pissing club, **Urolo-gnisten** in which the 2 female and 17 male members who live all around the country, liaise somehow on their favourite subject.

very own pissing club

▶ **Norway Addresses country code (47)**

125

Colorful People
PO Box 617, Sentrum 0106 Oslo

Cupido
Hverdag as, Postboks 9121 Grønland, 0133 Oslo (22) 42 94 50 fax 42 94 55

The Oslo Piercing Studio
Munkegt 1 (Gamlebyen) 0656 Oslo
☎(47) 22199265

SMil
Box 3456 Bjølsen 0406 N-Oslo 4
☎(47 2) 712342

Urolo-gnisten
Collector's Shop, Bok 201, 7001 Trondheim

travelling

philippines

manila

There is more guilt about sex in the Philippines than Thailand and places further south, because the Filipinos are mostly Catholic. There are also many violent crimes. However, much fun is still to be had, even though Ermita, the famous red light district of Manila is gone. Pacea is its modern replacement, near the Holiday Inn, and Mikati is still filled with jumping clubs along Jupiter

sabang

Street, especially at the **Papillon Club** and **Ritzy's** which has its own "Dave's Corner" for horny ex-pats. Sabang, on the beautiful isle of Mindoro, is dedicated to safe enjoyments. It has great

quezon city

discos with plenty of pretty, willing locals, who cater to your every whim and prostitution carries no stigma here. Quezon City has some of the best clubs, all open till 3am and customers in the Philippines are welcome to join in the bar sex shows. The girls of Daupan are said to give the best head. If you get to the Igorot tribal villages and pay your respects, you can be invited to attend to the needs of the young women who live in special huts until they get pregnant.

daupan

Poland has sex shops selling hard core, striptease at clubs and cafés, peep shows and sex cinemas in all large towns. Polish women seem to want to have fun freely with Westerners and hope that you bring in condoms as they hate their own brands. Brothels are illegal but ads in papers such as the daily *Zycie Warszawy* list them, as well as individual call girls, under "Social agencies" or *Towarzyskie.* *Mac Paraiadka,* an anarchist magazine, contains some hard core imagery. *Seksrety* is a home-grown sex mag with personals for all orientations including S/M. *Kontakt* is more for singles and marriage. *Filo* for gays in Gdansk, *Men* for macho guys in Warsaw. The gays are the best organised for sexual freedom — everything else is a bit of a mess with prosecutions taking place and pressure from the "Christian" parties. No clubs for S/M or swinging have yet been formed.

a home-grown sex mag with personals for all orientations

▶ **Poland Addresses**
country code (48)

Filo
box 733 80-958 Gdansk 50

Kontakt
Wojska Polskiege 78 70-481 Szczecin

Mac Paraiadka
PO Box 67, 81-806 Sopot 6.
Send cash donation

Men!
Warynsskiego 6 m,89, 00-631 Warsaw

Seksrety
PWU Baltyk box 65, 75-350 Koszalin 9

travelling

lisbon

People in Lisbon are generally eager to meet foreigners to demonstrate their hospitality and new liberal attitude. The avant-garde **Alcantora**, and the **Hypopotamus** and **Night and Day** are all good clubs to meet locals in. The **Elephanto Branco** is a relaxed and expensive girl bar with a good atmosphere and music. The **2+2** in Lisbon is a small disco with a restaurant section catering to liberal singles and couples.*Sexy Club* and *Sexologica* both carry hookers' and personal ads. There are about 200 whores on the rua Benformosa where it meets the Avenida Reis and rua Nova de Carvalho is still the place for little bars heaving with hookers, such as the **Texas** and **Oslo** bars. The **Tokyo Bar** in the midst of them is, by contrast, an upmarket disco. Biarro Alto also has many street walkers. To the north of Lisbon is Christine Stevenson's fetish holiday and retirement home, **Casal Do Sandre**, with special weekends for certain tastes.

▶ **Portugal Addresses**
country code (351)

Casal Do Sandre
Largo do Sandre No 8, 2500 Caldas da Rainha ☎(62) 23891 (& fax).

2+2
Praca Prof. Santos Andrea II, R/CD (ground floor right), 1500 Lisbon

little bars heaving with hookers

puerto rico

Men are respectful of whores here, that's why the brothels are so great. The **Black Angus** in San Juan is legendary, where exotic women cluster around you in the bar. San Juan has a street called "The Street of Demented Drivers". It's where all the sex motels are and all the cars have men talking away, as if to themselves, as their passenger crouches down so as not to be seen. If you want to try one of these motels, they are well-known by the taxi drivers, who will take you to a nice one, and you can pay by the hour or night.

russia

Club X is the new S/M and fetish club in Moscow and **Lis's** is a new huge club with a disco, gambling den and striptease joint. The red light district is near the Leningradskaya Hotel but you don't have to venture there to be propositioned. Thousands of women are on the game and a recent survey of Moscow schoolgirls showed over

permousova runs a school for stripping and has fifteen men on her course

half of them want to become hard-currency prostitutes. Hotel rooms are guarded by fierce *babushkas* but bribery will get your guest into your room, if only till 2am. The **Mezhdunarodnay** restaurant and **National Hotel** are both notorious.

The police go along with it all quite happily. There's a lively ex-pat scene at places like **Rosie O'Grady's**. **Alla Permousova** runs a school for stripping and has fifteen men on her course of 40 pupils. The Russian magazine **Cupidon** is a feeble copy of the Norwegian **Cupido**. 20,000 gays marched on Gay Pride in St Petersburg in 1994 and there's now an extremely arty and useful sexzine for gay men in Russian called **Partners** which reviews products and provides networking and contacts.

▶ **Russia Addresses country code (7)**

Partners
c/o Misha Gladkin, Glavpochtamt Do Vostrebovaniya, Moscow 10100

Rosie O'Grady's
ul. Znamenka 9, Moscow ☎ (095) 203 9087

Club X
Maxim Koltovoi, Seleznevskaiastrasse 30-2-3, 103473 Moscow

glasgow

travelling

Glasgow hosts a regular swingers' get-together on the first Wednesday of the month called **The Glasgow Grope**, a no-pressure laid-back night with little overt sex but much teasing and the odd sly wank in the corner. Varying their venues from pubs, clubs and saunas, they don't mind what age or shape you are but most are in their 30's and 40's and they welcome disabled people. They hold special parties for events such as the Worldcon Science Fiction convention (August '95 in Glasgow). Most of the women are passively bi, and safer sex is the norm. Many enjoy car sex (*not* called "dogging" up here) and seek out safe locations such as Stratchclyde Country Park, Fairlie Car Park and 'the bowl' where exhibitionists can have fun by leaving their interior car lights on and hope for an appreciative audience. The **Glasgow Forum Group** is similar but less adventurous. The local contact magazine is *Scottish Contacts*. The club scene includes several bi and gay clubs: **Club X** being popular with straights, bis and gays but very smokey. **Bennett's** is the famous gay disco. The longest running Friday night of alternative slamming is

over 1,500 women on the game in glasgow

Crash at the **Cotton Club.**
Most Glasgow saunas offer sex for sale where the workers are young, enthusiastic and offer a safe and straightfoward service. They are listed in Yellow Pages. There are over 1,500 women on the game in Glasgow and many of them are on the street and are junkies. They stand around Waterloo Street in the day and on Glasgow Green. TV cameras now operate in these red

much teasing and the odd sly wank in the corner

light districts 24 hours a day. The best prostitutes operate out of flats in the older part of Glasgow, offering a discreet and safe service, advertising in the *Daily Sport*. They are experienced and in control of their own lives, not to be messed with and their charges are moderate. Rent boys operate out of the **St Vincent's toilets** catering to covert bisexual men. Much of this activity is unsafe and violent. Exotic dancers, both male and female, offer hetero escort services through ads the contact magazines. Porn is available in the Barras market, where you can sometimes spot local amateur tapes. Edinburgh has better massage parlours and there's hardly any street action because the police are too heavy. **The Executive Sauna** is always highly praised and the Leith/docks area whores are not advisable because of health risks. The **Angel Escort Agency** and the **Eden** are OK. There's a new "gay quarter" around Leith Walk and the

edinburgh

> *the executive sauna is always highly praised*

gay clubs are the most interesting, with everybody going. Next door to The Playhouse in the Broughton Triangle is
CC Blooms, the new bar of this type, which has free entrance every night and dancing

downstairs. **Chapps Club Bar** is leather and denim. **Sessions** is a pick-up bar in Cowgate, but a bit rough, Leith has the most liberal licencing in the UK with bars staying open all day and late into the early hours. English girls work at one end of Aberdeen harbour's Regent Quay, and local girls at the other! The nearest sex shops and porn cinemas are in Newcastle. Stag nights are sometimes advertised in local papers around Scotland and you buy your ticket the day before. The Royal Bank of Scotland has stated that it is prepared to issue transvestites with two cheque-cash cards — one with their male persona photo on it and the other with the female persona.

aberdeen

travelling

▶ **Scotland addresses**

Bisexuals and TV dating line
☎ (0336) 426322

Body Positive Lothian
☎ (0131) 652 0754

CC Blooms
23 Greenside Place, Edinburgh

Chapps Club Bar
22 Greenside Place, Edinburgh
☎ (0131) 558 1270

Cotton Club
5 Scott Street Glasgow 3

Couples dating line
☎ (0336) 411290

Edinburgh Lesbian, Gay and Bisexual Centre
58a Broughton Street, Edinburgh EH1
☎ (0131) 557 3620

Executive Sauna
Rose Street, off Princes Street, Edinburgh

Glasgow Forum Group
c/o Forum Society, PO Box 418
Cardiff CF24XU

Scottish Contacts
PO Box 1396 Glasgow G4 9JJ

Sub/Doms phoneline
☎ (0336) 425404

Swingers Dating Line
☎ (0336) 426310

singapore

Singapore has everything available to the horny traveller, you just need to know where to look. It's the area called Gaylang, where grope bars, massage parlours and aquaria (brothels where you chose the whores through a window) thrive. There are no street hookers so you go to clubs and brothels. Censorship laws have been relaxed so erotic movies are shown in cinemas. Terror stories of Thai girls going to Japan for S/M clubs and never returning seem to keep local interest in S/M to a minimum. **Orchard Towers**, nicknamed "The HQ", houses fascinating whore bars: **Top Ten**, **Caesar's** (best for good-lookers, including transsexuals from Thailand, women also come here too to hire professional women for the night) **392** and **Payton Place** (best for Filipinos). There's a huge disco called

Zouk where young people go to find each other, gay and straight. **Xanadu** is the best place to find Japanese tourist girls who act like Essex girls on the Costa Brava and are known as 'squeakers'. For swinging, join the **Singapore Fun Club** run by Tommy Li & Nok. The Bugis Street transvestites and transsexuals have moved to

orchard towers, nicknamed 'the HQ', houses fascinating whore bars

Changi Village and the darker stretches of Orchard Road although they can still be found in the Bugis Street bars **Boom Boom** and **Ding Dong**, both of which are good fun.

▶ **Singapore addresses - country code (65)**

Caesar's
#02-46 Orchard Towers ☎ 737 7665

Boom Boom
2-4 New Bugis Street ☎ 339 8187

Ding Dong
☎ 339 1026

Singapore Fun Club
PO Box 218 Robinson Road,

Singapore 9004
Top Ten
#05 18A Orchard Towers ☎ 732 3022

Zouk
17-21 Jiak Kim Street ☎ 738 2988

south africa

porno, feather boas, tit clamps and gays snogging in the streets

With their new freedom, so much is developing so fast, any specific listings will be out of date before we turn round. The new explosion of sexual expression is beyond most South Africans' wildest dreams. You can see porno, feather boas, tit clamps and gays snogging in the streets. South Africa's proposed new constitution states "No person shall be unfairly discriminated against, directly or indirectly, and without derogating from the generality of this provision on. . . grounds of . . . sexual orientation." and the populace are being invited to write in with their views. Thai prostitutes and other illegal immigrants are flooding in. Durban, being the holiday area, has always had more entertainment than other cities and **Monk's Inn** has strip, the **Med** has wet T-shirt competitions and whores ply their trade in the **Smugglers Inn**. Swaziland has erotic sex shows, with the **Wild Coast Casino** showing blue movies.

durban

131

travelling

▶ **South Africa Addresses country code (27)**
Phoenix Society (for TVs)
PO Box 58 Wits 2050

spain

"Puta bars" advertise their services to motorists with huge red neon signs and prostitution is quite open here. *Sade* is the name of the Spanish S/M magazine which lets you know what's happening, which isn't a lot, because, so they claim, it's just too hot for dressing up in rubber and leather. However, they do have **Club VSA**, an S/M restaurant

madrid

Madrid no longer feels like a simmering cauldron of ecstasy it felt like in the late 80's. What was all-night self-discovery in clubs is now self-help groups and drag queens carrying ACT UP banners. The best live sex show is at **Rossy's Topless**, only 400 yeards from the Chamartin railway station. Gigolos and transvestite hookers hang out in the Pasea de la Castellana. For swingers, there's the **Acuarela Pub** with small room for sex and **Bar Trevi**, a swing bar which holds weekend parties. A very good hygienic luxurious sauna called **Ladys** has girls and transvestites to massage clients, and some nights it turns into a lovely orgy house.

Up in Bilbao, the people are completely different. Very physical, sexy and the women seem to have the upper hand.

bilbao

chickens and children and musicians and washing and whores all mill around

Being a single girl means you get a three tiered evening, squeezing in all your affairs in. Once married, you become surrounded by kids and family and hubby goes out for nooky. There's a fabulous red light street up the hill, behind the Station, where chickens and children and musicians and washing and whores all mill around. With lots of fun in the streets early evening with everyone drinking outside the bars,

off into the back rooms for "habitacion" together. At Privé, couples get formally introduced. Perhaps the best sex theatre in Europe is the **Bagdad**, with its Persian style décor and genial staff. The acts vary from elegant, almost balletic, screwing to bawdy blowjobs with the audience and outrageous kinky surprises. Married couples and business associates lap it up every night.

from elegant, almost balletic, screwing to bawdy blowjobs with the audience

travelling

barcelona

you can't fail to enjoy this pretty city. Barcelona's red light district has moved from the Ramblas to different areas all over town and it's difficult to recommend anywhere as this move is so recent, and nothing properly established. To find what you want, look in one of the local guides available in all kiosks, *Guía del Ocio* or the sexier one, *Guía del Ambiente.* Beware: if you get in a cab and ask for a club, this means a brothel here (as opposed to a disco). Cab drivers are not too sympathetic to women looking for a good time — they disapprove! Barcelona is not a nice place for women travellers. Swing clubs insist you come as a couple. The **New Kira** run by Eduardo Molina Arias is perhaps the best one to go to, as it is at least set up for sex, whereas the **Blau Nit** and **Rubens** have no beds, tissues or showers. At Blau Nit the husbands wear dinner jackets while the wives sing romantic songs and, somehow or other, couples decide to disappear

torremolinos

Many Spanish swingers go to the lovely naturist resorts on the Costa del Sol to enjoy themselves. **Costa Natura**, **El Portus Naturist Campsite**, **Vera Playa Naturist Campsite**, and the **Vera Hotel** which also gets German swingers in the summer. You can find ads for swingers, whores, dungeons and singles in the English language *El Sur*, which is free, under the heading Adult Relaxation. The **Club Cupido** in Torremolinos advertises here as being for couples only on Saturdays, and it's supposed to be good fun. **La Marioneta** is a holiday home for S/M, Subs/Doms and TVs near Alicante, run by an English woman. Fuengirola has a tiny red light area with **The Amsterdam** sex shop by the bus station and Malaga's girlie bar area is by the station where the trains arrive from Torremolinos. Just across the border from

costa del sol

fuengirola

malaga

la linea Gibraltar in La Linea, there are hundreds of whorebars and brothels, ask any taxi driver for a bordello.

Seville's Almeada de Hercules is the red light district with trannies on the NE side. If you walk up the streets north of here, you can have a competition as to who will be first to catch a whore who's still got a tooth left.

seville

On Mallorca, the official nudist beach is the pretty, if tiny, Platgo Mago, near Portals Vells, south of Magalluf. Sex shops here have slot machines to play porno videos which cost the same price as buying one (£25), and the "Top Less" bars have no topless women in them, just overpriced drinks to buy for the rather dreary looking hostesses.

mallorca

Ibiza is a much more sophisticated island. **Netty's Sun Paradise** has tiny self-catering swing & sun villas attracting a laid-back stylish European crowd, many Dutch and Germans

ibiza

who don't speak English. They mingle in the pool and at the weekly barbeques. The villas are surrounded by pine forests and only 12 mins from Ibiza Town. **Pikes Hotel**, owned by flamboyant playboy Tony Pike, has sexy rooms and is run with fun in mind. It has a restaurant overlooking the beautiful pool and poolside bar. Set inland, it's not far from Ibiza Town. All beaches are topless but the nude beach is quite the most relaxing and friendly, called Es Cavallet, 10 miles from Ibiza Town near the airport.

133

The island of Formentera has mud bathing, which some people find erotic, partly because, in the mud swamp, the clay, salt and sulphur rejuvenates your skin. You feel so weightless, young and look as if you're covered in rubber.

formentera

The messy enthusiasts in the *Reaching* section will tell you more. The loveliest beach on the island is Illetas and nude sun bathing takes place in sheltered coves.

travelling

▶ **Spain addresses - country code (34)**

Acuarela Pub
Paseo de la Chopera 9, Madrid
☎ (1) 473 4018

Bagdad
C/Conde del Asalto 103, Barcelona
☎ (3) 242 0777)

Bar Trevi
Las Fuentes 13, Madrid

Costa Natura
Carretera de Cadiz, Estapona, Malaga
☎ (95) 2801500, fax 280 2800

El Portus Naturist Campsite
☎ (68) 553052

La Marioneta
Calle Pare Pere 35, Denia 003700
☎ (6) 642 1175

New Kira
Font Honrada 24 (parallel to Pza Espana), Barcelona
☎ (3) 4263091 (1pm-2am)

Netty's Sun Paradise
Apt 55, Cala Llonga 0784 Sta.
Eulalia del Rio, Ibiza. b/Fax (71) 339 143,
or call Mike in London on
☎ (0171) 373 5388.

Pikes
San Antonio, Ibiza ☎ (71)342222

Privé
Paseo San Geruasio 1.1o, 2a, Barcelona

Vera Playa Naturist Campsite
Vera, Almeria ☎ (51) 456575

Vera Hotel
Carretera Garurcha-Palomares, Vera,
Almeria ☎ (51) 467475 fax 467413
POBox 21 41080 Seville

weightless, young
and look as if
you're covered in rubber

stockholm

To find out what's happening in Stockholm, head for the **Soho Erotic Shop**, open only Wednesday, Friday and Saturday afternoons and evenings, selling mags, videos and toys. Every Thursday, for example, there's **Extract**, a fetish club which meets in different venues. Any night of the week, a visit to **Hjarter Dam** will bring you into contact with local pervs. It's Madame Kertin's restaurant where slaves are sometimes tied to table legs and fed out of dog bowls. Mostly gay, they have special nights. Their 10th anniversary was celebrated in Stockholm on 28th May 1994, with a kinky party and their birthday is always celebrated. **Royal Madness** is the name of the new kinky party / dress code happenings in Stockholm. They happen about six times a year in a restaurant with a disco and are mostly for couples although visitors from out of town are welcome if they get in touch first. **Red Light** is a store with a torture chamber, spanking room, body painting, rubber & leather for sale and videos for hire. Its club is couples only on Saturday nights. **Sunrise** is the

gothenburg

biggest SM club in Sweden and holds parties in Stockholm, Gothenburg and a big summer bash in Linköping. **IPIS**, for pierced couples, meets six times a year at a private swimming pool and sauna, and visit nudist camps in southern Europe. **Black Women's Web** is the local fem dom/male sub group which experiments with erotica and rituals. **Raymond Och Maria** is the local

linköping

friendly swing club attracting young people. The Swedish drag show at **After Dark** is world famous, with Christer Lindarw as the top star. **Pride** is a restaurant café and disco run for and by gays. The local sex paper offering ads is *Aktuel Rapport*. The only sex show is a dull blue movie bar called **Bronx Non-Stop**. Sweden now has **Teleguide**, a computer bulletin board similar to Minitel.

a store with torture chamber, spanking room, body painting, rubber and leather for sale and videos for hire

Black Women's Web
Box 11489, 404 30 Gothenburg

Barbarella
kinky clothes Fjärde Langgatan 6,
413 05 Gothenburg

Hjärter Dam
Polhemsgatan 23, 11230 Stockholm
☎(8) 653 5739
IPIS
PO Box 710 S-114 79 Stockholm
☎(8) 747 1493

Pride
Sveavägen 57, Stockholm ☎(8) 315533

Raymond Och Maria
St Paulsgatan 23 Stockholm

Red Light Club
Roslagsgatan 43, 11354 Stockholm
☎(8) 612 5302

Royal Madness
RMC Box 1469 S-171 28 Solna Sweden

Soho Erotic Shop
Birger Jarlsgatan, Stockholm 15
☎(8) 611 43 93

Sunrise
PO Box 686, S-53116 Linköping
☎(510)17738

135

switzerland

geneva

Geneva is quite a centre for prostitution. Girls come from all over the world and sit in bars such as the **Velvet**, **Griffin** and **La Coupole** to entertain rich bankers and their clients. These are normal bars where everybody goes, so the sexual negotiation goes on quite publically. However, Geneva is unlike the rest of Switzerland and it's not covered in the Swiss sex "what's on" magazine, *SAZ,* otherwise an excellent source to find anything you want with its own guide to top sex salons. Nor is it included in the *SexFuhrer* which lists all the splendid brothels and which night of the week they hold their "open house" for group sex. They work on a rota basis so that, every afternoon/early evening, at least one of them offers a group sex orgy which adventurous couples and single amateur females attend as well as lots of horny men. At **N Stich**, in Zurich, a nice flat in a run-down block, a single man would pay 400 Swiss Francs to enter and orge with 5 call girls, 4 couples and 2

single girls. **Swiss Girls** has parties on Wednesdays and Saturdays, 7.30-10.30pm. The rota in *Sexführer* is under the name *Partyübersicht*. One incredibly gorgeous whorehouse called **Club Villa Merlin** offers itself as the new Wednesday swing venue between Zurich and Rapperswil, complete with pool, hot whirlpool, love-pavillion in the garden and sexy beds. Most of the hooker action in Zurich is in Niederdorfstr by the river. S/M is totally legal and professionals are said to be much harder here than elsewhere. The

travelling

work on a rota basis so that every afternoon/early evening, at least one of them offers a group sex orgy

Swiss S/M mag is called *Sadanas*. The annual **Eccentric Fashion**, the original grand fetish clothing event is still put on with humour every October in the mountains of Switzerland. On the swinging scene, **Fantasyland** throws frivolous couples nights in Zurich, where food and drinks are supplied.

▶ **Switzerland addresses - country code (41)**

Le Club 42
(S/M) Bahnhofstr 42, 8600 Dubendorf
☎(01) 281 8374

Eccentric Fashion Weekend
Postfach 1, CH 4857 Riken AG
☎(062)44 2221 fax 44 1181

Etablis Etablis
Stampflistr 47, Zurich ☎(01)462 9739)

Fantasyland
Marzenbuhlstr 14. CH 8102
Oberebgstringen/Zurich ☎(41) 7505750

N. Stich
Weststr 166, Zurich ☎(01) 272 2564

Sexführer
S-F Verlag Postfach 552, 8052 Zurich
☎(077) 63 45 03

Swiss Girls
Neugasse 84, Zurich ☎(01)-272 25 64)

Villa Merlin
Tödistrasse 9, 8700 Küsnacht
☎(01) 9109101

travelling

tahiti

There's little prostitution here as girls have sex with strangers so readily. Men say they've never been chased so hard (or determinedly). Papeete has plenty to do after dark, with young groovers frequenting the **Mayana Club**. Gillet Dan and Ruth welcome swingers from abroad, entertaining you in their luxurious swing house. They will fix you up with accommodation and contacts. On the other end of Papeete, the French military men dance with Tahitian transvestites at the **Piano Bar**, and the **Bounty** and **Lido** offer a colourful night of whoring. ▶

Tahiti Addresses

Tahitian South Paradise Islands Swing Club
c/o Dan & Ruth PO Box 2781 Papeete, SSP Tahiti

papeete

men say they've never been chased so hard

taiwan

taipei

Singles bars, dance clubs and sauna parlours have hit Taipei. The area between Chung Shan North Road and Lin Shen Street is known as the Combat Zone but most of the hostess bars have moved to Lin Shen North Road, particularly those catering to the Japanese, and Song Jiong Road, Tzang Tsung Road, Ge Lin Road and Min Shen East Road. The **S&M** is not a fetish bar but the name used for the **Sun and Moon**, a popular hangout on Taipei's Nanjon East Road! **Absolute** is the best disco, packed with stunning looking Chinese and open till 5am. Many of the street women are in their 60's and 70's, lonely and otherwise sex starved, still aiming at the good life. Nude performances are illegal but are quite common. They even have striptease at funerals! If you're brave, try the wicked treats down Snake Alley (although this is not popular with locals any more and they don't like letting white people in) and if you have time, venture up to Old Peitou for old-fashioned sex in the spas. Locals are now ignoring these areas, preferring instead to go to the sex motels, love motels, the modern saunas and relaxation and recreation clubs. Increasingly popular are the barbers' shops where hairdressing and cosmetics are provided as well as cockdressing and orgasmetics. Even some restaurants provide erotic services. Despite all this, though, locals go off to Thailand for sex!

old peitou

barbers' shops where hairdressing and cosmetics are provided as well as cockdressing and orgasmetics

137

travelling

thailand

thais are sexually soft and gentle

Thais are sexually soft and gentle, an attraction for many Westerners who feel worn out by aggressive sexual tension. Thai girls are considered by many men around the world to be the most beautiful flowers of creation. My advise is to miss Bangkok because it's such hard work. Pattaya is where the real sex-vacationers go, its **Marine Bar** (nicknamed the AIDS capital of the universe) is full of

pattaya

koh samui

amateurs, Phuket is similar but more up-market. Koh Samui is for sex with other holiday ravers. Krabi in the South has Thai and Malay girls (who you can find in bars) and they come home and sing in the bath to you. The incidence of HIV is high amongst professionals, so penetration is ill-advised and condoms should be brought from home.

Bangkok is a huge city and getting around is a nightmare. The tuk-tuk drivers take you

krabi

bangkok

where *they* want rather than to the club you ask for, and taxis are always stuck in traffic. Rumours about underage girls are mostly exaggerated — the main tourist bars, after pressure from the US, have banned all girls under 18. Underage is a Western definition, but one has to realise that this is a Mafia-run country where murder, corruption and exploitation are widespread. However, it's a fun

situation, so be warned. Stay on the street, or in recommended clubs like the **Touch Bar** which is fun for looking and flirting with stunning girls (but don't fuck here because many are junkies). On street level, drink in the laid-back open-air bars or see a go-go sex show at one of the delightful **Kings Castles**. If you fancy a girl in a bar in Thailand, you simply pay what is called a "bar fine" to take her off for sex. The **Rose Hotel**

place to visit: the Thais fall over backwards to satisfy tourists (admittedly for profit) and it's up to us to treat them well in return. The wonderful massage parlours used by locals are not in the red light districts, and hard to find. Don't bother searching for the legendary **Chao Phraya** parlour because the building recently fell down. When choosing one of the red light districts, try Sow Cowboy which is fun, Nana Plaza, which is handy or, late at night, in and around the **Thermae Turkish Baths Coffeeshop**. This is next to the Ambassador Hotel and where all sex-hungry souls end up — either still looking, or semi-satiated.

The famous Patpong has more colour and pace. Four streets, numbered Patpong 1-4 each have different flavours. 1 and 2 are for heteros, 3 is for gays and 4 is for Japanese and Taiwanese businessmen. Never allow a tout to tempt you upstairs to an exotic show because they will entice you, even if you are a woman, into a total rip-off

is a good place near Patpong where the girls feel comfortable. You must see a live sex show in one of the established theatre bars like **Queen's Castle**, **Lipstick** or **Supergirls**. In these theatres, girlies will come and cuddle men (or women) as you watch the live shows which demonstrate unique and amazing Thai stunts. With well-trained pussies from childhood, Thai girls can shoot ping pong balls across the showbar and snap things off inside themselves. Spectacular, yes, but erotic? You decide. Anyway, you can imagine how these muscular cunts would feel to the dick! Despite these tricks, hetero shows seem rather cold compared with Western sex shows but the gay performances are highly dramatic, with stunning orgiastic effects. They have more style and technique, hard, hot and horny. The **Taraka** is an established massage parlour where couples can go, or women or men on their own — all very pally and social. If you're travelling as a man-woman couple and want to have two girls in a parlour, pick one and then allow her to bring her friend. Otherwise you may get two who don't get along. Westerners might be confused about what to pay for sex, since you will not be asked for a sum directly. I suggest you pay the kind of money it would cost if you went out for a night out back home. English men have a reputation of being mean here. Don't be.

If you don't want to mix in the commercial scene but prefer to enjoy people in Bangkok without paying, hang out in **Brown Sugar** which has a good mix of Westerners and locals. Generally, Thais are fun, respectful and easy going although their own brand of entertainment is rather stiff, with garish singers on stage. Given the slightest encouragement, Thai men show an frantic desperation to screw Western women. However, they don't follow you or harass you. Travelling is safe for women and the prolific prostitution is not in your face. Two recommended massage parlours for women are the barber shop opposite the **Oriental Hotel** Bangkok, and the **Christen** in Phuket. Bangkok's **Monte Carlo** in the **Windsor Hotel** is renowned as the place for women to be seduced by tall, young Thai men. Thais do swing, and clubs are keen to welcome foreigners. There's the **Oriental Swing Club** run by an intelligent couple called Dr. Jim & Polly who are less commercial than

the **Oriental Swinging Club** which publishes several magazines and runs a singles club too. Their swingers meet weekly in a small bar, eyeing each other up, the women looking demure and the men totally unlecherous. Mr Kung Fu, the matchmaker, groups the couples together and packs them off to various sex motels where the swapping and gang bangs take place. Husbands seem to like seeing their wives

renowned as placed for women to be seduced by tall young thai men

serviced. Tours around Thailand are arranged specially when a couple from abroad arrives. Down in *pattaya* Pattaya, there's a little swinging resort called **The Sugar Huts** owned by a swinging doctor. Each hut *koh-samui* has its own pool.

Koh Samui is a blissfully sexy place for a holiday, although there's no nudity on its beaches. Nude beaches in Thailand can be found *haad rin* on Haad Rin or Koh Phengan and *koh phengan* other smaller islands, although local girls here won't undress. Up in the forests of Sila-Rang, an exquisite *sila-rang* resort called **Flower Town** is for gays only.

travelling

► **Thailand addresses - country code (66)**

Brown Sugar
Thanon Sarasinm, Bangkok

Flower Town
Sila-Rang ☎691 5769 ext 2206

Monte Carlo
Sukhumvit Soi 20, Bangkok

Oriental Swing Club / Dr. Jim & Polly
c/o Dr Apichet Nakalekha MD (Personal),

259/12 Patanakarn Rd, Bangkok 10250

Oriental Swinging Club
PO Box 6, Por-Thor-For Klong-Kum, Bangkok 10244 ☎(02) 5390355, fax 5399251

The Sugar Huts
391 Dat 18, Moo 10, Jomtien Road, Pattaya ☎427686

turkey

istanbul

The area of Yükselkaldirim in Istanbul, between the port and Galata towers, has been a red light area of brothels ever since the Empire of Byzantium. Today it has about 30 brothels and hundreds of girls working there, with a police check at the entrance to make sure nobody under 18 enters. Once inside, you can stroll around its narrow streets and look inside the brothels. In the 40's, Turkish authorities decided to control all brothels for better health standards. Designated areas and buildings were selected in each town, and top pimps were employed by the state to organise them. These continue today as the cheap public brothels. There are private and public brothels for men and women in every city. Young Turkish people use them for their first sexual experience.

Nightlife shuts down early but at the foot of the Divan Yolu Cad, you can have a nice time; Istiklad, north of the Horn, is for the more adventurous. Turkish baths are for male visitors only. An English couple run **Seaborne Safaris** flotilla sailing holidays on Turkish wooden-hulled boats for people who like naturism and freedom. Turkey is the first Moslem country to actually have a swing club for couples, and it advertises in the Turkish edition of *Penthouse*. A new group called **Sexual Liberties** is producing a sexual encyclopedia, led by Iskender Savisir, who is also helping Demet Demir in

her fight for the sexual rights of transvestites in Turkey. *Natasha* is Turkey's first home brew sexpaper and a private TV channel, ATV, broadcasts Inside Page Girls. The belated sexual revolution here has introduced private TV channels and legalised marriage for transsexuals.

▶ **Turkey Addresses**
country code (90)

Seaborne Safaris
c/o Independent Holiday Shop (UK)
☎(01962) 877327

Sexual Liberties
c/o Iskender Savasir, Hersey Yayinlari, Dostluk Yurdu Sok, 10/7 Sultanahmet, 34400 Istanbul Turkey ☎(1) 231 4080

public brothels for people who can't afford the private ones

travelling

new york

There are no less than seven sex guides to New York which gives you some idea of the level of erotic potential here. *Screw*, sold on every street corner is the brightest, funniest and makes all the clubs sound fab. *The New York Sex Guide*, *American Sex Scene* and *Climax Times*, all from the same publishers, PSI, list the brothels (here and all over America) with descriptions of the women, their phone numbers, and publish personal stories about their services; *Impulse*, fortnightly, is erotic, intelligent and responsible; *Brutus*, written in Japanese, bends over backwards to give the prices and is lavishly illustrated. Then there's *Mentertainment* which a sweet little magazine, edited by Sophie, on all the table dancing, go-go dancing, burlesque, show'n'tell and

banned vaginal intercourse in commercial clubs in New York City

bachelor/ette party news in New York, New Jersey (and clubs all over the States and Canada).

The state Public Health Council has banned vaginal intercourse in commercial clubs in New York City (oral sex and anal sex have been prohibited since 1985) but condoms are still provided (though often ignored) in **Le Trapeze**. The club gets packed although it's not very

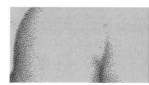

friendly and, if a girl won't play, the husband of the woman *her* husband is fondling, will pull her off him! **Anita's** is a new off-premises party in the Wall Street area. They hold erotic contests, and discreet discussions between interested parties in the dimly lit dining room. There's a new craze in America for bisexual swing clubs. These are mostly off-premises, with **Ambitions** being the first in New York City. **Couples** is a large, off-premises club for a young hip crowd with saucy contests and no pressure, on Saturdays and Sundays on Long Island. New York swingers can now meet up through the voicelines of *The Village Voice* and *New York Press*.

The **Hellfire Club** is now where The Vault used to be, open on Thursdays to Saturdays, your hosts *SM Express* and Leather Underground. The Vault has moved to a different cellar with dark corners with several extra rooms upstairs: special events are held in 'The Studio'. It's BYOB. Each night caters to a special crowd but they're mostly the 'Bridge & Tunnel' brigade wearing shorts and white socks, seemingly content with a rather poor standard of dominant. **Paddles**, New York's other fetish club, has lost its drinks licence but this means that total nudity is now allowed. However, there's a new 'no wanking' policy which enhances their casual couples atmosphere . Slave auctions take place on the third Saturday in the month. Most of the happening S/M in New York now takes place at private parties. Like all major US cities, New York has domination parlours where the client's fetish fantasies are catered to, sometimes with high-powered psychodrama and high energy fun. It's a favourite place to work for many women as they can play "in control" while acting out men's fantasies. There are many to choose from in New York. **The Nutcracker Suite** is the most hi-tech, with baby nurseries, clinical rooms, transformation salons and a Bastille room. **Paradise Lost** is an opulent dungeon with mistresses and a sub, selling psychological manipulation. Two girl at once costs $220 cash.

'body rub' includes prostate massage

New York's sex for sale is competive: 'body rub' includes prostate massage, at least at **Paradise on the Table**. **Aquiesce** is a New York swing club which allows single males in as well as couples and, for $120 men can watch and do what they want for three hours. Every cab driver will say he has a house of pleasure "just for you" and many of them are on Hudson Street. Street hookers can be found in the Theatre district, in Gramercy Park near Third Avenue and around Tomkins Square. You can seek them on foot or in a car. Girls will do it in back alleys if you don't have a car or the price of a

hotel. Otherwise, "short-stay" hotels are listed in *SCREW*. Prices range from $20 for a blow job on 11th Avenue (between 33rd and 24th Sts) to **Cafe au Lait**, an agency supplying young multi-ethnic women at $250 for the first hour to customers on Manhattan only. When you consider that New York women are always complaining that they can never get laid, it's surprising that the agencies hiring men out get so little custom.

wrapping their cards in phoney dollar bills

The **Mirage Agency** attracts a few husbands searching for studs to fuck their wives so they can watch, but gets few females paying for themselves. The sex phone lines are so incredibly competititve in New York that they use scams like wrapping their cards in phoney dollar bills and scattering them through the streets.
There are dozens of fancy Gentlemen's clubs such as **Stringfellows** where customers stuff money into dancers' garters. The ultimate is the **Paradise Club** where anything goes within the realms of Safer Sex including "erotic slow touch dancing", intimate cabaret and porn stars performing on stage. They even have a rock and roll stripper boutique called **Exotic Skinz**. **The Adult Entertainment Centre** is open 24hrs with its new "state of the art peep system". The **Show World Center** has peeps, headlining striptease and encounter booths, sometimes with absolutely dropdead gorgeous chics with dicks. The **All Star Harmony Burlesque** is a

lovely local theatre owned by Dominique who has now put a Mardi Gras (lap dancing) room in the basement so you can talk to the girls in a red-tinged dim light. Since the New York Planning Department began discussions on having just one red light zone in the city, Dominique and Rick Kunis of **Manhattan Video** set up the **Adult Industry Trade Association** in order to at least get the trade in on discussions and planning. The most famous topless/nude dance bar in Manhattan is the **Baby Doll Lounge**. Lunchtime strip is all the rage. Out at Queens there are hundreds of topless clubs where you can drink beer and sometimes get a free buffet. Chippendales is now called **Magique,** a large theatre where females look at muscular men putting on erotic acts never showing their dicks.

She-Male hookers bounce around the meat-packing district on 15th & 16th between 9th & 10th Avenues especially around 2am.The hookers on Eighth Avenue and 43rd Street are all drag queens wandering backwards and forwards from the TV club **Sally's II** up to **Eidelweis.** Eidelweis is open till 4am and has plenty of pre-op trannies (tits and dicks). You can be served by androgynous waiters at **Lucky Cheng's**. **Miss Vera's Finishing School for Boys Who Want To Be Girls** offers ambitious transvestites ballet classes, pedicure, voice training and tea, etc. The **New York Metro D&S Singles** welcomes out-of-town TV, TS, gay, bi, fetishist pagan S/Mers at their parties. The Witches' Ball is held annually on Halloween by **Enchantments**. The **Omega Institute** holds tantra workshops on a regular basis. **The Gay & Lesbian**

travelling

Visitors Center looks after its members when visiting NY or elsewhere, regardless of sexual orientation, age, ethnicity or ableism. **Goddesses** and **Large Encounters** are clubs for large women and men who admire them. *The Shadow* is NYC's Lower East Side's kick-ass underground paper. The East Village is as trendy as ever with the **No Tell Motel** attracting the naughtiest; its sleazy impressario claiming that she matches people up. **Tenth Street Lounge** is an intimidating experience. There's hopping nightlife with clubs like **Squeezebo X** (Friday nights at Don Hill's), **Jackie 60** and **Green Door.** Jackie-60 is a mixed club with female dom/fetish themes and experimental performances such as kinky puppet shows and its own arty publication, *Verbal Abuse*. You can see Robert Mapplethorpe and other outrageous artists' work in the **Whitney Museum**. If you just want to stay indoors, there's sex on cable TV: **Robyn Bird** at 1.30am, **In and Out with Dick** at 12.30 on Channel U and

Screw's **Midnight Blue**.
Manhattan Video is the best video store, **Kinematics** the most fascinating porn shop, **Come Again** the best stocked sex boutique (which also puts on some fun events too). **Saturday Night Lingerie** is the best undie store, **Sizzling Sensations** is good for erotic clothes for men and women, **The Noose** the best bondage store, **The Leather Man** the best leather store for men, and **A Woman's Touch** has the most amazing array of clothing from S/M outfits, go-go outfits to bridal gowns for both women and men. **Purple Passion** sells fetish clothing, jewellery, corsets and toys. **Body Worship** sells fetish fashion and erotica. **Tattooed Love Child** is the best tattoo parlour with special events on Thursdays. The body-mod shop called **Venus Modern Body Arts** offers piercing and branding. There's a jubilant annual "Rated X" Exhibition photo show at the **Neikrug Photographica**.
The Commack is a busy sex motel with waterbeds, jacuzzis and videos out on Long Island and the **Winslow Motor Lodge** is strictly for sex only — complete with mirrored ceilings, sex videos and liberal management. It lies between Philadelphia and Atlantic City, 90 miles from New York City.

jubilant annual 'rated x' exhibition

travelling

▶ **New York addresses**

Acquiesce
☎ (212) 644 1020

Adult Industry Trade Association
c/o Manhattan Video 60 W 39th Street
☎ (212) 354 6890

All-Star Harmony Burlesque
279 Church Street betw Franklin
& White Sts

Anita's
c/o 244 North Avenue #104, New Rochelle,
NY 10808 ☎ (914) 576 4773

Beginnings
(swing) PO Box 851-D, Rahway, New Jersey
07065 ☎ (201) 388 9106

Body Design
☎ (516) 986 8847

Body Worship
112 East 7th Street, NYC 10009
☎ (212) 614 0124

Cafe au Lait
☎ (212) 714 9784 / (0800) 801 9784

Charldene Club
(swing) PO Box 4631 Schenectady NY 12304
☎ (518) 895 2372

Come Again Erotic Emporium
353 East 53rd St, NY ☎ (212) 308 9394

Couples
PO Box 718, Levittown, New York 11756
☎ (516) 5793828

The Commack
2231 Jericho Turnpike, Commack,
New York 11725 ☎ (516) 499 9060

Condomania
351 Bleeker Street, New York NY 10014

Don Hill's
511 Greenwich St ☎ (212) 334 1390

Enchantments
541 E 9th St, New York NY 11105

Eidelweiss
48 W 20th St betw Sixth & Broadway
☎ (212) 255 2829

Eulenspiegel Society
PO Box 2783 Grand Central Station,
New York NY 10163 ☎ (212) 633 8376

Eve's Garden
(feminist boutique) 119 West 57th St,
Suite 420 ☎ (212) 757 8651

Gauntlet
☎ (212) 229 0180

Hellfire
28 9th Ave, between 13th & 14th
☎ (212) 647 0063

Impulse Magazine
7 Oak Place Montclair, NJ 07042
☎(201) 783 4346, fax 783 5057

Jackie 60
on Tuesdays at 432 W 14th St, betw 9th
& Washington, NYC ☎(212) 366 5680

Kinematics
61 W 37th St ☎(212) 944 7561

Large Encounters
☎(212) 836 9000

The Leather Man
111 Christopher St, NY 10014
☎(212) 243 5339

Lesbian & Gay Visitors Center of New York
135 W 20th St, 3rd Floor, NY NY 10011

Love 'n' Kisses Boutique
220 Hempstead Tpke, West Hempstead
NY 11552 ☎(516) 486 5683

Lucky Chengs
1st Ave and 1st St

Magique
1110 First Avenue at 61st St
☎(212) 935 6060

Manhattan Video
60 West 39th St ☎(212) 354 6890

Mentertainment
Box 9445 Elizabeth, NJ 07202
☎(908) 558 9000

Le Mirage Agency
☎(212) 831 5200

Neikrug Photographica
244 East 68th St, New York 10021
☎(212) 288 7741 fax 737 3208

New York D&S Metro Singles
3395 Nostrand Ave # 2, Brooklyn NY 11229
☎(718) 648 8215

The Noose
261 W 19th St, NY 10011 ☎(212) 807 1789

No Tell Motel
167 Avenue A. ☎(212) 475 2172

Nutcracker Suite
☎(212) 674 2294

Omega Institute
☎(914) 266 4444

P. & Pleasure
43 Overidge Road, Latham NY 12110
☎(518) 785 6643

Paradise Club
42 West 33rd St, between 5th & Broadway
☎ (212) 279 0179

Paradise Lost
☎(212) 947 2959

Paradise on the Table
☎(212) 684 6494

Pink Pussy Cat Boutique
161 W 4th St, NY 10014 ☎(212) 243 0077

Pleasure Chest
156 7th Ave South, NY 10014

Purple Passion
PO Box 1139 New York, NY 10113

Sally's II
252 W 43rd Street, NY ☎(212) 944 6000

Saturday Night Lingerie
119 St Marks Place NY 10009
☎(212) 675 3070

The Shadow
($2 each or $15 for 10) Shadow Press,
PO Box 20298 NY NY 10009

Show World Center
669 Eighth Ave at 42nd Street
☎(212) 247 6643

Sizzling Sensations
276 West 43rd Street, NY 10036
☎(212) 819 0080

Stringfellows
East 21st Street

Tattooed Love Child
380 Lafayette St at Great Jones
☎(212) 529 3300

Tenth Street Lounge
212 E 10th St ☎(212) 473 5252

Le Trapeze
17 E 27th St, (betw 5th & Madison) NYC
☎(212) 532 0298

TOM
male j/o group PO Box 10514 Rochester
NY 14610

The Vault
28 Tenth Ave btw Little W 12th & 13th St
New York ☎(212) 255 6758

Venus Modern Body Arts
199 4th Street ☎(212) 473 1954

**Miss Vera's Finishing School for Boys Who
Want To Be Girls**
Veronica Vera, Dean of Students, New
York City ☎(212) 242 6449 / 1-800 844
VERA

A Woman's Touch
124 N Wood Avem Linden NJ 07036 ☎(908)
486 8022

Winslow Motor Lodge
Route 73, Winslow, New Jersey 08095
☎(609) 651 6200 fax 567 9340

travelling

boston and the north east

boston

Kim Airs runs two sex shops in the Boston area called **Grand Opening** which are setting the area alight. They can let you know the hot/cool places to hang out. Mistress Diana and Mistress Bianca hold the annual **B&D Ball** in Cambridge, where dressing up is a must, and they also run small monthly parties.The New England D&S and leather scene is documented in *Diversified Services* which has a calendar of forthcoming events. **Fantasy Nites** is a fetish night every Friday at Manray in Cambridge. Police decoys work the red light district so be warned. For street girls, look in Boylston Street at Newbury, from Atlantic Avenue to Arlington. Pleasure houses are in Charles Street and in Cambridge, and cab drivers know. In the Combat Zone around Washington Avenue, dancers can strip right down. The best clubs are the **Naked I Cabaret** and the **Glass Slipper**. Outside the Zone such things are forbidden. The *Boston Phoenix* has all the ads you'll need. **Moonlight** in is the bisexual swing club, while straight swinging takes place at **Sterling.** There's a sex motel worth visiting: **Creative Pines** which delivers happy service to guests in your huge beds, providing with porno, mirrors and jacuzzis.

connecticut

Connecticut has interesting swing clubs: the **By-Gals Female Mating and Dating Club** and **Senior Service**. **The Grantmoor Motorlodge** has a range of rooms including a gel-bed room and a fantasy disco bedroom. **Cape Exchange** is where they swing club in East Wareham.

happy service in your huge beds

▶ **boston and mass addresses**

B&D Ball
PO Box 1039 Everett, MA 02149 ☎ (617) 397 2853 Modem (617)394 0814

Cape Exchange
PO Box 285 East Wareham MA 02358
b(508) 759 1579

Creative Pines Motel
1518 Memorial Drive, Chicopee
☎ (413) 533 2776

Diversified Services
PO Box 35737 Brighton, MA 02135
☎ (617) 787 7426

Fantasy Nites c/o Diana,
PO Box 1039 Everett, MA 02149
☎ (617) 397 2853

Glass Slipper 16 La Grange Street, Boston

Grand Opening
318 Harvard Street, #32, Brookline, MA

02146 ☎ (607) 731 2626 / in summertime:
3 Freeman St, Provincetown, MA 026570
☎ (507) 487 6655

Innovations in Leather
581A Tremont Street, Boston MA 02118
☎ (617) 536 1546

Naked I Cabaret
666 Washington Avenue, Boston
☎ (617) 426 7462

Northampton's Pride and Joy
erotic boutique in Northampton
☎ (413) 974 8985

Sterling
PO Box 542 Needham Heights, MA 02194
☎ (508) 586 4442

Vernon's TV wear
386 S Moody St, Waltham MA
☎ (617) 894 1744

By-Gals Female Mating & Dating Club
PO Box 778 Branford CT 06405
☎ (203) 481 6448

The Grantmoor Motorlodge
3000 Berlin Turnpike, Newington,
CT 06011. ☎ (203)666 5481

Senior Service
PO Box 2290 Darien CT 06820
Bareware Boutique
3323 Lake Ave, Rochester NY 14612
☎ (716) 621 9355

Club Erotique
PO Box 350 Falls Sta, Niagara NY 14303

R.I. Connection (swing)
PO Box 29097 Providence RI 02909
☎ (401) 351 0165

Middle Door Parties (Swing)
42 Cutts Street, Portsmouth NH 03801
☎ (603) 436 7085

Peter's Palace (fetish store)
Rte One Bypass N, Portsmouth NH 03801
☎ (603) 436 9622

147

travelling

usa
philadelphia and pennsylvania

philadelphia

Philadelphia street girls are rare but can be found lurking in Broad Street and Penn Square. Sex newspapers in street racks list call girls. An old-fashioned brothel where the girls are friendly called **Sophisticated Hideaway** is located in the Society Hill area and **Four Seasons** supplies outcall girls whi will do S/M. **Queens** supplies pre- and post-op trannies. **People Exchanging Power** in Philly is a hot group. *S&M News* comes out of Philadelphia and lists all the local (as well as international) services, including a domination parlour

called **The Pocono Palace of Pleasure and Pain**. **Dressing for Pleasure** is an international held event every November in the Pocono mountains, with treats such as pony races, with prizes for the fastest, best form and best cart as well as many other attractions. **Mr Fashions** is a pervert's dream, tucked away in North East PA, with all sizes of clothes & goods. **The Cottage** is an on-premises swing house with fireplaces and Jacuzzis and nearby skiing at Ski Liberty, welcoming couples for the weekend. They put out a newsletter called *Cottage Times*. The **Sunny Rest** naturist club in Pennsylvania, open only in the summer, has a similar ambiance to **Paradise Lakes**. One correspondent old me that his wife thinks that the men at Sunny Rest are even hornier! **Pocono Paradise** is Pennsylvania's lovely retreat with fantasy rooms and dirty dancing

> **treats such as pony races, with prizes for the fastest, best form and best cart**

parties. Orgy clothes welcome. Jim is in charge. There's a outdoor dance floor and pool at the **The Mountain Retreat,** a log cabin on the top of a mountain, where you can party with other visitors, then sleep in your own camper/tent. Art Rosenblum is setting up his own community called **Germantown Peace Factory** for peace and social change with an open lifestyle

The **Roman V** is the Pittsburg downtown massage parlour, open 24 hours a day where you can get the works for 100 dollars but without much joy. Manual releif is available at the **Shogun Health & Fitness Spa** for about the same. The **Dolphin Bar** on the corner of Broad and Tasker is a rough and tumble inner-city titty joint but over the bridge, on Admiral Wilson Blvd, whores line the highway. Kensington has a wide range of girlies too.

pittsburg

travelling

148

▶ **phiiladelphia and pennsylvania and addresses**

The Cottage
PO Box 3713 Gettysburg PA 17325
☎ (717) 334 0882

Dressing For Pleasure Gala Weekend
c/o Constance Enterprises PO Box 43277
Upper Montclair, New Jersey 07043
☎ (201) 746 4200 fax 746 4722

Fair Exchange (swing)
Pittsburgh ☎ (412) 864 7388

Fetishes for Her
525 S 4th St (at South St), Philadelphia
☎ (215) 592 1617

Four Seasons
1319 Arch Street, Philadelphia
☎ (215) 854 9281

Images Kustom Tattooing & Erotic Piercing
Rt 715 Readers ☎ (717) 629 3029

Mr Fashions
1255 Sans Souci Highway,
Wilkes-Barre 18702. ☎ (717) 829 2224

Germantown Peace Factory
c/o ARF,
5620 Morton Street, Philadelphia PA 19144

Moutain Retreat (swing/nudist)
PO Box 86 Brier Hill PA 15415
☎ (412) 246 8012

North Hills News
(porn & video booths) 7600 McKnight Rad,
Pittsburgh PA 15237 ☎ (412) 367 8182

Our Special Place
(swing) Newcastle
☎ (412) 658 7151

PEP
PO Box 812 Morrisville PA 19067
☎ (215) 552 8155

Pocono Paradise
POBox 411 Wind Gap, PA 18091.
☎ (717) 629 0804 (10am-4pm Mon-Fri).

Pocono Palace of Pleasure and Pain
c/o CSP
PO Box 727 Pocono Sumit PA 18346

Pocono Paradise (swing)
PO Box 441 Wind Gap, PA 18091
☎ (717) 692 0804

Queens Philadelphia
☎ (215) 627 8706

Shogun Health & Fitness Spa
2013 Penn Avenue, Pittsburg
☎ (412) 261 5504

Sophisticated Hideaway Philadelphia
☎ (215) 829 0889

Sunny Rest Lodge
RD1, Box 1050
Palmerton PA 18071
☎ (215) 377 2911 fax (215) 377 9477

Roman V
801 Liberty Avenue, Third Floor, Pittsburg
☎ (412) 391 9870 / 391 9739

S&M News Carter Stevens Presents,
PO Box 727 Pocono Summit, PA 18346

Someplace Special (swing)
Pittsburgh ☎ (412) 898 3063

Stormi Steel Body Piercing
RR#2 Box 2689A, Factoryville PA 18419
☎ (717) 945 7039

washington dc, virginia, maryland and the carolinas

dc

DC Street girls can be found near the Lincoln Memorial and Washington Monument and after 10pm on K Street and Georgetown. Many of the girls here use electronic mail to find clients. Calls girls are listed in sex papers in racks in front of all the main hotels. At **Kimberly's Bath House** you get a bubble bath with the girl of your choice. **Dixie's Escorts** provides a wide range of services from sweet Southern Belles. **Le Marquis** is for domination and fetish fantasies. **The Oriental Spa** is in Elkridge. Many houses have opened up after recent clamp downs. **TLC** events are held for curious and experienced swinging couples betw NYC & DC. **Fantasy Black** caters mostly to black swingers and **Cleopatra's Brother** is the new bisexual swing club. **Party Place** is a fabulous swing house up in Baltimore, with a massage room, a fantasy swing, X-rated movies, seven bedrooms and 5 acres of garden to play in, admitting singles on Fridays and couples on Saturdays. The **Black Rose** offers warm S/M camaraderie & networking and Washington hosts a **Living in Leather** event with competitions for the title of

baltimore

heart-shaped and waterbeds, private jacuzzis

American Leatherman, American Leatherwoman and American Cowboy. The **Great Southern Tattoo Co** is run by liberal and experienced people.

fayetteville

Beck's Motel in North Carolina's Fayetteville has a swingers' noticeboard in the lobby, heart-shaped and waterbeds, private jacuzzis, and friendly staff. The sex parlours here are all traditional massage parlours, the best two being in North Carolina: **Debbie's** in Rocky Mount and **Obsessions** in New Bern. **Rick's** is the place for strippers and star features. **Cathy and Kent Craig** welcome swingers in Raleigh, although they no longer run a club as such. The nicest swing club in Charlotte is **Carolina Friends**, a non-profit club which holds introductory seminars and feverish parties. **Rising Moon Books & Beyond** sell multicultural erotic books for gays, lesbians and straight.

rocky mount

raleigh

charlotte

travelling

149

▶ **dc, virginia and maryland and addresses**

Black Rose
PO Box 11161 Arlington,
Virginia 22210-1161 ☎ (310) 369 7667

Capitol Couples (swing)
PO Box 1000, Ste 262, Merrifield VA 22116
☎ (301) 369 6758

Dixie's Escorts
Washington DC ☎ (919) 220 1452

Dream Dresser Boutique
PO Box 3787, 1042 Wisconsin Ave NW,
Washington DC 20007 ☎ (202) 625 0377

Fantasy Black
PO Box 10083
Washington DC 20018-0083

Good Guys (strip)
2311 Wisconsin Ave NW ☎ (202) 333 8128

Great Southern Tattoo Company 9403
Baltimore Blvd, College Park, MS 20740

Kimberly's Bath House
7616 Georgia Avenue NW, Washington
☎ (202) 829 7293

Living in Leather Jose Ucles,
3281 S Stafford St # A1, Arlington VA
22206-2018 ☎ (703) 931 7407

Majic Moments
erotic boutique in DC ☎ (202) 529 1469

Le Marquis
Washington DC ☎ (202) 842 2006

Oriental Spa
6325 Washington Blvd, Elkridge MD
☎ (301)796 0030

Party Palace
822 Guilford Avenue # 185,
Baltimore MD 21202

PEP
Baltimore ☎ (410) 385 3341 and
Washington ☎ (301) 369 7667

Pleasure Dome (swing)
PO Box 12126 Norfolk VA 23541-0126
☎ (804) 552 1739

Virginia Friends
PO Box 29 Highland Springs VA 23075
☎ (804) 527 6607

TLC
PO Box 322 Claymont, DE 19703

▶ **the carolinas addresses**

travelling

Beck's Motel
5401 Raeford Road, Fayetteville, North
Carolina 28304 ☎ (919) 425 2108

Debbie's US
301 South Bypass, Rocky Mount, NC
☎ (919) 985 2028

Carolina Friends
PO Box 561294 Charlotte NC 28256-1294
☎ (704) 784 3766

Cathy & Kent Craig
PO Box 36070 Raleigh NC 27606-6070

Obsessions
1100 Highway 70 East, New Bern, NC
☎ (919) 636 9601

Paradise International (swing)
PO Box 8825 Rocky Mount, NC 27804

Rick's
417 Hay Street, Fayettville, NC 28301
☎ (919) 471 2599

Rising Moon Books & Beyond
316 East Blvd, Charlotte, NC 28203
☎ (704) 332 7473

usa

miami and florida

south beach miami

Florida is strictly censored. The names of men accused of soliciting prostitutes are even read out on prime-time TV! While most of the inhabitants want things this way, the rest really enjoy the sun and sexy clubs that thrive here. There's plenty for the man with raging hormones and for swinging couples too, but the only two truly liberal areas are South Beach Miami and the

gay town of Key West. South Beach has become free much like Ibiza was ten years ago, with a large gay community as a result of its local gay rights legislation. It also has plenty of drag and everybody dresses wildly. The annual Erotic Art Expo is

**cat fighting, body
piercing, fusion
friction dancing**

**Erotic entertainment
every night from midnight**

Get turned on!

put on at the **Griffin Gallery** in South Beach and, if you're looking for somewhere to stay, there's a seaside art-deco hotel designed by "Biba" Barbara Hulanicki in fantasy style called **The Marlin**. Miami Beach has no street scene.

Miami's street action is along Collins Avenue where they also sell sex papers with ads. The Yellow Pages lists whores under *Models* and *Escorts*. North Miami has some brothels which the cab drivers know about. The sexpaper *Florida Xcitement* is brimming over with cat fighting, body piercing, fusion friction dancing, interactive role-playing booths, whip cream machines, and joke ads showing "Tri Sara Topps with three breasts". **Alley Cat** is the risqué romper room of Miami, with a shower dance grotto, four-poster bed shows, porn, S/M bondage stage acts, and balloons everywhere. The hoarding outside the **Solid Gold Club** has semi-naked cut-out girls sitting on top of it — Florida fun *is* blatant. **DejaVu Showgirls** has good lap dancing but no couch dancing. **Gold Baby's** is the Beach's only licenced table and couch dance (where you can fondle yourself as well as the dancer) and where the girls strip naked. **Club Rolex** has lap dancing performed by black and latino girls, some of whom will go home with you. Playhouse South was demolished by a hurricane but now they have a new club called **Menage**, more of which later.

In Fort Lauderdale, there's a seedy sex motel with a certain character of its own called the **Bon Soir**. The **Club Chic** is for swingers with amateur strip on Wednesdays; **Fallen Angel**, for custom bondage

leatherwear; and the **Apropos Art Gallery** shows erotic art, much of which has been censored elsewhere in America. Pompano Beach's **Cheetah 111 Lounge** is a super sex strip bar where the girls make the customers feel like kings. The Orange Blossom Trail is the Orlando sex area, with fabulous striptease emporiums such as **Pure Platinum**.

Newsracks along Beeline Expressway sell magazines where the sex establishments are listed and downtown you can find hookers around the Church Street Station Complex. They are also in Turkey Lake Road and Sand Lake Road. The penalty for soliciting is very stiff and lots of prostitutes get arrested. **Kathy Willets** made a name for herself by defending a prostitution charge by asserting herself as a nymphomaniac. *Body Scrub* is big in Orlando, on offer at

asserting herself as a nymphomaniac

sex parlours such as **Roosters**. The **Parliament House Motor Inn** is the world's largest all-gay resort and entertainment complex with theatre, pool and lovely rooms. **Club Paradise**, the large, exuberant clothing-optional resort, is where they set up a record of 307 people in a hot tub (since superceeded). Naturist by day but, once the lights go out… ! **Florida Fun** is a modern castle in Kissimmee, where swingers enjoy fake orgasm contests and other such laughs.

Tampa offers men a-plenty in the way of wild sex parlours, dressed up as things such as adult toy demonstrations (at **Sugarbaby's**

VIP), hot tub demonstrations (at **Ecstasy Spa**), wet modelling photo shoots (at **Thee Retreat**), lingerie modelling (at **Sheer Pleasures**) and 'body scrubs'. The **Tanga Lounge** was featured in *Cheri* as one of the best clubs in the country where good looking dancers will also dance with male customers. There's a naughty little nude-dance bar called **Lipstixx** which offers lap dancing (also called *friction dancing* in this area). Take

travelling

your condoms for dicky-do dancing in the back rooms. The area from Naples towards the Everglades is becoming an alternative weekend scene for New York commuters. Between Orlando and Tampa, the **Full Moon Bar** provides a saucy BYOB bottle club for modern-thinking couples and singles on Friday and Saturday evenings which has very lively young people — many of them female and wearing outrageous skimpy garments, making it wild and wonderful. It is not to be confused with the **Full Moon Saloon**, a gay leather and uniform bar back in Orlando. **Parties Unlimited** has hot tub and weekend parties in the Tampa-St Pete area. Run by Charlie & Carolyn, their house rule #10 is "Have Fucking Fun".

Swing clubs are different in Florida. The older on-premises clubs such as **Club Ménage**, a wild adult bottle club, the fabulous **Deenie's Hideaway** and the old Rendezvous (now called **Zanadu**) are erotic playgrounds where anyone can just drop by and get into the action.

They're laid back and have few rules. **Zanadu** has B&D on the last Thursday in the month. By contrast, newer clubs take their swinging extremely seriously. **Club Sensitivity** which finished when Bob Adler died, is continuing in the same vein with his wife Nancy's **Anakosha** project, a whole village of freedom. They believe that people need to be prepared so they can really let their hair down for scorching hot orgies. Nancy throws monthly house parties with her new fiancé. A swing club owners' cooperative meets to discuss the aims of swing clubs — how to help people overcome guilt and focus on self exploration and appreciation. Tom & Lynda Gayle, organisers of couples-only **Perfect Pairs**, also run **Club Relate** for fantasy playshops and put on a January swing convention, **Reflections** on Daytona Beach. **Visions** is another swing convention which takes place in Orlando. Now there's **The Centre for Shared Experiences** offering a four hour discussion to orientate people into the swinging lifestyle. Many locals and visitors prefer to swing at the naturist haven **Paradise Lakes**, now called **Club Paradise**, mentioned above, where you can find the people you like and just get on with it. The **Black Orchid Society** and the **Florida Leather Association** put on events called **Fetish Explosion** in Lauderhill, and the **Black Orchid** has fortnightly parties and bi-weekly non drinking meetings: no smoking at any events. **Margo & Joey** hold bondage parties which are also drug and alcohol free. **The Queen** operates her corporal correction from the **Theatre of Arts**, and **Madonna's Castle** provides subs as well as doms for singles and couples with special requests.

Adult Businesses In the State of Florida And Abroad
☎ (305) 779 1700 / (813) 874 2030

Alley Cat
3875 WS 41 St at Shipping Ave,
Coral Gables ☎ (305) 446 8346

Analosha
2338 Immokalee Rod, #146, Naples,
FL 33942 ☎ (813) 658 2239

Apropos Art Gallery
701 East Las Olas Blvd, Ft Lauderdale
FL 33301 ☎ (305) 524 2100 fax 524 1817

Black Orchid Society
PO Box 451592 Sunrise, FL 33345
☎ (305) 437 5176 ext 9655

The Bon Soir
2731 N Federal Hwy (US1) Fort Lauderdale,
FL 33306 ☎ (305) 565 1893

Center for Shared Experiences
PO Box 680687 Orlando FL 32868

Cheetah 111 Lounge
497 NW 31st Ave, Pompano Beach
☎ (305) 971 2600

Chic Club
3720 N Andrews Ave, Ft Lauderdale
☎ (305) 563 1066

Christine's Fantastic Lingerie
202-4 Building E, Bigtop Flea Market 1-75
Fowler Ave, Tampa FL 33613 (Sats & Suns)
☎ (813) 971 8182

Contact Socials
PO Box 12457, Port St. Lucie, FL 34597
☎ (407) 460 6649 fax 466 7294

DejaVue Showgirls
2004 Collins Avenue, Miami Beach
☎ (305) 538 0355

The Dollhouse
(strip) 1010 N Westshore Blvd, Tampa
☎ (813) 281 9389

Erotic Art Expo
c/o *Sarasota Arts Review*, 130 2nd St, Miami
Beach FL 33139 ☎ (305) 534 0303 (also fax)

Ecstasy Spa
3911 West Waters Avenue, Tampa
☎ (813) 935 9449

Fallen Angel
3045 N Federal Hwy (SW corner of Oakland
Prk Blvd) Fort Lauderdale ☎ (305) 568 0471

Florida Fun
PO Box 24835, Lakeland FL 33802
☎ (813) 967 7444/407 846 9702

Full Moon Club
6763 Land O'Lakes Blvd, Land O'Lakes
FL 34639 ☎ (813) 681 4709

Full Moon Saloon
500 N Orange Blossom Trail, Orlando,
FL 32805 (407) 648 8725

Gold Baby's
255 Sunnyside Isles Blvd ☎ (305) 948 3087

Lipstixx
Dale Malbry Hwy & Martin Luther King
Drive, Tampa

Madonna's Castle
☎ (305) 941 1244

Margo & Joey
2651 N Federal Hwy, Ft Lauderdale
FL 33306 ☎ (305) 566 3723 / 568 0471

The Marlin
1200 Collins Ave, Miami Beach, FL 33139
☎ (305) 673 8770 fax (305)673 8770

155

travelling

a whole village
of freedom

Ménage
9551 SW 168th St, Miami FL 33185
☏(305) 233 9721

The Mint Lounge
(private dancers) 2510 NW 187 Street,
Miami ☏(305) 624 8876

Club Paradise
Box 750, Land O' Lakes, 34639
☏(813) 949 9327 fax 949 1008

Parliament House
Motor Inn 410 North Orange Blossom Trail,
Orlando, FL 32805 ☏(407) 425 7571
Fax 425 5801

Parties Unlimited
☏(904) 775 2372

Pure Platinum
(strip) 3411 N Federal Hwy Ft Lauderdale
☏(305) 565 4557 and 5581 S Orange
Blossom Orlando ☏(407) 851 8115

Reflections/Relate/Perfect Pairs
POBox 681687, Orlando, FL 32868-0687.
☏(407) 656 1393, fax 656 3963

Thee Retreat
Dale Mabry, West Waters ☏(813) 886 5808

Club Rolex
12001 North West 27th Avenue, Miami
☏(305) 685 7408

Roosters
676 S Highway 17-92, Longwood Lakes
Shopping Center, Longwood ☏(407) 830
1161 (also branches in Ft Lauderdale)

Scarlett's Men's Club
East Courtney Campbell Causeway, Tampa
☏(813) 289 0520

Sheer Pleasures
8457 North Florida Avenue, Tampa
☏(813) 993 7340

Sugarbaby's
4516B Mest Martin Luther King Blvd,
Tampa ☏(813) 875 6711

Tampa After Dark
sexshop 3830 South 50th St, Tampa
☏(813) 248 3829

The Tanga Lounge
6333 W Columbus Drive, Courtney
Campbell Causeway Highway 60, Tampa
☏(813) 886 0468

Theatre of Arts
☏(305) 685 5899

Visions
PO Box 12457 Ft Pierce, FL 34979
☏(904) 473 9876 (3-10pm their time)

Kathy Willets
☏1-900 288 52849

Zanadu
PO8, 120 McNab Road, Pompano Beach,
FL 33060 ☏(305) 941 5566

travelling

usa

the midwest and rockies

Many of the hundreds of strip joints around Detroit, such as the wild **52nd Showbar**, are on the city's Michigan Avenue. Regulations concerning who may touch what in massage parlours varies from one district to another and, if you're lucky, a man gets manual release once he has convinced his masseuse that he's not a cop. The **Tokyo Oriental Spa** across from the Pontiac Mall is your best bet and the **Polynesia Fitness** over in Kalamazoo is the most liberal parlour. For an orgy education, swingers can visit **Friendship & Frills**. Swingers come from Detroit and further, for campouts at the **Cherry Lane Nudist Park**. The **Noir Leather** store will let you know about fetish nights. In Cleveland, **The Robin's Nest** swings in a glamorous house in seven acres of garden; in Columbus, **Sensations** shows videos

detroit

*who may
touch what*

cleveland

columbus

and provides a hot tub for non-threatening on-premise swinging; and in Toledo, the **Tender Times Socials** does hot dancing and camp-outs. **Fit to be Tied** is rave-olution, techno-shamanistic, morphogenetic-resonating House Culture of the 90's. It's put on by Randy Lee Payton, editor of the *Roc Out Cencorship* rag. **Body Language** is the Cleveland store

can see topless stage and table dancing. **Club Rio** has amateur strip nights, oil wrestling and special contests. **La Plase** in Indianapolis is the bona swing club. It has a huge party house with large Jacuzzi, eleven private rooms (two of which have two-way mirrors) a love swing, and enthusiastic plans for more rooms on the roof. It's terrific, and owners Charlie and Lee run it with pride. Frank and Ann run **Reel One**,

rave-olution, techno-shamanistic, morphogenetic-resonating

indianapolis

where you might hear about events in Ohio on the S/M and gay scene.
Indianapolis has a thriving commercial sex industry, ranging from **A-AAA Escorts** who do private sessions and strippograms, to the chi-chi **Brad's Golf Club**, where you

another great club. The **Ponderosa** nudist campsite is the home of the Miss Nude Pageants.
Chicago's Rush Street is the liveliest late-night place to hang out, hookers and everyone mixing in its fun bars. South Halston and Clark Streets have strip joints, porn booths and peep shows. The *Chicago Reader* is the paper with all the outcall ads but, take note that some of the agencies are wary of people they don't know. **Babes in Boyland** provide a reasonably priced escort service. Street hookers are evident near the Hilton hotel. The ancient **Admiral Theater** has topless and nude dancers, table dancing but no touching and, at **Bare Assets**, the girls spread their lips.
The swing convention, **Conclave**, in Chicago is becoming a bi-annual event with **Conclave II** happening in the autumn, holding fewer workshops than the original March event, and starting at a later time to give people who fuck all night a

chicago

travelling

two-way mirrors, a love swing

chance to catch up on sleep! **The Hitching Post** provides swing love and fun for everyone in Chicago. Men wanting to dress in lingerie, high heels, wigs, make-up and perfume should go to **Stiletto's**. The **Leatherworld Weekend** is held in Chicago, a laid back event that takes place within a hotel — you just dress up and indulge. The annual **Ball of Whacks** is put on by the amazing store, **House Of Whacks**, hosted by

toledo

parlour and, Southeast of Toledo, the **Utopia Spa** is a busy dive with hot tubs and lovely ladies. All kinds of sexy resorts are hidden away in middle America. One such is **The Sun Spot**, a naturist resort open all year which is more of a sex camp than a nudist camp.

Undercover cops stalk the streets of Minneapolis to

minneapolis

you wanna cry?
I'll give you something to cry about

travelling

domina Maitresse d'Arcy. Their theme is along the lines "You wanna cry? I'll give you something to cry about". Not so new, and still meeting regularly is the **Chicagoland Discussion Group** which is for singles and couples to discuss and try out S/M. For a professional, try **Mistress Diamond** who now has a fully equipped dungeon in Chicago. **Mad Jack's** is where to go for piercing and tattooing. Chicago has a lovely little leather, S/M fetish, cross-gender bod-mod shop called **No Hope * No Fear** and you shouldn't miss the erotic love boutique called **Cupid's Treasures**. **Tabou Tabou** is for trashy

dayton

glamourwear and **Translucere** for trannies.

There are little brothels in outlying areas such as Calumet City and you may need a taxi driver to help you.

In Dayton, the swing club **The Seekers** provides female attendants for single men, and whoring goes alongside the swinging. In Columbus, **Delilah's** is a good massage

columbus

arrest men looking for whores. Once caught, their cars are taken away and they get fined $700! The **Deja Vue**, **Solid Gold** and timeless **Payne Reliever** provide erotic naked entertainment. **Knights of Leather** hold fun bondage weekends in the

the feminine spirit is
extremely lively

woodlands nearby. The **L&L Society** holds non-profit fetish parties & helps with networking from Bay City. **Dream Haven** is the erotic book store which can fill you in on local fetish events. The **Minnesota Party Connection** holds sexy parties for swingers on the second Saturday in the month; **Club H** have hedonistic parties and camp-outs for couples & females and runs its own bulletin board; and the **Golden Phoenix Social Club**, the well-established couples-only swing club in St Paul, is renouned for its extremely lively females.

st louis

There are street hookers and brothels along St Louis' Fourth Street and the brothels are listed in the local sex papers. Police patrol at weekends.

total debauchery for bikers from all over the world

hot-tub fun at **Ladies En Confidente**. **The Dance Studio** has mistresses and slaves. At **Diamond Cabaret**, near the

customers go topless

stylish Larimer Square, business deals are conducted while the men watch table dancing. Plenty of other strip clubs compete: **Mile High Saloon**, **PT's** (Pop your Tops, where

Over the border in Brooklyn, the **Fantasy House** provides all kinds of pleasures that you cannot find in the city. **Extra Special People (ESP)** holds monthly swingers' dances in St Louis, and contribute to the **In Touch** swing convention every November. **Friendship 100** and **The Party Club**

kansas

provide swinging opportunities in Kansas. The **Black Hills Motorcycle Rally** is a week of total debauchery for bikers from all over the world.

south dakota

There are still contests for the most daring women but police control has sadly quietened things down a bit. Denver's local sex mag, the *Rocky Mountain Oyster* has plenty of ads for hookers and sex stores. Denver has lingerie

denver

playgrounds where you can watch pretty girls try on panties and things (but not much else!). **La Fantastique** is one such place. You get nude shows, one-on-one striptease, D/S, cross-dressing, couple swapping and

customers also go topless), and **Shotgun Willie**'s. Denver's street girls stand on Market Street, Grant Street, Glenarm Place near the Holiday Inn and Colfax Avenue. **Rocky Mountain Connections** holds weekend swingalongs, dirty dance fests & bawdy kicks. One of the country's oldest swing clubs, **The Golden Circle**

travelling

boulder

in Arvada, had its 25th birthday party in 1994. Couples can try the **Ultimate Fantasy Club** and **The Retreat**, which also accepts singles.

Denver's finest adult motel is **Mon Chalet**, a 24-hour sex, swing and quickie resort with whirlpools, bidets, pool, spas, a "love machine", a swing (their own version of the Taiwan basket) and a swingers'

colorado springs

registry. In Boulder, **Bus Stop** is the strip joint and Colorado Springs has the **Dejá Vu** strip palace. People go nude skiing in the Crested Butte ski resort at Easter.

A swing club called **L'Amour Club** has got going in Utah, and **The Million Dollar Club** in Salt Lake City puts on striptease.

utah

weekend swingalongs, dirty dance fests & bawdy kicks

travelling

the midwest and rockies addresses

▶ **Detroit & Michigan addresses**

52nd Showbar
7443 Michigan, Detroit ☎(313) 842 9756

Cherry Lane Nudist Park
11600 North Adams Road, North Adams, MI 49262 ☎(517) 287 4760

Friendship & Frills
PO Box 6049, Ann Arbor, MI 48106 ☎(313) 4344782

Noir Leather
415 South Main Street, Royal Oak ☎(313) 541 3979

Polynesia Fitness
563 Portage Street, Kalamazoo ☎(616) 388 4590

Safety Girls
female erotic boutique in Ann Arbor ☎(313) 668 0647

Tokyo Oriental Spa
2411 Elizabeth Lake Road, Pontiac ☎(313) 683 2630

▶ Cleveland & Ohio addresses

Amber House
(strip) 13311 Brookpath Road, Cleveland
☎(216) 267 0132

Body Language
3291 West 115th Street, Cleveland
OH 44111 ☎(216) 251 3330

Dayton Swing & Social Club
PO Box 2144 Dayton OH 45401
☎(513) 890 6277

Dejá Vu
(strip) 135 Byrne Road Toledo
☎(419) 531 0329

Fit to be Tied
c/o Randy Lee Payton, Coalition, POB 436
New Philadelphia OH 44663
☎(216) 364 2705

Robin's Nest
POBox 602671 Cleveland OH 44102
☎(216) 251 5101

The Seekers
3609 North Dixie Drive, Dayton
☎(513) 276 3220

Sensations
PO Box 292169, Columbus, OH 43229
☎(614) 885 2266

Tender Times Socials
POB 235, Swanton, OH 43558 Toledo

Tokyo Health Spa
4040 Belmont Avenue, Liberty,
Youngstown ☎(216) 759 9778

Toy Box
(strip) 2922 Westerville Road, Columbus
☎(614) 476 3706

▶ Indiana & Indianapolis addresses

A-AAA Escorts
Indianapolis ☎(317) 788 1248

Brad's Golf Club
3551 Lafayette Road, Indianapolis IN 46222
☎(317) 293 7908

La Plase
POBox 26676 Indianapolis IN 46226

Ponderosa Box
305 Roselawn 46372 ☎(219) 345 2268

Brandy's
(strip) 3011 W Coliseum Blvd, Ft Wayne
IN ☎(219) 484 3991

PT's Show Club
7916 Pendleton Pike, Indianapolis
☎(317) 545 5783

Reel One
POB 51412 Indianapolis IN 46251
☎(317) 240 3373

Club Rio
5054 West 38th Street, Indianapolis,
IN 46254 ☎(317) 297 2705

Scuttlebutt
(strip) 9148 Milton Road, Portage
IN ☎(219) 938 3959

The Sun Spot
RR#1 Box 320, Lake Village, IN 46349
☎(219) 345 2000

▶ Chicago & Illinois addresses

Bare Assets
318 Clark Street, Chicago ☎(312) 661 1894

Big Al's
(strip) 519 Main St, Peoria ☎(309) 673 9893

Babes in Boyland
Chicago☎(312) 670 2449

Chicagoland Discussion Group
CDG Dungeoneer, 3023 N Clark St, # 806
Chicago, IL 60625 ☎(312) 281 1097

Conclave
c/o Executive North, Box 110 Mt Prospect,
Chicago IL 60056 ☎(708) 297 4711

Cupid's Treasures
3519 North Halsted, Chicago IL 60657
☎(312) 348 3884

Dejá Vu
(strip) 3270 Lake Plaza Drive, Springfield
☎(217) 529 1281

Delilaha's
2836 Johnstown Road, Columbus
☎(614) 476 8512

Heavenly Bodies
(strip) 1300 S Elmhurst Road, Chicago
☎(708) 806 1120

The Hitching Post
POBox 2261 Des Plaines, IL 60017

House of Whacks
1800 West Cornelia, Chicago IL 60657
☎(312) 761 6969

No Hope * No Fear
1579 North Milwaukee Avenue # 306,
Chicago IL 60622

Mad Jack's
613 Weat Briar, Chicago IL 60657

Tabou Tabou
854 Belmont, Chicago IL 60657
☎(312) 548 2266

Translucere
2652 North Lincoln, Chicago IL 60614
☎(312) 835 3468

Leatherworld Weekend
Paradise Entertainment, S&L Sales, 2208
North Claybourn Ave #470, Chicago
IL 60614 ☎(312) 528 0041

Mistress Diamond
c/o POB 12597 Ft Pierce, FL 34979-2597

Stiletto's
Silver Jaguar, 117 West Harrison Bld
Suite 622, Chicago IL 60605

Utopia Spa Massage
1600 Woodville Road, Milbury
☎(419) 836 9945

▶ Minneapolis & Minnesota addresses

Club H
PO Box 581515, Minneapolis MN 55458-
1515 ☎(612) 566 1212
modem (612) 566 0693

Deja Vue
315 Washington Avenue North,
Minneapolis ☎(612) 333 6333

Golden Phoenix Social Club
PO Box 75972, St Paul, MN 55175

Knights of Leather
Box 582601, Minneapolis, MN 55458-2601
☎(612) 529 5622

L&L
PO Box 2145, Bay City, MI 48707
(send 2 IRCs) ☎(517) 892 3519

Minnesota Party Connection
c/o MPC PO Box 580069, Minneapolis
MN 55458-0069

Payne Reliever
899 Payne Avenue, St Paul ☎(612) 771
4215

Solid Gold
115 South 4th Street, Minneapolis
☎(612) 341 4524

Kansas, St Louis & Missouri addresses

Extra Special People
POB 8 Staunton Il 62088. ☎(618) 635 3328

Fantasy House
Brooklyn, IL (618) 271 1777

Friendship 100
PO Box 4088 Kansas City KA 66104 ☎(913) 287 4934

In Touch
c/o Palmetto Society, PO Box 1075 Hartwell GA 30643 ☎(706) 376 8022

The Party Club
PO Box 240097 Kansas City MO 64124 ☎(913) 299 9081

South Dakota addresses

Black Hills Motorcycle Rally
c/o Jack Pyne Gypsy Club, PO Box 627 Sturgis, ND 57785

Denver & Colorado addresses

Bus Stop
4871 Broadway, Boulder ☎(303) 440 3911

The Dance Studio
5454 N Washington, Unit 8, Denver ☎(303) 292 2814

Dejá Vu
2145 B Street, Colorado Springs ☎(719) 576 7724

Golden Circle Social Club
POB 128 Arvada CO 80001 ☎(303) 325 1568

Ladies En Confidente
5921 N Broadway, Denver ☎(303) 292 0302

La Fantasique
1725 E 69th Ave, Suite C, Denver. ☎(303) 289 7653

Mile High Saloon
Virginia Avenue Boulder ☎(303) 440 3911

Mon Chalet
12033 E. Colefax, Aurora, CO 80010 ☎(303) 364 2643

PT's
1601 W Evans, Denver ☎(303) 934 9135

The Retreat
PO Box 275 Eastlake, CO 80614 ☎(303) 234 0508

Rocky Mountain Connections
4559 Wadsworth Blvd #127, Wheat Ridge, CO 80033 Denver

Rocky Mountain Oyster Mountaintop Publishing
Box 27467 Denver CO 80227 ☎(303) 985 3034

Shotgun Willie's
490 Co Colorado Blvd, Denver ☎(303) 779 8127

Ultimate Fantasy
Social Club 5977 N Broadway, Denver CO 80216 ☎(303) 293 8629

travelling

Utah addresses

L'Amour Club
PO Box 550 American Fork, UT 84003. ☎(810) 756 9399

Lace
(strip) 1847 Wall Ave, Ogden ☎(801) 394 4757

Million Dollar Club
1037 3300 S,E, Salt Lake City ☎(801) 486 0100

the deep south

arkansas

In Arkansas, **Eagle Lake** is a private inn and plush resort for swinging members of Rendezvous International. Little Rock has two other swing clubs: another whole resort called **The Natural State** and a club called **Touch of Class**. The Clintons must have set things off in Little Rock! **Gi Gi's II** on the Stagecoach Road has exotic dancing girls. **Gig** is one of the few alternative bars in the State, with groovers mixing and making out till

straight and fetish sex. The **Classic Cat** has feature dancers, 60 strippers and many of its visitors come from the nearby convention centre. **Deja Vu** also has sexy shows in Nashville, the **Boobie Bungalow** has them in Elkton and there's another **Deja Vu** in Memphis.

memphis

atlanta

Naughty Girl Lingerie is one lingerie bar in Atlanta where girls may do nice things to boys, but most of the lingerie bars here are 24-hour-a-day rip-off

> **the clintons must have set things off in little rock!**

chattanooga

5am. There's a wild alternative haunt in Eureka Springs called **The Crescent Hotel**.

The **Scenic Motel** is a charming, well equipped, and popular swingers' motel beside a river and beneath a mountain near Chattanooga. **Elite International** offers Nashville Southern hospitality & horniness at their swing club and they go off for 'Funtime' weekends in Pensacola Florida. **Southern Lights** holds bawdy intimate swing gatherings of young people. Other swing clubs include the **Free Spirit Lounge** and **Tennessee Social Club**. **Onynx**. **Leather and Lace** hire women for

eureka springs

joints, their sole purpose being to tease money out of men. Atlanta is also a difficult place to find an escort agency with willing girls, but the **Distincively Exquisite Escorts** are the exception. The **Gold Rush Show Bar** heats up in the evenings and at weekends with almost 50 girls dancing on stage (but no extras) and porn stars sometimes make appearances. Sunday nights at **Blakes** is gospel drag. **Backstreet** is a wild mixed/gay disco which is open 24 hours a day. The yuppy area of Buckhead has a pick-up place called **Revolution**. **Masquerade** has a fetish night on Wednesdays, which is in Little Five Points, near some other

> **gays intermingle with everyone else**

alternative venues **The Point** and **The Starr Community Bar**. Atlanta is a very gay city and the gays intermingle with everyone else although lesbians have their own little suburb of Decatur. Cobb County is an uptight area, to be avoided. The well-established swing club, **Palmetto Socials,** run by George and Joan host the swing convention **In Touch** annually and a summer 'Pool Party & Cookout Social'.

Two teenagers in Bossier City, Louisiana, were arrested for having sex on a bed in a department store and though they said they were sorry, they were taken to court to face prison sentences. So don't try that here! New Orleans (known as NOLA to the locals) has a black magic tradition with shops selling skulls and potions. **Maison de la Lune Noir** provide a pagan bed & breakfast run by Mishlen & Louis of Black Moon Publishing. **Jewel's Tavern** attracts the leather, chains and nipple-ring groovers and the local fetish shop is called **Second**

Skin. To find the horny singles, head east to Metarie or south to the more hip University area. **Bourbon Burlesque** is in the main touristy French Quarter and has some high class strippers who will sit and chat with you before doing their collection for money in a jar. **Hot Rocks** is a newer theatre and sometimes has stunning strippers. The transvestite bar **My O My** has been putting on a good show for over 50 years. **The Silver Frolics** (also called **Cajundale's**) has male and female strippers. **Female Amateur Wrestling** can be fun. New Orleans is full of music joints. Horny, wealthy fishermen drive down to Grand Isle from all over the country to the **Tarpon Rodeo** on the last weekend in July, showing off their semi-naked cuties in the car parades in between the fishing contests.

showing off their semi-naked cuties in the car parades

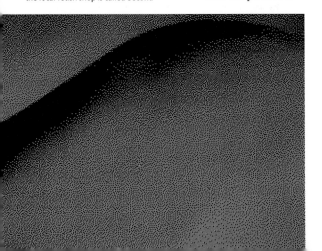

the deep south addresses

travelling

▶ **arkansas addresses**

The Crescent Hotel
Eureka Springs, AR 72630 ☎(501) 253 9766
fax 253 5296

Eagle Lake
PO Box 15608, Little Rock, AR 72231

Gig
201 East Street (Highway 71 South)
Texarkana AR 75502 ☎(501) 773 6900

Gi Gi's II
11800 Stagecoach Road, Little Rock,
AR 72209 ☎(501) 455 4499

The Natural State
PO Box 165118 Little Rock AR 72216

Touch of Class
PO Box 1424 NLR AR 72115
☎(501) 791 0223

▶ **nashville and tennessee addresses**

Deja Vue
1214 Demonbreun Street Nashville
☎(615) 248 1926 and 2532 N Watkins
Memphis ☎(901) 358 8642

Elite International
PO Box 22728 Nashville, TN 37202
☎(615) 355 7244

Free Spirit Lounge
302 Hermitage Avenue, Nasville

☎(615) 251 9130 or 244 0064

Onynx
PO Box 25045 Nashville TN 37202

The Scenic Motel
2000 Cummins Hwy, Chattanooga,
Tennessee ☎(615) 821 1071

Tennessee Social Club
☎(615) 244 2438

▶ **atalanta and georgia addresses**

Backstreet
845 Peachtree, Atlanta

Blakes
227 10th Street NE, Atlanta

Distinctly Exquisite Escorts
Atlanta ☎(414) 255 1062

Gold Rush Show Bar
2608 Stuart Avenue, Northside, Atlanta

Naughty Girl Lingerie
1891 Cheshire Bridge NW, Atlanta
☎(404) 872 2055

Palmetto Socials
POB 1075 Hartwell GA 30643
☎(706) 376 8022

PEP Atlanta
Atlanta ☎(404) 621 7961

Revolution
293 Pharr Road, Atlanta

Bourbon Street Burlesque
327 Bourbon, NO

Female Amateur Wrestling
514 Bourbon, NO

▶ **new orleans and louisiana addresses**

Hot Rocks
418 Bourbon NO

Jewel's Tavern
1207 Decatur St, NO ☎(504) 523 9237

Maison de la Lune Noir
726 3rd Street, New Orleans, LA 70130

My O My
Iberville & Chartres, NO

Second Skin 519 St Phillip, NO

Silver Frolics / Cajundale's
427 Bourbon, NO

Southern Lights
PO Box 77912, Baton Rouge,
Louisiana 70817

Tiffany's Cabaret
(strip) 4312 N State Street, Jackson, MS
39206 ☎(601) 366 5203

texas

Texans really go for whatever they are into in a horny way and are very hospitable, so visitors are made welcome to join in their kinky hot nights. Dallas is probably the most hopping city, were **Suntanz** offers both male and female masseuses but swinging hopefuls. The **Lido Theater** gets couples playing in the little rooms downstairs or joining the main porn movie audience on Fridays and Saturdays.

The intersection of Harry Hines and W Northwest Highway has great

put your shit-kickers on before venturing to _billy bob's_

dallas

some of the girls flagging male drivers down on the Dallas LBJ Freeway are cops, so beware! The Fairmont Hotel and surrounding area (Main and Market Streets) are where to look more safely. Dallas has more swing clubs than you could shake a stick at. Some state no fatties, blacks or gays so are being omitted from this guide. Here are the best: **Creatures of the Night** is somewhat exclusive and runs parties & trips; **Real People,** now called **Rumours,** holds wonderful sexy Texan nights in their big Tudor-style club house; **Sans Souci** is a frenetic off-premises club catering to yuppies; **Jet Set** and **Jet Set II** are also off-premises; **Clark & Margie's** is up in Garland, **Seclusion** provides swingers with an ultra plush playhouse; **Club Chapango** caters to a mixed crowd; **Kalino's** holds on-premises parties for singles and couples; **The Play Pen** is on-premises for couples and singles on Wednesdays thru Saturdays. Tub clubs such as the **Oasis** and **Paradise** also attract

stripclubs like the **Baby Dolls Saloon** which, like many Texas clubs, requires guests to arrive in collared shirts and proper shoes — call clubs in advance to find out the dress code. **Caligula XXI** is down the block. The extravagantly designed **Wild Orchid** is a gentleman's club deep in the heart of the clubbing district of Greenville Avenue. Strip enthusiasts say that Dallas only _thinks_ it's the cowboy town; Forth Worth is the real thing, and recommend you "put your shit-kickers on before venturing to Billy Bob's Texas", the world's largest (of course!) sex show bar, and **Sinbad's. Fantasy Foxx** is the only totally nude club and you have to bring your own booze. The Metroplex of Dallas/Fort Worth lists over fifty escort services in its phone books. **Skin and Bones** do body piercing and **Leather by Boots** is a fetish store. The **Spankee's Club** welcomes singles and couples for their 'kick back, let your hair down, hold me tight, swing your partner' dances and **Lone Star PEP** is the S/M club. Dallas has an erotic art gallery

travelling

called the **Fantasy Emporium** which also sells sexy books and gifts. Houston has never had many swing clubs but couples find the action in the porn cinemas and sex motels. The **Star Theater** has a balcony where you can watch the movie and get hot and sexy in the group fun. **Hot X** is another porn theatre packed with swingers every night of the week. The **First Monday Club** is the best swing club. **Baby Dolls**, in the centre of the sleaze district, and **Colorado** both have exotic dancers and there are more up-market gentlemen's clubs like **Heartbreakers** where there's topless dancing, the girls don't hastle guests and big groups come along for fun. Allens Landing at Main and Commerce Street is the red light district, so is the area around the Houston Center. The newsracks along Main Street sell sex papers with ads.

houston

A city with many gay venues and romantic river trips for tourists, San Antonio's sleaze is discrete. **Tiffany's Cabaret** has exotic dancing on four stages and presents feature dancers. **Top O' Strip Showgirls** and **Ziegfelds** both have individual tabletop dancing. The **Texas T Party** is a huge weekend event for transvestites put on by the local

san antonio

Boulton & Park Society
Even before *Slacker* and *The Butthole Surfers*, Austin had a reputation as the liberal, free-thinking oasis of Texas. There are hundreds of clubs to choose from. Sixth Street shakes with Jell-O shot emporiums, sleazy discos and the **Black Cat Lounge**, a boozer for models and bikers. The **Blue Flamingo**, a downtown Mexican drag bar, attracts 'a curious mix of people' according to thier publicity. You can try the local sexy dance called kicker dancing at **The Broken Spoke**. **Sugars** is the conventional strip club and **Club Decadence** is Austin's local swing club. The latest scam to dodge the prostitution law here is 'Adult Tanning Salons'.

austin

El Paso's swing club **Gentle Quest** has been successful for years. The town has several nude dance bars such as the **Candlelight** on Pershing Drive. To the south, **Lower Rio Grande Valley Socials**, a swing club which has been going for ages, has just started to hold parties down in Guadalajara which are proving very popular with both their regulars and the Mexicans. They admit couples and single ladies only.

el paso

the liberal, free-thinking oasis of texas

▶ **texas addresses**

Baby Dolls
3700 Westheimer, Houston TX 77057
☎(713) 266 4012 and 3700 Hwy 157, Forth Worth (817) 267 7701

Baby Dolls Saloon
3039 West NW Highway, Dallas TX 75220
☎(214) 358 5511

Boulton & Park Society
PO Box 700042 San Antonio TX 78270
☎(512) 545 3668

The Black Cat Lounge
309 East Sixth Street, Austin
☎(512) 441 4677

The Blue Flamingo
617 Red River Street, Austin
☎(512) 469 0014

The Broken Spoke
3201 South Lamar Blvd,
Austin ☎(512) 442 6189

Caligula XX1
282 8 W NW Hwy Dallas ☎ (214) 350 264

Candlelight Club
3810 Pershing Drive El Paso
☎(915) 5651333

Club Chapango
2912 McKinney Ave, Dallas TX 75204
☎(214) 855 5465

Clark & Margie's
PO Box 477852 Garland, TX 75047
☎(214) 686 7830

Colorado
6710 SW Freeway, Houston, TX 77071
☎(713) 781 1122

Creatures of the Night
PO Box 551117 Dallas 75355-1117

Crystal Pistol
(strip) 3211 W NY Hwy Dallas
☎(214) 351 6212 and 907 Amarillo Blvd.
East, Amarillo TX 79107 ☎(806) 371 9620

Club Decadence
POB 162000 # 149, Austin, TX 78761
☎(512) 473 7115

Fantasy Black
(swing) 13030 North Borough, #201,
Houston TX 76110

Fantasy Emporium Erotic Art Gallery
11211 Ables Lane, Dallas ☎(214) 991 3321

Fantasy Foxx
Lindale & South Loop 820, Fort Worth

The First Monday Club
PO Box 19035 Houston TX 77225

Gentle Quest
PO Box 4594 El Paso, TX 79914
☎(915) 821 1997

Forbidden Fruit
erotic boutique in Austin ☎(512) 478 8980

Heartbreakers
3200 Gulf Freeway, Dickinson TX 77003
☎(713) 337 4091

Jet Set
3136-B Routh Street, Dallas TX 75201
☎(214) 520 6969

Jet Set II
2629 Oak Lawn, Dallas TX 75219
☎(214) 520 6969

Kalino's
Dallas ☎(817) 792 3329 ext 8878

Leather by Boots
4038 Cedar Springs, Dallas ☎(214) 528 3865

Lido Theater
7035 John Carpenter Fwy, Dallas
☎(214) 630 7127

Lone Star PEP
PO Box 810715 Dallas, TX 75381

Lower Rio Grande Valley Socials
LRGVS PO Box 1021 Edinburgh
TX 78540-1021

Paradise Tub Club
Highway 121, Frisco ☎(214) 248 9388

The Play Pen
Dallas ☎(817) 792 3339 ext 5037

Rick's
(strip) 3113 Bering Drive, Houston
☎(713) 785 0444

Rumours
9009 Sovereign Row, Dallas Texas 75247
☎(214) 951 1837

Oasis Tub Club
1621 N Haskell Avenue, Dallas
☎(214) 823 1489

PT's
(strip) 111 NW Loop 410, San Antonio
☎(512) 344 6601

Sans Souci
Dallas Texas ☎(214) 350 9656

Seclusion
3527 Oak Lawn, Box 435, Dallas Texas
75219. ☎(214) 528 5920

Suntanz
Dallas ☎(214) 495 1911

Sinbad's
8128 Highway 80 West, Fort Worth

Skin and Bones
☎(214) 826 6647

Spankee's Club
6750 Shadybrook Lane, Suite 110, Dallas
TX 75231

Sugars
404 Highland Mall Blvd E, Austin
☎(512) 451 1711

Tiffany's Cabaret
8736 Wurzbach, San Antonio
☎(512) 614 3919

Top o' Strip Showgirls
6415 San Pedro Avenue, San Antonio
TX 78216 ☎(512) 342 8088

Wild Orchid Cabaret
5201 Matilda (at Lovers Lane & Greenville)
Dallas, TX 75206 ☎(214) 373 1111

Ziegfelds
2525 NE Loop, San Antonio TX 78217
☎(512) 646 6311

west coast & hawaii

In the Bay area, a free-and-easy attitude blends with heavy networking, making sure everyone evolves sexually at a steady pace. San Francisco is the home of swing, but their new clubs now suffer from the same problem as the rest of the world: too many eager men and not enough eager women. The safer sex **Mother Goose Parties** have gone downhill as a result of this discrepancy, and only the private safer sex party clubs, which insist on equal numbers, are succeeding. However, on a good night, **Edgewater West,** a liberal motel near Oakland Airport, which leaves things to chance, gets a brilliant collection of people piling up and can be absolutely fantastic. Most of the swinging goes on down the coast around San Jose.

Wednesday is the night to go out in San Francisco. It's when the **Faster Pussy Cat** opens to cool cats of all persuasions; **The Kit Kat** holds its Banana Eating Contest; and **Bondage-A-Go-Go** takes place at the Bridge Night Club, where girls who are prepared to be handcuffed to the bar get free drinks and bikers arrive wealding bullwhips. All these are listed in *The Spectator*, a fabulous local sex tabloid giving you news, views and reliable details of what's on. As well as the usual whores' ads, they have the occasional ads placed by male prostitutes but the only men who get replies, apparently, are the male dominants — masochistic women

a brilliant collection of people piling up

call them when they feel like a good beating! *The Spectator* is sold in slot machines on street corners. *Black Sheets* is a hot, multi-sexuality magazine with personal accounts and reviews. **The Eros Center** was set up specifically to offer Safer Sex education, recreation & parties for all persuasions. Most of the events are gay but some are bi or mixed. **Differences**, a local dungeon, holds a fetish play party every first Friday in the month. **QSM** puts on fascinating workshops where you can learn anything from "Branding with a hot Knife" to "The Fantasy and Reality of Caning" and "Fisting for Beginners". The local fetish club, **Backdrop**, has a slave auction every Friday night, parties & demonstrations run by Master Robin. **Gemini** is for dominant men and submissive women. **Petrucio** is more private and **Serpent's Lair** is a new S/M fetish party offering safer sex supplies and welcoming responsible

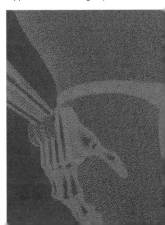

novices and experienced players. **Pat Califia** runs S/M workshops and play parties for women. The **Janus Society** provides exploration of consensual dominance & submission. **L/SM Round-up** is for sober & drug-free fetish parties & workshops for those into "recovery". **Stormy Leather** is the local "get the buzz of what's going down" fetish shop that throws groovy parties. Sessions can be booked with **Fantasy Makers**, one of the many fetish playgrounds for adults. **Raelyn Gallina** who has been providing piercing, scarification and mixed media body modification for over ten years is available for rituals. **Fakir Musafar** provides shamanic S/M journeys and professional piercing instruction. **Frank Moore** is more of a free-love shaman. **The Gauntlet** does piercing in a hitech setting and sell New Age jewellery. The **San Francisco Sex Information Line** is a free service offering any kind of help you need including club information. **The Pacific Center** is also volunteer-based aimed at helping sexual minorities. There are some

san francisco sex information line is a free service

fascinating sex shops in the area. **Fetters** gear is now stocked at **Mr S**.and their own store. **Romantasy** is a lovely shop and holds all kinds of events including slumber parties. **Good Vibrations** has a video library, a vibrator museum, erotic reading circles and trained assistants to give you good advice. **Passion Flower** will impress you, it's such a luscious erotic store in Oakland. The **Temple of Sacred Sensual Arts** offers to open you up to ecstasy and **Covenent of**

smut fests are still performed

The Goddess puts on Ancient Ways festival. **Jwala** offers Sacred Sex Tantric weekends, women's breath orgasm, and extended orgasm workshops sometimes in conjuction with the gay erotic energy school, **Body Electric**. **Harbin Hot Springs**, a clothing-optional new-age resort is where the water-borne experience of Shiatzu massage, Watsu, originated. San Francisco has many alternative groups dating back to the hippy days and communes are common, the **Kerista** being one, with an open sex policy but fidelity within its own group.

San Francisco has a new gentleman's club called **Centrefolds** on North Beach, as well as the old splendid down-town sex theatres: the **O'Farrell**, **New Century**, **Regal Show World**, **Crazy Horse Theatre** and **Lusty Lady**. They offer shows, lap dancing, private one-to-one booths, torch peeping and a video dome. **Lusty Lady** has man-woman live sex shows and vintage porn in its booths. The **Mini Adult** is a seething sex cinema in the Tenderloin. Street hookers hang around Union Square and along Market Street. Jennifer Blowdryer's **Smut Fests** are still performed, even after ten years! Erotica COYOTE's sexy benefit parties and the Exotic Erotic Balls — let-your-hair-down knees-ups at New Year and Halloween — are put on by Stephen Parr.

There used to be sex stores in San Jose until the last one, **L'Amor Shoppe**, was closed down, a victim of the local anti-red-light ordinance. However, the town is not completely dead. **Leatherfest**, the local leather pride is held here, sponsored by **Leathermasters**. **Bay Cities Socials** hold huge dance parties for swingers, in hotels. **The Forum** is a female-initiated swing club which has lively parties and "Strip for Your Man" contests, which swing till 4am. The only swing clubs between Stockton and Los Angeles are the **Central Valley Social Club**, which holds its monthly dance at the Crazy Horse Saloon at the Hacienda Convention Center in Fresno, and the **Central California Social Club** run by Chris and Katrina at Clovis. They also hold monthly dances. Fresno's tranny prostitutes have a bad name for robbing and beating up their clients. The famous **Madonna Inn** is not to be missed. It has beautiful themed rooms, quality and charm. You are allowed to move

fresno

travelling

waterfalls, huge beds and fireplaces

rooms every night during your stay, to experience them all. There are waterfalls, huge beds and fireplaces. They don't take credit cards and you must book in advance. Nearby are sulphur hot tubs and springs such as **Avila Hot Springs**, off Highway 101. Los Angeles houses America's most notorious dungeon, **The Chateau**. Like many venues here, it has moved address since the earthquake. You get manual relief as well as kinky sex or you can jerk off. Lawyers and stars arrive looking harassed and leave, after severe beatings, looking revived. The

los angeles

lawyers and stars arrive looking harassed and leave, after severe beatings, looking revived

Janus S/M club is now called **Threshold** and meets privately on a montly basis and on the first Sunday of the month it's open to the public. **Rubber Ranch**, a local latex mail order outfit, holds S/M action get-togethers and **Atavar** puts on lectures on S/M. **Dressed to Thrill** is the **Versatile Fashions** extravaganza in May, with under-table entertainment and fashion shows. **Siren** is Andy Wilkes' stylish rubber fashion store. There's a Saturday night fetish club in LA called **Sin-a-Matic**. **Entre Nous** is a horny dance club for women only. **Him 'n' Her** is LA's first bisexual swing club. **Freedom Acres** holds laid back wild parties on Saturday nights and people enjoy the **Gemini Club** which has several private rooms, videos and dancing. Dick Drost's **Naked City**, two hours South of Los Angeles, enjoys swinging nights and naked days, with monthly contests throughout the year including the Nude Olympxxx.

Los Angeles' drag queen bar is the **Drag Strip**. TS whores hang out on Santa Monica Boulevard. Beverly Hills pros are very expensive and Hollywood and Sunset Boulevards

are heavily policed. The girls in Echo Park are younger but more likely to be druggies. Figueroa near the Hilton and around Chinatown, and the mall near Century Plaza Hotel in Rodeo drive are OK but Sepulveda Boulevard between Roascoe and

men sit waiting for their massage and hand jobs beside little old ladies waiting for their hair to be done

Devonshire is where you'll find most of the street action, still watched by police to a certain degree. Much of the street scene has moved out into the Valley. Some of the sex establishments are undercover — like the hairdressing salon **Leo's**, where men sit waiting for their massage and hand jobs beside little old ladies waiting for their hair to be done! There are are also some swanky places like **Platinum** which supplies delightful women for $300 an hour. Striptease is usually tame but at **Jumbo's Clown Room**, a heavy metal disco, you can see some wild acts and the **Tropicana** has oil and

sex-starved hollywood widows with handsome young hunks

mud wrestling.
Women hire nude cleaning boys from **Maid in LA**. They dust the house beforehand. A new agency has just become successful, matching wealthy sex-starved Hollywood

widows with handsome young hunks. Called **Mutual Admiration**, they hold weekly parties for introductions. **Pink 'n' Blue Christmas** is the event when porn stars party in the **Toy Box** sex shop. The *LA Star* still has sex ads but most of them are for phone sex. *LA Weekly* is better. *Choice* is another local rag to find swingers, singles, TV and TS whores and any sex for sale. If you're single and want to find a partner at night, **Cheesecake Factory** has several singles bars but mostly people aim for the exclusive **Roxbury**, **Vertigo** and **China Club** to find rich stars. There's a tantric bed and breakfast hotel called **Sensual Environments** promoting love, intimacy, pleasure & spirit, close to the beaches of Santa Monica. The **Quoduoshka** (Cherokee) way of love is taught in Malibu. **Sun West** is one of the more pleasure-oriented nudist groups.

san diego

There's a book on San Diego's underground called *Sin Diego* compiled by FM Phillips and Roger Warren, with forwards by Nina Hartley and San Diego's sex idealism tycoon, Captain Sticky. The city is conservative but its nightlife is great and the petty laws (such as no drinking in all-nude clubs) don't really spoil the sexual fun available. There isn't a sleaze district any more but the main street-girl areas are Midway, El Cajon Avenue and Hill Street/Mission Avenue in Oceanside, North County. The oriental massage parlours do the works for a hundred bucks, the nicest being perhaps the **Tokyo** out at Mesa. **Dirty Dan's** became the posh **Pure Platinum** and now the best girlie bar is **Nitelife Uptown** thanks to its naturally friendly girls (without tit implants).

Unlicenced nude bars include **Deja Vu** and **Cheetah's**. The Yellow Pages lists escorts for men and women. Whores and dominatrices advertise in the the swing mags such as *Swing* and *Friends and Lovers*. **Tessara Moore** is the town's most highly regarded dom. The classy club **Hillside** draws attractive couples who wish to enjoy an open sexuality party, **Expressions** is more middle class, both contrasting with **Thad's** wild parties which have been moving location, to dodge the law, for almost two decades. He encourages zany sex fun, in and out of the Jacuzzi and offers the ultimate chocolate experience! The **Annual Leatherfest** of the National Leather Association is held in San Diego. The Gaslight district, once the red light area, is now full of trendy clubs.

offers the ultimate chocolate experience

Young people, often using fake IDs in order to go clubbing, hang out in Pacific Beach. There are clubbing hotlines such as **SIN**, **Playscool** and **The Statik Line**. Bisexuals meet for lively discussions around sexuality at the **Gay and Lesbian Center**. Drag is very popular, with 'Ladies By Choice' appearing at the **Brass Rail**. **The Learning Annex** puts on erotic courses and provides possibilities like photographing *Playboy* playmates.

flamboyant gatherings & couplings take place on black's beach

Condom Plus sells nice sexy gifts. **Cat** does torso sculpturing, preserving your beautiful body for ever! Flamboyant gatherings & couplings take place on Black's Beach which is down a long steep climb, putting it into a world of its own.

Carousel Connection, up in Sacramento, holds classy, couples-only dance nights and the **Bangkok Tanning Center** offers a full service to men. The **T&A Times** must be one of the trashiest sex tabloids in the world but it will give you porno stories and ads for hookers and clubs around Oregon. South West Broadway from Salmon to Washington is Portland's red light zone, near the bridge. Avoid Yamhill Market whores. **Orgasm** holds incredibly hot S/M parties, and the **U & I Tavern** allows both singles and couples at their swing parties.

Kinky Couples is an exciting attraction of the Northwest when all the kinky people from miles around congregate in the beautiful swing house, **New Horizons**, a swing house of hedonism caringly run by Carmie. Architecturally inspiring, it has devoted guests, beautiful grounds where you can camp, occasional S/M parties and an action-packed annual Northwest Swing Celebration Convention in mid July. The *Seattle Gay News* provides information of interest to anyone seeking alternative nightlife and you can always ask at the fantastic store called **SIN**. **Tattoo You** is a well established tattoo parlour. The **Apple** is one of those sex cinemas where hands are busy.

Up in Seattle, they do "couch

'couch dancing' instead of table dancing

dancing" instead of table dancing. There are hundreds of parlours for sex and the street girls are around Pike Market Place (after 9pm) and in North Pioneer Square. Police are fierce at weekends.

The Red Rooster over in Las Vegas provides an 11,000 sq-ft home with exotic decor to orge in, and the people are very friendly. The famous brothels of Nevada are open 24 hours and listed in the yellow pages. None are in the main cities but they operate a limo service to pick you up. They are called ranches but look like shacks. Inside you get offered a menu by a topless girl which may include specialities such as *Nero Sex* (she puts little chocolate replicas of her organs on her real ones and you can lick them off) or *Scandinavian Water Toys* (prickly balls or gloves filled with oil which are rubbed on the body). Girls work long hours and

service around ten clients a day. At the **Green Lantern** you can pay to be with a girl all night and sleep-in with her in the morning. Most ranches are quite small but the old **Mustang Ranch** employs 100 girls, and a

prickly balls or gloves filled with oil which are rubbed on the body

175

support team of 60! **Mabel's** is more luxurious than most. Upstate they are called *Saloon brothels* and the service is more basic. Back in the towns, freelancers advertise in the phone book under Entertainment or Nude Dancers. The nightclubs in Las Vegas sometimes hint at providing professional services but these are all rip-offs. **The Oasis Motel** in Las Vegas has 24-hour sex movies and special three-hour room rates. **Shirley Sez** is a great sex store.

plush padded bedrooms, a hot tub, 24 hour service

The **Great Alaskan Bush Company No 2** which owns some of the most sparkling strip joints in Phoenix and elsewhere has been under attack from the law over the snakes they keep for their acts, even though the club claims they keep them under the best possible conditions! The top whore agencies are in Scottsdale. Phoenix hookers walk the University Drive at Tempe and near Squaw Peak although, the police do, too. **Home Lodging** is a nudist B&B just outside Phoenix with plush padded bedrooms, a hot tub, 24 hour service, and welcomes swingers, nudists, and people looking for group sex. The **Mohave Social Club** is a club for swingers. Scottdale is where The **Love Academy**, the future home of the **ZEGG Centre for Free Love and Free Thought,** publishes their magazine *COM-PER-SION.* The **Kriya Institute** puts on seminars in Tantra for singles & couples including the 'cosmic cobra breath' both here in Sedona and in other cities.

albuquerque

Mr Peepers Adult Video Sales & Rentals has opened a 60-seater adult theatre in Albuquerque which has private viewing booths as well as kinky gear. It is open 24 hours a day. The city is disappointing with regard to parlours and men are advised to use outcall services such as **Absolutely Addictive**. Swingers can meet up **at Roses of the Desert**. The **Happy Trails Show Club** puts on sexy shows in Continental Divide, as does the

continental divide

Palamino in Alburquerque and **Cheeks** in Santa Fe. In Hawaii, **Pure Platinum** has a table dancing gentleman's club in Waikiki but for real striptease go to **Club**

Rockza, **Femme Nu** or **Club Rose.**

hawaii

Dancers is on Sand Island near the Pearl Harbour base, and **Club Cheri** in Honolulu has porn stars over from California to perform. The **Kahua Hawaiian Institute** offers Tantric instructions to the rhythms of nature and experiences with whales and **Body, Heart and Soul** run as 'Art of Being' programmes. **Mana Kai Maui** have honeymoon-style vacation seminars on Tantric sexual energy to uplift your relationship. Alternative lovestyles parties are held for swingers by **Pacific Velvet, The Playhouse** and **Club Aloha. Select Friends** is Anchorage's cosy swing club which has its own

honolulu

anchorage

magazine *Personals Only*; **Chilcoot Charlies**, commonly known as Coats, is the fun pick-up bar for everyone; and **The Great Alaskan Bush Company** is the best of the numerous sex show theatres.

west coast & hawaii addresses

Alcoholics Leather AA
150 Eureka, San Francisco (Fridays 8pm)

Ancient Ways Festivals
PO Box 1226 Berkeley, CA ☎94704

Backdrop
☎(415) 552 6000

The Black Book
PO Box 31555 San Francisco CA 94131-0155

Blush Entertainment
erotic boutique ☎(415) 861 4723

Body Electric
6527A Telegraph Ave, Oakland, CA 94609
☎(415) 653 1594

Body Manipulations
254 Fillmore SF CA 94117 ☎(415) 621 0408

Bridge Night Club
520 4th St, at Bryant, San Francisco
☎(415) 495 6620

Pat Califia
2215-R Market Street, San Francisco CA
94114 ☎(415) 333 1723

Celebrations of Love and Tantra
45 San Clemente Drive 200B, Corte
Madera, California 94925
☎(415) 924 5483 fax 924 4214

Crazy Horse Theater
980 Market St ☎(415) 771 6259

Differences
☎(415) 585 9662

Edgewater West
10 Hegenberger Road, Oakland
☎(510) 632 6262 fax 562 3187

Eros Center
2051 Market St, San Francisco
☎(415) 2554921

ETVC
(TV/TS/TG) PO Box 426486 SF CA 94142
24-hour hotline: ☎(510) 549 2665

Fantasy Makers
San Francisco ☎(510) 234 7887

Faster Pussy Cat
The Clubhouse, 3160 Sixteenth St,
San Francisco ☎(415) 561 9771

Raelyn Gallina
PO Box 20034 Oakland CA 94620
☎(510) 655 2855

Gauntlet
2377 Market (just E of Castro, south side of
Market) SF CA 94114 ☎(415) 431 3133

Gemini
Box 282719 San Francisco CA 94128

Good Vibrations
1210 Valencia St, at 23rd, San Francisco
CA 94110 ☎(415) 974 8980

Harbin Hot Springs
POBox 782 Middleton CA 95461
☎(517) 287 4760

Janus Society
PO Box 6794 San Francisco CA 94101.
Hotline ☎(415) 848 0452

Kerista
543 Frederick Street, SF CA 94117
☎(415) 759 9508

The Kit Kat
907 East Arques Ave, Sunnyvale
☎(408) 733 2628

L/SM Round-up
POBox 525547 San Francisco CA 94142-
5547 ☎(415) 764 2990

Lusty Lady Theater
1033 Kearny, San Francisco CA 94133
☎(415)391 3991

Mini Adult Theater
Jones & Golden Gate, San Francisco

Frank Moore
(shaman) PO Box 11445 Berkeley CA 94712

Mother Goose's Jack & Jill-Off Parties
PO Box 3212 Berkeley, CA 94703 (SASE)

Mr S
PO Box 460122 SF CA 94103
☎(415) 863 7764

177

travelling

Fakir Musafar
PO Box 42168 San Francisco CA 94142-1668
☎(415) 324 0543

NNS (Not Naughty Seminars)
NSS Seminars, PO Box 620123 Woodside N,
CA 94062 ☎(408) 336 9281

Nurse Anice Von Enema
San Francisco ☎(510) 601 5808

Pacific Center
San Francisco ☎(510) 841 6224

Stephen Parr
☎(415)558 8112

Passion Flower
1647 Sanchez St, Oakland ☎(510) 601 7750

Petrucio
PO Box 12182 Berkeley CA 94712

QSM
PO Box 882242 San Francisco CA 94188.
☎(415) 550 7776

Romantasy
199 Moulton Street, San Francisco 94123

☎(415) 673 3137

Sacred Sex
☎(415) 995 4643 / 927 2543

San Francisco Sex Info Line
☎(415) 621 7300

Serpent's Lair
☎(510) 532 1744

The Smut Fest
c/o Eastern Time Productions, PO Box 102,
New York NY 100009

Society of Janus — see Janus Society

Stormy Leather
1158 Howard Street ☎(415) 626 1672

Temple of Sacred Sensual Arts
POBox 9424 San Rafael, California 94912.
☎(415) 492 9377 /1402

Two Plus Two
(swing) PO Box 193376 San Francisco
CA 94119 ☎(415) 749 2582

▶ san jose, and down the coast addresses

Bay Cities Socials
191 Harder Road, Suite 138, Hayward,
CA 94544 ☎(510) 746 4809

Central Valley Social Club
(800) 21-SWING

Central California Social Club
POB 597 Clovis CA 93613-0597
☎(209) 443 6244

The Forum
☎(408) 776 9265 / (408) 776 9275

Leathermasters
969 Park Avenue, San Jose ☎(408) 293
7660

Lupin Lodge
naturist resort PO Box 1274, Los Gatos,
CA 95030 ☎(408) 353 2250 fax 353 2250

The Madonna Inn
100 Madonna Road, San Luis Obispo,
CA 93401 ☎(805) 543 3000 fax 543 1800

▶ los angeles addresses

Atavar of Los Angeles
8033 Sunset Blvd, # 747, LA CA 90046

The Chateau
7310 North Atoll Street, between
Coldwater Canyon, and Fulton Street,
North Hollywood ☎(818) 503 3034

China Club
1600 N Argyle, Hollywood

Choice
1614 N Cahuenga Blvd, Hollywood
CA 90028 Fax ☎(213) 466 9106

Church of the Most High Goddess
PO Box 1704 Canyon County, CA 91386
☎(805) 2514747

Drag Strip
2500 Riverside Drive ☎(213) 969 2596

Entre Nous
2214 Stoner Avenue, West Los Angeles
☎(310) 477 1485

Freedom Acres
PO Box 6024 San Bernardino, CA 92412
☎(714)887 8757

Gauntlet
8720 Santa Monica Blvd, Los Angeles
CA 90069 ☎(310) 657 6677

Gemini Club
PO Box 105 Claremont, California 91711
☎(909) 622 8544

Jumbo's Clown Room
5153 Hollywood Blvd, Hollywood

Leo's
N Hillhurst and Los Feliz, Hollywood
☎(213) 664 3029

Los Angeles Sex Education Resources
(LASER) (213) 486 4421

Maid in LA
(310) 398 6243

Mutual Admiration
☎(310) 217 7666 or (213) 665 3190.

Dick Drost's Naked City
PO Box 551, Homeland, CA 92548-2000
☎(909) 9262264, fax (714) 926 1737

Platinum
☎(213) 288 6206

Quoduoshka
☎(213) 739 3904

Roxbury
8225 Sunset Blvd

Rubber Ranch
1250 Long Beach Ave, Unit 127C,
Los Angeles CA 90021

Sensual Environments
☎(310) 822 1181.

Sin-a-Matic
7969 Santa Monica Blvd ☎(213) 463 7868

Sun West
PO Box 85204 Los Angeles CA 90072-0204

Threshold
2554 Lincoln Blvd Suite 381 Marina Del Rey
CA 90291 ☎(310) 371 6504

Toy Box
☎(714) 982 9407

Tropicana
1250 N Western Ave, Hollywood CA
☎(213) 464 1653

Vertigo
333 S Boyleston

Versatile Fashions
1145 W Collins Ave, Orange CA 92667
☎(714)538 0257

▶ san diego addresses

Black's Beach
PO Box 12255 La Jolla, CA 92039-0620
☎(619) 278 7106

The Brass Rail
3796 Fifth Avenue ☎(619) 298 2233

Cat
☎(610) 563 4052

Cheetah's
8105 Clairemont Mesa Blvd
☎(619) 277 2339

Condoms Plus
1220 University Avenue, Hillcrest
☎(619) 291 7400

Deja Vu
5520 Kearny Villa Road (along Hwy 163)
☎(619) 279 GALS and 2720 Midway Drive
☎(619) 224 4757

Expressions
☎(619) 471 5185

Gay and Lesbian Center
3916 Normal, San Diego

Hillside
PO Box 462923 Escondido, near San Diego,
CA 92046 ☎(619) 738 8284

The Learning Annex
344 Kalmia Street, San Diego CA 92101
☎(619) 544 9700

Tessara Moore
8895 Towne Center Drive, Suite 105,
San Diego CA 92122 ☎(619) 491 4422

National Leather Association
PO Box 3092 San Diego CA 92163
☎(619) 685 5149

Nitelife Uptown
4307 Ohio Street ☎(619) 284 7435

Playscool
☎(619) 286 PLAY

Pure Platinum
4000 Kearny Mesa Road ☎(619) 278 2230
and 2431 Pacific Highway ☎(619) 233 7359

SIN
(310) 364 0315 / (714) 254 0891
/ (619) 685 7542

Sin Diego
PO Box 620219 San Diego CA 92162
Fax ☎(619) 239 8700

The Statik Line
☎(619) 685 8449

Swing and **Friends and Lovers**
Dawn Media PO Box 33148 San Diego
CA 92163 ☎(619) 299 0500

Thad's
☎(619) 237 8849

Tokyo Oriental Massage
7016 University Avenue, Mesa
☎(619) 466 2555

travelling

▶ sacramento addresses

Bangkok Tanning Center
☎ (916) 920 1629

Carousel Connection
PO Box 348551 Sacramento CA 92412
☎ (909) 887 8757

Crimson Phoenix
sex boutique Portland ☎ (503) 228 0129

It's My Pleasure
erotic boutique Portland ☎ (503) 236 0506

▶ portland and oregon addresses

Orgasm
PO Box 5702 Portland OR 97208

T&A Times
STV Publishing PO Box 3992 Salem

OR 97302 ☎ (503) 373 0590 or in Portland
☎ (503) 790 0590

U & I Tavern
6910 N Interstate, Portland OR 97217

▶ seattle and washington addresses

Apple
Pike and Boren Street

Kinky Couples
Seattle ☎ (206) 244 4612

Loveseason
erotic boutique in Lynnwood
☎ (206) 775 4502

New Horizons
PO Box 2188 Lynnwood, WA 98036
☎ (206) 745 3156

Seattle Gay News
PO Box 22007 Seattle WA 98122-0007
☎ (206) 324 4297

Tattoo You
1017 East Pike Street, Seattle WA 98122
☎ (206) 324 6443

SIN
616 East Pine Street, Seattle WA 98122
☎ (206) 329 0324

Toys in Babeland
erotic boutique in Seattle ☎ (206) 328 2914

▶ las vegas and nevada addresses

Fantasy Faire
erotic boutique Reno ☎ (206) 682 0167

The Oasis Motel
1731 Las Vegas Boulevard, S. Las Vegas,
NV 89104 ☎ (702) 735 6494

Green Lantern
95 High Street, Ely, Pine County
☎ (702) 289 9958

Mabel's
Nye County ☎ (702) 372 5574

Mustang Ranch
10 miles East of Reno,
just off I-80 in Lockwood

Red Rooster
6405 Greyhouse Ln, Las Vegas, NV 89122-
0575 ☎ (702) 451 6661

Shirley Sez
PO Box 12574 Las Vegas NV 89112

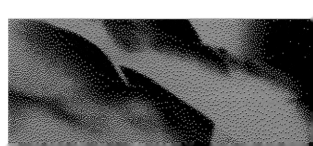

▶ **albuqerque and new mexico addresses**

Absolutely Addictive
☎(505) 888 4024

Cheeks Lounge
2841 Cerrillos Road Santa Fe NM 87501
☎(505) 473 5259

Happy Trails Show Club
1-40 Exit 47, Continental Divide NM 87312
(505) 862 7645

Palamino
2900 Coor NW, Albuquerque NM 87112
☎(505) 831 2020

Mr Peepers
4300 Edith NE (1 blk W of 1-25),
Albuquerque ☎(505) 343 8063

PEP Albuquerque
414 Loussana SE Suite 2, Albuquerque
NM 87108 ☎(505) 260 1324

Pussywillow
erotic boutique in Albuquerque
☎(505) 242 3531

Roses of the Desert
Albuquerque ☎(505) 877 3061

▶ **arizona addresses**

HomeLodging
George, PO Box b, Mesa, AZ 85274
☎(602) 831 6758

Kriya Institute
55 Sinagua Drive, Sedona AZ 86336

Love Academy
POB 14183 Scottsdale AZ 85267-4183 fax
☎(602) 474 9916 $39 sub, tel in Germany
☎(49)33841 59510, fax (49) 33841-59512

Mohave Social Club
PO Box 3510 Bullhead AZ 86430

▶ **hawaii addresses**

Club Aloha
PO Box 931 Hoanaunau HI 96726
☎(808) 328 8420

Body, Heart and Soul
PO Box 269 Paia HI 96779

Kahua Hawaiian Institute
PO Box 1747 Makawao, Maui, HI 96768
☎(808)572 6006 fax 572 6666

La Femme Nu
1673 Kapiolani Blvd, Honolulu
☎(808) 947 3444

Mana Kai Maui
PO Box 69, Paia, HI 96779 ☎(808)572 8364

Pacific Velvet
Box 23073, Honolulu, HI 96823-3073

The Playhouse
1164 Bishop Street-124, Honolulu HI 96813
☎(808) 923 7529

Pure Platinum
2301 Kuhio Avenue, Honolulu
☎(808) 922 5566

▶ **alaska addresses**

Chilcoot Charlies
24-35 Spenard Road, Anchorage AK 99503

Great Alaskan Bush Company
631 International Airport Road, Anchorage
AK 99518 ☎(907) 561 2209

Select Friends
1317 W Northern Lights Blvd, #555-SSC,
Anchorage AK 99503

travelling

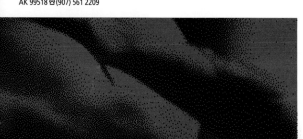

venezuela

curaçao

The whole of the centre of town on Curaçao seems like a swinging red light area but the authorities try to keep it clean by hiving all the activity off into a special police-controlled area called **Campo Alegre**, the official red light district out by the airport. Many of the night clubs and discos have happy hours and there is a great spirit of sexual adventure. **La Guaira** has lots of fun for the single man at the Holiday Inn. **Circulo Moderno de Amistad** is a long-standing, hot swing club in Caracas.

▶ **Venezuela Addresses**
   country code (58)

Circulo Moderno de Amistad
Apartado Postal 75082, Caracas 1071A

a special police- controlled area called *campo alegre*, the official red light district

vietnam

saigon

Saigon's night life is exuberant. The **Hard Rock Café** has a motley collection of backpackers, expats and good-time girls, and the busy downtown disco **Thai Son** has girls on supply. Massage parlours in hotels can be forthcoming but overpriced, for example, at the **Rex**. Sex for sale is marred by sporadic clamp-downs but it's cheap and plentiful for those men who want to slum it. The cafeterias of Hai Ba Trung are hard core brothel bars. **No 47** Hai Ba Trung Street has an upstairs balcony where girls beckon you up. **The Casino**, popular with Australians, has 40 girls who speak good English. Don't let the cyclos (motorcycle taxis) take you to tourist traps like the **Snake Bar** or the **Tulip Bar**. Go down by the port, past the two water towers, past the sailors' bars **Tuc Trung** and **Nhut Yet** where street walkers are cheap, and carry on over the big blue suspension bridge where, below, short-time brothels such as **Tran Xan Sioan** have really cute girls. If you don't want to venture this far, another low-life area is opposite the **HMC Museum** and to the right are excellent friendly short-time brothels. Going towards the animal market, in the opposite direction to the floating hotel, you can crawl in the pitch black under the old Cau Mong bridge and have a knee trembler. This is for true degenerates only. More so, if you continue to the little

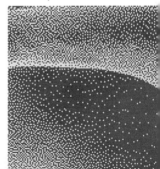

park where you can get a shag for 50 cents. Liberal hotels, where you meet women or take lover back to, include the **Mini Hotel**, **Thai Bing Duong**, opposite and very clean, **Phong Phu** around the corner, **The Queen** and **The Saigon**. Freelancers working outside the old American Embassy wear flattering miniskirts and halter necks. Le Huong Puong (pronounced lay hung vung) is the old red light district for locals where you can enjoy yourself too if you have a Vietnamese escort, who insist you get quality. They also have a secret brothel called **Nga Ba Sung Suong** up past the zoo in a side street called **Ngo Tat To**. You'll need to be with a local to be let in through the portal. The **Volvo** and **Superstar** cater to rich Chinese businessmen and **Candle Street** is full of lovely young girls selling ciggies' under lamp-posts. Boys are for rent in the cafes on **C.T. Quoc Te**. The English pub **Shakes** has the best disco. **Down Under**, opposite the Floating Hotel. Although a two-tier price system exists so that foreigners pay more for sex than locals, foreigners are liked and you can easily find a lover or someone to go out with.

▶ **Vietnam Addresses**
   country code (84)

Mini Hotel
(Thai Binh) 181 Nguyen Thai Binh, Saigon

Queen Hotel
Duong Nguyen Tat Thanh, Saigon

Saigon Mini Hotel
opp Floating Hotel Saigon ☎ 24 038

Saigon Hotel
66 Duong Nguyen Tat Thanh, Saigon

Thai Son
66 Duong Khoi, Saigon ☎ 23 267

183

travelling

sex travel companies

Advance Travel
Ron Johnson, PO Box 237, Oakton VA
22124, USA ☎(703) 352 2440 fax 591 0340
*Provides naturist travel packages for
singles, couples and groups worldwide*

Alternative Travel
6910 E Alabama Road, Ste 284, Woodstock,
Georgia 30188, USA ☎(404) 924 0968
A couple-only travel club and service

Forum Society
PO Box 418 Cardiff CF2 4XU, UK.
Swingers' trips to Holland and France

Lesbian & Gay Visitors Center of New York
135 W 20th St, 3rd Floor, NY NY 10011,
USA
*Provides unbiased gay-friendly tourist
information and personalised travel
services to all subscribers regardless of
sexual orientation, ethnicity, age or
ableism*

Lifestyles Tours and Travel
2641 W La Palma Ave, Ste A, Anaheim CA
92801, USA (714) 821 9939, fax 821 1465.
*They take swingers from Los Angeles to the
Enchanted Gardens in Ocho Rios, Jamaica,
Hedonism II, New Horizons in Washington
State, Pepe's Paradise in Mexico, and Costa
Rica. They also put on Windjammer Cruises
and Houseboat Getaway weekends***Naturist
Video Club Naturist Leisure**
POBox 65, Leighton Buzzard, Beds LU7 8TJ,
UK.
*Sexy Susan Mayfield's trips to Spain and
weekends in UK, making naturist videos.
Her Naturist Update features some of the
trips*

Oriental Cupid Tours
Box 4132 Medford OR 97501, USA Fax (503)
536 2827.
*Inexpensive tours to the Orient for
marriage and exotic fun with ladies (non
underage). $2 photo info packet*

Peng Travel
☎(01708) 471 832
*Takes Brits to parts of the world where
they can relax & be themselves*

Sunmasters Travel Service
66 Oakmount Road, # 312, Toronto Ont
M6P 2MP, Canada ☎(416) 763 5830

Tantra Society
67 Maple St, Newburgh, New York 10159,
USA.
*Ancient Tantric rituals every full moon on
clothes-free Caribbean cruises*

Wicked Travel Club
*Taking sex-starved Brits to foreign parts to
let rip*
☎(0843) 869390

184

travelling

FETISH STYLIST by S. SIN

PARA *diso*
B O D Y W O R K S
CREATE YOUR FETISH WONDERLAND with
RUBBER, LEATHER, PVC, LACE, TOYS, and
MODIFY YOUR BODY WITH JEWELLERY
41 OLD COMPTON STREET, SOHO, LONDON W1V 5PN
tel. 0171 287 2487

4
SHOPPING

Betty Dodson

< the minute I threw the switch on the vibrator,
my brain waves were in alpha, and they stayed
there throughout my entire sexual build-up...
just before the median orgasm ...
my brain waves dipped down to theta ...
the EEG data confirmed what I intuitively knew
— masturbation was

a delightful form of meditation. >

This is an alphabetical listing of utterly wonderful suppliers and unique products omitting things easily obtainable from shops

SEXTOYS +
gadgets

187

shopping

Adam's Sensual Whips & Gillian's Toys $2 mail order catalogue from POB 1146 New York NY 10156. ☎(516) 842 1711 / (212) 686 5248 11am-8pm. Huge variety of rods, paddles, cats and straps, etc., in nylon, rubber, miracle plastic, deer, elk, lamb and cowhide. Their Whipperware parties are held every 4th Saturday in the month at Paddles.

Big Sex Outfitters sell dog tags and chokers with labels such as "slag" on them. 147 Second Avenue, Suite 905, New York NY 10003

Birch Bottoms and Lovitt make unique toys and clothes to order, all sizes and specifications welcome. London ☎(0181) 886 5801

Blow-up doll with vagina and bum hole called *Miss Perfection* from **Pink Star**, 176 Bd Vincent, Auriol, 75013 Paris

Bondage Beds in rustic and heavy duty materials. **Barry Clune** PO Box 86686 Portland OR 97286, USA ☎(503) 771 6136

Cakes that Seduce from **Sweet Sensation** in London ☎(0171) 727 3359

Cassettes for self-help on sexual problems both audio and video from **Focus Therapy Company** PO Box 82 Chertsey, Surrey KT16 8YH, UK

Cats and Floggers in deerskin, bullhide, cowhide etc., custom orders welcomed from **Lashes** 2336 Market Street #39, San Francisco CA 94114, USA ☎(415) 621 6048

Chastity belts are available from Centurian, for both men and women. Made of steel or leather, they look as if they would work so well you'd be worried about the key getting lost.

you'd be worried about the key getting lost

The penis chastity belt is $195. Centurian PO Box 459 Orange CA 92666, USA

Cock Strap and Ball-Spreaders

can be eagerly ordered from **Voyages** PO Box 78550 San Francisco CA 94107-8550, USA

Dante Amore's inventions such as Electric Butt Plugs, Cock Head Stimulators (Sparkler) from **Paradiso Electro Stimulations** PES 3172 N Rainbow Boulevard, Las Vegas Nevada 89108, USA ☎(702) 656 9641. These implements may be able to help men and women with paralysed bodies. Be careful not to buy such equipment from dodgy sources and NEVER USE ELECTRICITY ABOVE THE WAIST.

Dismantleable Bondage Furniture

such as whipping posts, cages, St Andrews Crosses from The Tie Rack PO Box 1521 Youngstown Ohio 44501-1521, USA

The Drummer Store sells hard-to-find S/M toys, including wooden ones. The 'leather pride' flag adopted by the S/M community for marches etc. is also stocked. It has black, blue and white horizontal stripes with a red heart in one corner. 24 Shotwell Street (between 14th & 15th) San Francisco CA 94103 ☎(415) 252 1195

Enema, Vaginal Examination and Urinary Equipment is best bought from a medical supply store which isn't prudish about the erotic implications. **Mediquip** is one such company. You can choose one of many sizes of catheter gauges, nurses uniforms, vagina specula, vaginal dilators, gloves and smooth bore connectors. **Mediquip (SW)** North Road Industrial Estate, Okehampton Devon EX20 1BQ credit card orders: ☎(01831)3710. **FPN6D Services** sell the above plus suction enlarging equipment and suspension gear from **Mark Ensinger**, PO Box 1014 Novi MI 48376, USA ☎(& fax) (313) 348 5332

Eroteak's hand-made dungeon and sexy furniture has now reached amazing standards with beautiful objects available which really work for the clients who want them. Unit 2a Norwich Road Industrial Estate, Lowestoft, Suffolk NR32 2BN, UK ☎ (01502) 519222

smooth bore connectors

Fetters is a wonderful group of friendly people who make bondage and fetish gear caringly and with empathy. 40 Fitzwilliam Road, London SW4 0DN ☎(0171) 622 1356 & 310 Seventh Street, San Francisco CA 94103, USA ☎(415) 863 7764

Flicker Machines, dreamachines, brainwave synthesisers or synchronisers as they are variously called, are hallucinogenic and can offer self therapy, psychological growth meditation and mystical experiences. From

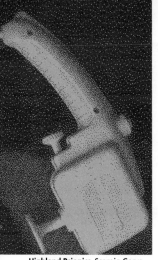

Highland Psionics, Scoraig Garve, Ross-shire Scotland IV23 2RE Oliver Krieger's erotic furniture such as phallic candle holders and fetish-leg lamp stands can be ordered from him at Brackwanderstr 15, D-73572 Heuchlingen, Germany

Heartwood Whips of Passion at 412 N Coast Highway # 210, Laguna Beach, CA 92651, USA ☎(714) 376 9558. Jeanette Heartwood's famous hand-made whips with fully balanced handles, multi-coloured braiding and exciting embellishments. $5 for a catalogue

Jane Hess' Love Eggs made to help women exercise their vaginal muscles are 550 KR by post from her at **Mabella**, Vesterbrogade 21, 4600 Copenhagen ☎(45) 53 65 63 61

House of Gord make trolleys and other bondage contraptions. **HG Publications** PO Box 27 Welshpool SY21 0ZZ, UK

multi-coloured braiding

Incontinence Care Products catalogue and helpline: **Milton Stay-Dry,** Granby Court, Weymouth, Dorset DT4 4YD ☎(01305) 785108

Insider Handelsagentur, Postfach 2144, 2914 Barsell 2 Germany. All kinds of erotica including boots and dungeon equipment

JK Perfect Personal Products PO Box 13383 Scotsdale AZ 85267-3383, USA. Rubber mattress covers, waterproof vinyl panties, good selection of adult pishers, etc.

Kinky Joe's Erotic Furniture Box 174, Westchester Station, Bronx, NY 10461, USA. Oral sex chairs, kinky headboards, deluxe penis back chair with scrotum seat and vibrating bar stools

vibrating bar stools

The Little Old Strap Maker POB 10184, Portland, ME 04104, USA. Makes all types of disciplinary straps including the Razor Strop, the Tawse, discipline bras, ECT, and paddles in leather and rubber

Lovelocks heavy engravable solid brass heart shaped locks in a gift box with red felt, to be worn or used to secure handcuffs etc. From **Romantasy** 119 Moulton Street, San Francisco CA 94123, USA ☎(415) 673 3137

Lucifer's Armory sells Vampire gloves, hardware and sportsheets with velcro restraints. Mail order from 874 Broadway, Box 808, New York NY 10003 USA

shopping

Mouse pads with erotic designs: Olivia DeBernadinis's *Panther Lady 11* or *Zebra Lady* 11 cost $23.95 from **Contact Eurocorp Computer Services** in Americab ☎(1-800) 843 9497

Party Pete is a blow-up penis which becomes four feet tall, balls included available from any good sex store

The Psychic Vampire Company supplies 90-minute audio cassettes of bawdy R&B classics PO Box 2473 New York NY 10009, USA

Real Touch artificial vaginas in the *Family Jewels Collection* of **Real Touch Products** Box 413966 Kansas City MO 64108

Restraints used by hospitals and law enforcement agencies can be obtained from **JuRonCo** PO Box 5992 Peoria IL 61601, USA ☎(309) 673 7854

anchor pads are for advanced play

Rubber Sheets and specially printed rubber from **Big Box** Studio 1, Maws Craft Workshops, Ferry Road, Jackfield, Telford, TF8 7LS ☎(01952) 883994 and from Moko, also in the UK ☎(01676) 533418

SandMutopia Supply Co excellent range of bondage and torture implements, including needles and electrical appliances. PO Box 410390 San Francisco CA 94141-0391, USA

Scorpio Silicon Dildos beautiful feel, colours and shapes. Available from all good sex stores. List of retailers or wholesaling: **G.B.D. Scorpio Products** 117 West Harrison Bldg, 6th Floor, Suite D-313, Chicago IL 60605, USA. They are available in the UK from Get Wet, BCM 3564 London WC1N 3XX ☎(0171) 627 0290

Second Skin Metal Company makes stainless steel and chrome plated bronze butt plugs and bondage equipment for men and women. 521 Rue Saint Philip, New Orleans LA 70116, USA ☎(504) 525 SKIN, fax 525 8167

Sensual restraint accessories are sold from **Noelle Nielson** Software Box 69826 Los Angeles CA 90069, USA

it really works for leverage

Sex Swing and other fantasy furniture from Fantasy in Furniture Box 798, 4119 N State Road 7, Ft Lauderdale FL 33319, USA ☎ (1-800) 647 0739

Shiatsu Massage Chair made of leather which massages your back, bottom and legs comes from Japan and is sold at **Good Vibrations**, 1210 Valencia Street, San Francisco ☎ (415) 550 7399 and **Coré** in London

Sportsheets are soft velcro bondage kits for people who want to keep each other secured down on the bed. Anchor Pads are for advanced play. If this appeals, write for more info from **Sportsheets** PO Box 7800 Huntington Beach, CA 92646, USA

Sybian Abco Research Associates, PO Box 329 Monticello, IL 61956-0354. Age statement required. A vibrating stool for women to sit on to get off.

Temporary Tattoos by Temptu, a wonderful range put up by a high spirited company Unit 17 Jubilee Market, London WC2 ☎ (0171) 981 0336 fax 981 8639

The Thigh Harness is a unique way to attach the dildo to your body so that it really works for leverage. Manufactured by Socket Science Labs, Marketing HT, 4104 24th Street #187 San Francisco CA 94114, USA

Triple Knob Butt Plugs and bondage equipment from **Motail** PO Box Pangbourne, Berks RG8 8LW UK

Vaginal Trainers (to be used in conjunction with sex therapy treatment) for women with vaginismus, a condition which makes entry seem impossible, from **Amielle**, Owen Mumford, Freepost Woodstock, Oxon OX20 1RB, UK ☎ (01993) 812021

Vibrators which Plug into the Mains are best. You can buy them from the electrical departments of major department stores but there are specialist vibrators available. The Thumper is heavy duty and very powerful and available in medical stores. The Hand Massager can be purchased from hairdressing suppliers like Barber Styles in London ☎ (0181) 965 7527. The infamous Hitachi Magic Wand, the Wander Wand, G-Spotter and other gems are all available from **Good Vibrations** in San Francisco. Their mail order address is **Open Enterprises**, 938 Howard Street, Suite 101, San Francisco CA 94103 ☎ (415) 974 8985 fax 974 8989

191

Waist Clinchers from **Paul C Leathers** PO Box 285 Prospect Heights, Illinois 60070 ☎ (312) 508 0848

Unusual materials in bondage equipment are in the range of toys from **Sorodz**. They use fibreglass, neoprene and Teflon as well as leather, fur and horsehair. Custom orders are encouraged, age statement required. **Sora Counts**, PO Box 10692 Oakland CA 94610, USA ☎ (510) 839 2588

CLOTHES +
adornments

Antique underwear and sexy clothes from **Echoes** Hebden Bridge Road, Todmorden, W Yorks

Axfords have a 64-page catalogue of corsets in many styles costing £7. 82 Centurion Road, Brighton Sussex ☎ (01273) 27944

Baby clothes for adults from **Precious Baby Wear** 3 South Hill Road, Gravesend, Kent, UK ☎ (0634) 571 296 and **Especially for Me** 113 North First Avenue, Upland CA 91786 ☎ (909) 964 6251

Batman's capes & masks, and screen printed rubber from **Rubber Developments** Unit B4, Maw's Craft Workshops, Ferry Road, Jackfield, Telford TF8 7LS ☎ (01952) 883994

Bedspreads in gleaming black with chains, pockets and D-rings designed by Jane Kahn from **Khaniverous** in London

BR Creations sell all styles of corsets in leathers, brocades, satin & metallic. Monthly newsletter and catalogue. PO Box 401 Mountain View California 94040, USA

Catwoman hood with ears from **Versatile Fashions** PO Box 1051 Tustin, CA 92681, USA

Cocoon Clothing to cocoon you in rubber, including inflatables and made-to-measure garments. Mackintosh House Green Street, Kidderminster DY10 1JF ☎ (01562) 829419

The Clit Clip is the name for jewellery for the labia and other tender parts which clips on rather than pierces. **Judy Kirk**, 13428 Maxella Ave, Ste 314D Marina del Rey, CA 90292, USA

Cocks in Silver on a Leather Rope purchased from **Sign O' The Times** gives £1 to The Terrence Higgins Trust, from 17 Ranby Road, Greystones, Sheffield, South Yorkshire S11 7AN, UK

Conflicto make the most bizarre fantasy clothes and costumes for anyone who wants to bring frou-frou and sensationalism into their fetish wardrobe. 1 Johnstrups Allé 1st TH, 1923 FRB C Copenhagen Denmark ☎ (31) 350380

Customised clothing for tattooed and pierced people (exposing their finery) is made by Bridie Przibram for **Cat's Whiskers** 94c Old Church Street, Newton Heath, Manchester M40 2JS, UK ☎ (0161) 681 7255

Dark Garden is a new corset maker in San Fran, offering many of the original authentic designs and concepts. 2229A Market Street, San Francisco, CA 94114, USA

Extreme Fashion Footware from Terry de Havilland's endless creativity can be ordered from him at **The Magic Shoe Company** Unit 4 88 Mile End Road, London E1 4UN ☎ (0171) 791 3352

Fashion Fantasy Mail order company with specialist catalogues e.g. for large people. 12423 Hedges Run Drive, Suite 200, Woodbridge, VA 22192 ☎ (703) 791 2670

Fetish badges with bondage and S/M logos on them are being sold by **Boutique Minuit** PO Box 1400, 1000 Brussels 1, Belgium ☎ 223 10 09 and **Le Scarabée d'Or** 61 Monsieur le Prince, 75006 Paris ☎ 46 34 63 61

Fetish Fashions are featured and listed in all major fetish magazines. The most international listings are in *Marquis* Felnsburgerstr 5, 42655 Solingen, Germany ☎ (212) 58651 and from **Una Diva** PO Box 1426 Shepton Mallet, Somerset BA4 6HH

Fetish Shoes and Boots from the source: **The Little Shoe Box** is the original incredible manufacturing shop at 89 Holloway Road, London N7, UK

Handcrafted Erotic Body Jewellery in stainless steel, niobium and gold from **Silver Anchor Enterprises** PO Box 760 Crystal Springs, Florida 33524-0760, USA ☎ (813)788 0147

shorts that show your bulge

Hardline make simple sexy rubber outfits for men including snazzy T shirts, shorts that show your bulge, rubber sleeping bags and collars. The mail order address is Contact Versand, Postfach 401960 D-80719 Munich, Germany. Catalogue DM12

High-Heeled shoes and Boots for trannies and women from **Ritual Shoes** 29 Brewer Street, London W1 ☎ (0171) 287 2096

Gloves – Mr Hammer custom-makes gloves in any fabric 7210 Melrose Avenue, Hollywood, CA 90046, USA

Luminescent Lingerie *(useful for the Planet Sex Ball fluorescent room)* is on sale from the spanish company **Things** San Pablo 32-34 Apartado correos 7300, 50003 Zaragota, Spain ☎ (976) 44 63 62

Military Uniforms are sold at **Blunderbuss Antiques** 29 Thayer Street, London W1

Modern Armour's embossed latex sculptured jackets , chaps and full-length wrap-over coats are shown in Los Angeles and London. 3 Kimberley, Letchworth Herts SG6 4RA, UK

193

shopping

▶ created by Jeff Willis

The Naughty Victorian unique custom-made Victorian clothing and implements from 2315-B Forest Drive, Suite 68, Annapolis MD 21401, USA ☎ (410) 626 1879

Sexy Underwear The best shops are: **Wendy Jane** 62a Station Road, March, Cambs PE15 8NP ☎ (0352) 661467 (catalogue £4); **Coré in London**; Phylea 61 rue Quimcampoix, Paris 75004 ☎ 42 76 01 80 and **The Trashy Lingerie Store** 402 N La Cienega Blvd, Los Angeles CA 90048 ☎ (213) 655 5437

Regulation sells the wildest and weirdest range of gas masks, anti-gravity high altitude suits, 60's pac-a-macks alongside stylish rubber ball gowns and suits. 17a St Albans Place, London N1 0NX ☎ (0171) 226 0658

St Michael's Emporium sells leather attire of the Middle Ages through to Armageddon, plus poet shirts and wedding dresses! 156 E Second St, Suite One, New York NY 10009, USA ☎ (212) 995 8359

Spandex – thick, sensual full body sheaths and isolation hoods from **Mark I** Chester, POB 42501 San Francisco, CA 94101, USA ☎ (415) 621 6294

Swingers' ID Pins from Dionysian Designs PO Box 1086 Greenfield, MA USA and **Lifestyles** PO Box 7128 Buena Park CA 90622-7128 ☎ (714) 229 4870

Tentacle make erotic fetish wear with an inspiration that comes from ritual performance and female surrealism (rather than just displaying your bits) PO Box 20 Grantham Lincolnshire NG33 5RB

Wildcat International has now opened a huge showroom for wholesale and retail customers in Brighton from which they sell the world's most exciting range of things for body decorations, including fluorescent and other exotic piercing jewellery. 16 Preston Street, Brighton, UK ☎ (01273) 323758. *Warren*, offering expert piercing at **Perforations** on the same premises, can be contacted on ☎ (01273) 326577

shopping

fluorescent and other exotic piercing jewellery

▶ *created by Jeff Willis*

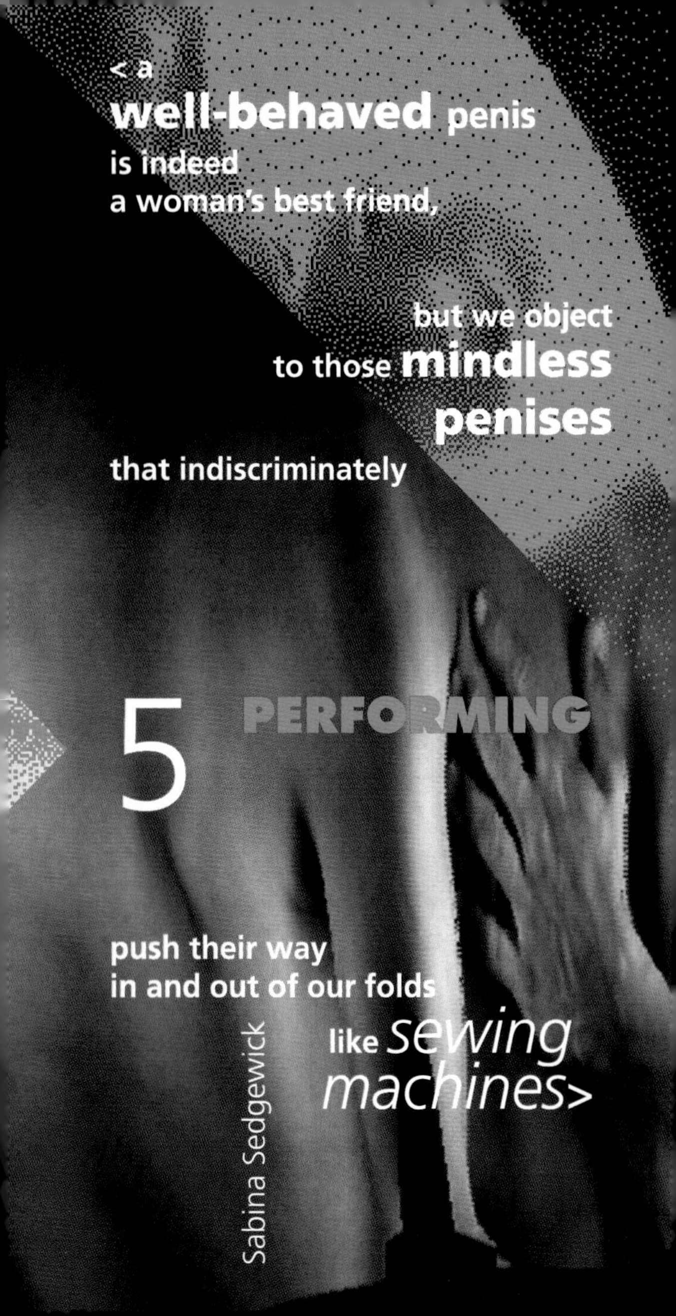

< a
well-behaved penis
is indeed
a woman's best friend,

but we object
to those **mindless**
penises
that indiscriminately

5   PERFORMING

push their way
in and out of our folds
like *sewing*
machines>

Sabina Sedgewick

The Performer Within You

We have all seen erotic pictures, images, and performances and thought "that could be me — that's how I feel when I'm sexy". Well, it *can* be you.

There's a performer lurking inside nearly all of us but, for all those who have realised their potential, millions of others never even make the first step. Shyness and lack of confidence obviously hold people back but what most people need is encouragement from someone, usually someone they love. Once you realise they like watching you, they can tease more and more exhibitionism out of you,

a new capacity for arousal

opening you up to a whole new area of eroticism. Carol Queen described the experience as a new capacity for arousal. Women of all shapes, sizes and ages are saying such things today, but men rarely seem to get that far. The norm is the female stripper, and men see no place for themselves as erotic performers, being afraid that they could not even look, let alone act, sexy.

Men

Many cultures have specific times of the year when people get to let their hair down, like Carnival and Mardi Gras. Men get relaxed enough to

dress flamboyantly and women find themselves enjoying what they see. In Britain, some men have found an outlet through drag and tranny clubs, wearing clothes and make-up normally used by women, either to look female or to create their own look. This has had an interesting spin off, in that they sometimes do it so well that women feel inspired to make their own attempts to out-camp the boys!

Fetish fashion has offered men — and women — the chance to dress up, dress down, and expose their bodies. Wearing only a few leather straps is cool in fetish and even some swing clubs. Exposing your body and being exhibitionistic has become a form of safer sex. The average man, however, still feels uncomfortable parading around like this. Sometimes this repression creeps into their lovemaking. Men are especially prone to attempting to "perform" during sex. This is called spectatoring; the goal being to

wearing only a few leather straps is cool

impress rather than to enjoy. They may even imagine some fictitious person is in the room, watching them make love. Spectatoring has a devastating effect, leading to performance anxiety and even loss of erections, to coming too soon and feeling too awkward. The cure is to learn how to let yourself go, and sensate focus often helps. This is a strict sexual regime where you forget any kind of lovemaking for a few weeks, except the simple act of touch. You take it in turns with your partner to touch each others' bodies with your hands, concentrating on the sensations, tuning-in like you tune-in a radio, so that you increase your physical awareness. You may describe how it feels to each other, or remain silent. If you find it difficult to concentrate, just try harder. Many people find sensate focus very challenging, but the end result brings sexual liberation. It will probably make you more aware of your body so you'll want to show it off.

Naturism

Most people equate the naked body with exhibitionism but this is usually far from the truth. Exhibitionism is a conscious effort of sexual exposure whereas naturism is not about showing off. People who have never been to a naturist beach or club presume that sex is the *raison d'être* of nudism, but if and when they do go, they realise that the naturists there simply accept each other's bodies. The enjoyment comes from feeling free, enjoying the sun and air on their bodies, rather than sexual. This doesn't mean to say that the sexy ones don't get aroused, just like anybody anywhere.

Only particular clubs cater to sexy encounters (and these are the ones listed in this book). Naturists, on the whole, are family-oriented. They wish to "improve" their reputation and fear that sex endorses the false image that has been thrust upon them by the ignorance and greed of the media.

performing

198

Female Exhibitionists

Female exhibitionists often say that they had no idea that they could enjoy performing until they happened to have a camera or camcorder pointed at them and which opened up the exhibitionist side of themselves. Even shy and retiring types report this transformation. Women who work in peep shows report similar experiences. What they thought might be just a means of earning some cash changed their entire sexual conception of themselves. They find themselves enormously turned on and do things they never thought was in them.

Once women start showing off they

a mother and daughter team took part and 385 men were serviced

can get really carried away. Performance records are always being set up at swing clubs. An early nomination was from **Plato's Retreat**. **Tara Alexander** got 78 gents off vaginally, orally and manually and was taped doing so. After this, the Dutch contact-magazine **Chick** held a sex marathon inviting women to see who could keep at it the longest. Four girls including a mother and daughter team took part and 385 men were serviced in all. **Jenny Van de Hoole** took the record with 145 men. Now, **Linda Murrie** of Humpty Doo in Australia's Northern Territory has set her heart on taking the world record away from Jenny and she's in search of 150 men (premature ejaculators will be ideal, she thinks) and volunteers should contact her at her company, G-String Services in Darwin. Back in Europe, at the club Le Cheminée in Paris, our Suffolk Poke-a-Rama girl Rona took 38 different men, some of whom had come back for second helpings, the first young man coming back for six! She now wants to beat the record at Club Paradise in Amsterdam. The French swinger and porn star of the 70's, Sylvia Bourdon wrote an account in her autobiography of having over 70 men in the Bois de Bologne. Nina Harley conducted a wall-to-wall fuckathon at one of the Lifestyles Conventions with the spontaneity and fun to make one of the best orgy videos on the market, Welcome to My Orgy, marketed by Video Alternatives. A new porn star, Annabel Chong, legendary for her performances in Depraved Fantasies 3 and Anal Queen, is offering the public the chance to fuck her on screen to see how many she can take in one film. This is an equal opportunities offer, and fluffers are being employed to make sure all participants go on set stiff. Condoms will be worn. Volunteers can write to her c/o Fantastic Pictures, 21528 Osborne Street, Canoga Park, California 91304. Such contests are not always limited to women, and at the annual ten-day Ballybunion Bachelor Contests of the 70's and 80's in Ireland, one of my readers scored with no less than 25 different women, representing County Limerick in a contest against 22 other bachelors from other counties.

Thankfully, most sexual performance is not competitive. Here are some of the many forms it takes:—

Striptease

Stripping is an under-rated art. So often, shows take place in down-trodden pubs and sordid little sex theatres. The audience sometimes enjoy the sleazy aspect but it can make the strippers feel like social outcasts instead of stars. It also means that few women go, stunting their erotic education. Trendies these days wouldn't dream of adding strip to their sex repertoires although perhaps after reading this you might consider becoming a

you might consider becoming a jungle cat at home

performing

199

jungle cat at home. All you have to do is decide who will put themselves in the position of voyeur, while the other dresses provocatively and puts on an act. It can build up a new tension and excitement between you. Teasing, flashing, turning away before exposing, unbuttoning slowly, thrusting bits out and playing with yourself, bending over to offer different views, dancing slowly and moving your body enticingly, using a mirror to add narcissistic spice, shimmering up towards your partner and allowing them to feel through silky underwear — all these manoeuvres are part of the normal striptease routine. If doing it alone together ever gets dull, you can always head off to the local amateur strip night, and perform to a crowd. Professional male strippers usually put a lot of humour into their act and provoke the women by inviting one of them to suck them off under a cloak and by making other wicked suggestions. Female strippers also play with their audience and some even offer hand jobs using baby lotion or talcum power. Stag nights get quite blue, and female strippers should be warned that going to private homes to do a stag will normally end up with the men expecting a gang bang.

Live Sex Shows

You both have to be ambitiously exhibitionisitc to make love on a stage or in front of friends at a party. You need to consider how to position yourselves so that people can see the action. Most theatres have revolving beds so that the angle is constantly changing. You have to be spontaneous because the man may take some time to get a hard-on or lose it, getting distracted by nerves or the audience. At these times, kiss and do a little simulated sex until it goes up again. Most couples fuck or play to their favourite music to help them along. The music usually dictates the pace. There are many different styles, but usually the sex is slow, acrobatic and sombre. Sometimes the audience are invited to join in. The man in the audience with the most bravado needs little encouragement to rip all his clothes off and make an idiot of himself, so this part of the show is normally more amusing than erotic. It's better if the performers can chose someone from the audience who would be more receptive to their seduction, but these types are usually too nervous to go out in front of the audience.

his friends on either side of him can have a grapple too

Lap Dancing

Many strip clubs throughout America feature lap dancing, called *Mardi Gras* in New York, and *friction dancing* in Tampa. It's performed by girls wearing stockings, suspenders, panties and bras, exposing their cleavage and bottoms but protecting their tender parts. The dancer is invited, by the wave of some money in the form of a crisp note, to dance on the gentleman's lap and shimmy up against his crotch. The more money he tucks in her bra and stocking-tops, the more she will let him grope, but he knows not to push the boundaries or he will be deserted. Sometimes a man will pay a bit more so his friends on either side of him can have a grapple too. Good lap dancers distract the entire audience's attention from the main show by their flamboyant flirting and gyrating. Lap dancing has developed into couch dancing in some clubs, especially in Florida and Washington State. On the couch, the man can get his dick out and play with himself as well as the performer.

Table Dancing

This has just hit London, brought over by Peter Stringfellow. It's big in Australia, America and Canada. There is no touching, the dancer just wiggles her tits and bum very very close to the man's nose. It's either done on a one-to-one basis or the dancer stands on a table surrounded by seated men. The money offered

makes the girl feel appreciated and she tucks it in her underwear. The atmosphere becomes highly charged due to the intense teasing.

Belly Dancing

Belly dancing has become very popular in the West, both with men and women. You have to isolate parts of your body so you can move them independently of one another. The slow, sensual belly rolls are highly erotic to perform and to watch, as the movements look so like the hip movements we making during sex, only exaggerated and extremely enticing. Traditional dances change pace several times throughout the routine. Chiffon veils and beaded fabrics in vibrant colours add visual excitement and the eyes are used to lure the imagination of the audience. Belly

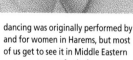

dancing was originally performed by and for women in Harems, but most of us get to see it in Middle Eastern restaurants or at festivals.

The Peeps & Booths

Most red light districts have peep shows: a round space surrounded by a corridor with little windows that go up when you put a coin in, and down again when the money runs out (usually just when it's getting interesting!). If you continue to feed your slot you will get the attention of the girl who is performing on the inside. She will be feeling safe to flirt with you and knows you want to see

her pussy and be seduced. The corridor has to be hosed down to clean the spunk off the walls and floor. More interesting is the one-to-one booth. Booth babies enjoy their work more because they can build up some rapport with the man who has paid to watch. She can do as he asks and what *she* wants too. Showing off to a stranger inside your own safe environment with a glass wall between you, being as provocative as you like, knowing he is jerking off, is many an exhibitionists' ideal. It's a similar situation to producing custom-made

the performer gets turned on and masturbates too

videos for friends or clients, except that this is much more immediate. Sometimes the performer gets turned on and masturbates too which is all the more fun for the viewer.

Padded Booth Dancing

This is a new craze to hit America. The dancer is inside a padded booth and can be touched but not seen by the audience, who put their hands through holes in the booth wall.

put their hands through holes in the booth wall

Radical Performance Art

Politically-motivated performance art was all the vogue in the 60's and 70's, and is just becoming so again. The Vienna Action Group in the late

60's was renowned for people pissing, shitting and having orgasms on stage and Otto Muehl continued his show, taking a live goose on stage, killing it, and then sticking its neck up people. In the mid 70's, Coum put on sexually shocking shows in London with Genesis P Orridge and Cosey Fanni Tutti did piss acts and a notorious Prostitution show at the ICA. Lindsay Kemp was running a sexually explicit dance group which become a great influence on stars such as David Bowie, Derek Jarman and Marisa Carr. The biggest star of our time is Annie Sprinkle whose performances have transformed the way many people think about sex and pornography. She began performing in Jennifer Blowdryer's Smut Fests which led her to do a one-woman show, the tale of her life of prostitution, burlesque and experimentation, which includes an invitation for the audience to examine her cervix through a speculum. Her work is subversive. She thought "everyone wanted to look at my pussy so I decided to let them see right inside". Fun and powerful, magical and orgasmic, her shows have inspired many other performers and artists, both

"everyone wanted to look at my pussy, so I decided to let them see right inside"

professional and amateur. She has given people who have something to say about sex the confidence to perform on stage. The Brighton Festival will be having erotic performance artists in 1995 as part of their fetish theme. In America, shows are getting more and more outrageous. David Aaron Clark performed with his girlfriend at a venue in New York in 1994 and upset the audience by drinking her piss then spraying it all over the audience from his mouth.

performing

202

▶ addresses

Australia and New Zealand After Dark
reviews and lists Antipodal performers, theatres and table dancing antics.
People Magazine, ACP Pty Ltd, 54 Park Street, Sydney ☎ (02) 282 8000

David Charles
hires strippers and imaginative shows for stag nights and events in the UK
☎ (01442) 64402

Divinity
covers subversive performance art and film
POB 108 Stockport Cheshire SK1 4DD, UK

Exotic Dancer
200 pages in full colour offering a detailed description of the US and Canadian strip clubs. It also has a special VIP card deal and a dance contest every year in December.
ED Publications Inc, 3437 West 7th St, Suite 209, Fort Worth, TX 76107, USA

The Exotic Dancers Reunion
is an annual event featuring legends from burlesque's golden era.
Exotic World, 29053 Wild Road, Helendale, California 92342, USA ☎ (619) 243 5261

Headpress
Interviews with and articles on radical performers.
PO Box 160 Stockport, Cheshire SK1 4ET
☎ fax/phone (0161) 796 1935

Bill Margold
is a wonderful agent for erotic performers.
8231 Delongpre Ave, Suite 1, West Hollywood, California 90046, USA
☎ (213) 560 7121

Mentertainment
keeps enthusiasts up-to-date on the contests and circuit of Go-Go, topless and nude dancers in America.
Box 9445 Elizabeth, NJ 07202, USA

The Official Strip Joint Guide
comes out twice a year at $17 per issue and provides critical reviews of clubs in North America.
William A Harland, OSJG, PO Box 568 Quincy, Illinois 6306, USA

Rainbow
is the main striptease agency for London and the South of England
☎(01305) 852215

Sisters of Perpetual Indulgence Inc
is a gay theatrical group confronting attitudes, to 'epiate, stigmatic guilt and promulgate universal joy.'
584 Castro St #392 San Francisco CA 94114, USA ☎(415)8646722 USA. Monthly nuncheons are held at Central Station, 37 Wharfdale Rd, London N1, UK

The Smut Fest
Eastern Time Productions, PO Box 102, New York NY 100009, USA or The Leydig Trust PO Box 4ZB London W1A 4ZB

Stripper
reviews and lists the American clubs and agents.
Fax ☎(212) 399 0439

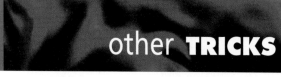

other **TRICKS**

performing

Despite my warnings about performance during sex, there are some things people can perfect to increase their sexual enjoyment

Female Ejaculation

Some women ejaculate naturally when climaxing, others can learn how. The first thing to do is to get your pelvic muscles toned up, squeezing like you do when you have to stop peeing. Learn where your G-Spot is. You can sometimes

this means you are about to spurt

feel a little spongy lump, especially when you're aroused, just 2-3 inches up the front wall of your vagina. If this area is rubbed during sex, you may get a 'wanting to pee' sensation. Try masturbating the area around your pee hole, just in front of your vagina. You may feel the glands filling up and this means you are

about to spurt. Use the other hand to press down on your lower belly. Bear down. Ejaculate may come out in jets or waves. Once practiced, you might find it happens automatically but you may need some months before this happens. Even then, some women just don't.

Male Multiple Orgasms

With perfect ejaculatory awareness, most men can come many times. You need to become extremely aware of your organs and how they work. Get your pelvic floor muscles in trim by tightening (like when you do to stop peeing) and relaxing them. Be experimental with masturbation and learn to differentiate between the various sensations. Become sensitive

keep coming again and again

to that time just before the 'point of no return'. When you feel your balls tightening, learn how to relax them. Come very slowly. Attempt orgasm without ejaculation. Exercise, awareness and your resultant enthusiasm will enable you to keep your erection after your first orgasm, and keep coming again and again, either with or without ejaculation. There will be less spunk each time you come.

Coital Arousal Technique

This has been described by Nobile and Eichel to help men fuck in a way which encourages women to experience clitoral orgasms. With the man on top, resting his torso gently on the woman, he rides her high, so the upper part of his cock grazes her clit. She keeps her legs down and thrusts her pelvis into him. A rocking movement is set up directed by the woman, while he hardly moves.

The Perfect Enema

Pleasurable in itself and a pre-requisite to handballing or fisting, this is best done near a lavatory. You need a two-litre enema bag with a long tube, a tap and nozzle. You can buy such things from a medical company (look in the Shopping section). They can also supply an enema solution or you can use Simple Soap, by pouring boiling

put a funnel into their bum and piss in it

water over it (one slab dissolving for 2 minutes). Don't use booze. When the liquid is body temperature, put it in the enema bag, let the bubbles out, then tighten the tap. Your partner kneels down, you grease their arse hole with KY and hang the enema bag about two feet above their bottom. Insert the nozzle and encourage your partner as you let the liquid into their body. Remove the nozzle and engage in sex play. The pressure from the liquid will add pleasure to their arousal. When they can hold it no longer, let them rush off to the toilet. A happy alternative is to put a funnel into their bum and piss in it. Serious enema play requires a Balloon Enema which prevents the liquid coming out, but is not available in the UK.

Handballing

A spiritual and sensual activity, involving intense intimacy and trust. It takes months of practice to even start fisting, and needs great care and knowledge to ensure you don't cause damage. The book *Trust* is devoted to teaching people and it is listed under *Handballing* in the Reaching section. Here is a short outline of what to do. The person to be handballed should, for the 36 hours before, eat only things that pass through the body quickly: fruit, vegetables and grains. They should take a laxative the night before and eat very little that day, just have cold drinks. Take another laxative two hours before starting and lie down in a relaxed state. A sling is the best place to recline. The handballer should trim their fingernails and put on a glove. If using a latex glove, you should only use water-soluble lubricants. Establish rapport so that you know which terms mean what. It's a good idea to agree that "stop" will mean stop and "Out" will mean that you withdrawn your arm slowly.

ecstatic and reach orgasm and you may wish to do this at the same time, being careful to keep the arm inside quite still. Beyond the rectum, lies the S-shaped sigmoid colon, which takes a double turn, then there are a series of loops opening into the descending colon. Only proceed if the loop gives way to your probing. Take extreme care and move very

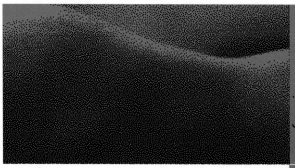

Kiss and fondle them in the sling, to make them feel adored. Lubricate your glove and give your lover's arse a good coating too. Enter with your hand in the 'swan's head' position, and wait for your lover to suck it in. Firmly massage the walls of the orifice. All movements should be slow. Rest. Then feel around to find out where your hand is going. The rectum swings forward towards the navel, back, then forward again. If your lover's legs are at 90 degrees, it will be easier to negotiate the bends. You can play with yourself as you proceed, as this is a sexual adventure. Your lover may become

slowly indeed. Experienced people can allow elbows and beyond although this can seem awkward. If you decide to use a foot for a change, never put the heel in as it can get locked inside.

Screwing Yourself (men)

Oil your bum with KY and get a semi-erection. Slide your testicles to one side, push your cock back, and ease it into your arse. Slowly does it. Once inside, you can get a little stiffer but not so much that your erection forces it forward and out. Even if you can't do it, don't discount the idea. I have seen a photo of my friend Grant doing it. He used to swear that, before safer sex was essential, the experience was even better when he got someone else's cock inside too, at the same time.

massage the walls of the orifice

Sucking yourself off
(men)

Men with long, inflexible backs will find this impossible but it's worth getting a supple back for. Sit on the floor near a solid wall so that, when you lie back, your head is propped up against the wall. Swing your legs over your head so your toes touch the wall and then adjust your position so that your cock is pointing towards your mouth. When you lift your buttocks up, yummy, it's in!

Twirling tassels
(women)

When strippers twirl tassels on their nipples, it looks incredible. The tassels must be the correct weight and on pivots. Shoulder shimmy so they twirl the *same* way. To reverse them and make them twirl in opposite directions, click your heels up and down.

if he *is* looking, he'll be mighty impressed

Shooting Ping Pong Balls
(women)

You need to train your pelvic floor muscles, and this was described earlier under female ejaculation. Kneel on all fours and lower your stomach, and drawing in, as if you were sucking in air. Insert the balls and tighten your abdomen tightly. Bear down, as if to fart at the same time as squeezing the muscles around your cunt. The Horse Sutra yoga position would help you learn this technique where you stand in water, draw it in, then shoot it out again.

Putting on a Condom
with your Mouth

Prostitutes are used to doing this with customers who might not wish to use a condom. Take the tip of the condom in your mouth, unroll it with your fingers, stretch it a little, put the tip of the penis to your lips and release the condom over the cock. The dick needn't be fully erect. If he's not looking he'll think he's just getting a blow job and if he *is* looking, he'll be mighty impressed.

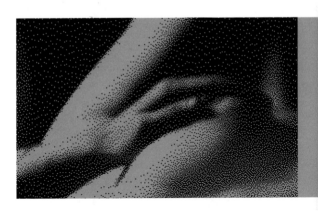

**THE
PORN REVIEW
MAGAZINE**

BNI appears
magically through
your door when
you subscribe

$2 per issue, $3 for
furreners - checks
to Richard Freeman -
we trade for the
unusual and if it's
unusual enough,
we review it.
Send us your writing
and home movies.
We'll use them.

Batteries
Not Included

130 W. Limestone St. Yellow Springs OH 45387 USA

< the purpose of pornography
is to show us a world we'd like to see

pornography serves sexual fantasy
the way science fiction serves
utopian social fantasies –

LOOKING

6

pornography should
not be
documentary,
but *dream-like* >

Larry Tritten

visual *desire*

Beautiful sexy people are great to look at but there's more to voyeurism than that. Commercial porn has become cliché and dull and people are becoming more conscious of visual desire, seeking more experimental imagery, using models who fall outside the young, twenty-year old female stereotype.

Talented photographers no longer seem ashamed of trying their hand at sexy pictures and some amazing erotica is emerging. In the new *Scenario* magazine, the celebrated photographer China Hamilton claimed "eroticism is a most demanding subject and it is at its best if it can convey both overt and subtle messages on many levels." Confused between trying to avoid "lookism" and having your fantasies stuck in old-age clichés? Many people are, but why not appreciate both?

Women want to enjoy looking at men the way men have always looked at women. A British group of female photographers called Exposure run workshops to help people explore their "erotic gaze". The last few years have seen many sex magazines and novels aimed at women. Few of these have actually moved the barriers forward but least they made women sit up and think about what they *do* want to see and discuss their differences.

Some people are into video, some prefer novels, others glossy magazines, arty books, fanzines. The choice yours. The following listings will hopefully open you up to the possibilities that you may not already know about. On the video front,

there is much crap to sift through to find anything worthwhile. Videos are churned out, often three being made in the same week to the same formula, using the same studs and stars. Sadly, taking more care and using imagination doesn't pay off, as it costs more and brings in no more income. Safer sex is rarely used on set, they just test porn stars for HIV on a regular basis. Don't follow their example! I hope the lists will help the discerning viewer. When ordering videos from abroad, remember the different incompatible systems: PAL in UK, Western Europe (except France) and most Commonwealth countries, Australia and New Zealand; SECAM in Eastern Europe, France, and North Africa; NTSC in USA, Canada, Japan, Philippines, Korea, West Indies and Central America. The wrong system will not work on your video player — best to get a multi-system machine next time you replace your old one. British customs, who used to allow you to keep a couple of sexy videos or magazines, are now being more stringent. Ordering by post is also risky. Whereas the stuff just used to get seized, purchasers are now getting police visits and being prosecuted for possession.

looking

209

overt and subtle messages on many levels

The Advertising Archives include much erotica especially from the 40's and 50's. London. Fax ☎(0171) 837 8701

The Best American Erotica 1993 edited by Susie Bright is an incredible collection of stories which will open your mind. Macmillan Publishing Co, 866 Third Avenue, New York NY 10022. $12

Bibliothèque Nationale in Paris has restricted access to its collection of erotic Greek pottery, prints and sexually explicit literature by Pièrre Louys, Octave Mirabeau, Restif de la Bretonne , Picasso and casts of other French artists

The British Library in the British Museum holds an enormous collections in various departments, some in Oriental Antiquities but most are in the restricted section. You have to know what to ask for before being allowed to view it, and you will be watched as you do. Museum Street, London WC1

The Delta Collection in the Library of Congress in Washington has a large collection of older erotic books seized in customs collections. It is open to anyone over 18 but they will not let you browse through their catalogue; you have to know what to request

The Sexuality Library is in the feminist sex store, Good Vibrations where you can hire hardcore books, toys and videos which. They also have a Sexuality Library Jr., a mini catalogue for educational books for use by children, adolescents, parents and teachers. 1210 Valencia Street, San Francisco CA 94110

Spirit of London Life Library at the London Life League in Montreal stores articles, catalogues, texts, books and magazines on corsets and tight lacing. Photocopies are available to members. PO Box 1319 Place Bonaventure, Montreal Canada H5A 1H1

The Edward Nikola Collection of Erotic Art was left to the City of Vienna in 1905 and includes works by Egon Schiele and Gustav Klimt

The Institute for the Advanced Study of Human Sexuality has over two million erotic books, magazines and videos which can be viewed by the public by appointment. They are attempting to get it all onto CD Roms so it will be available to all. 11523 Frankin Street, San Francisco CA 94109, USA ☎(415) 928 1133

The (Kinsey) Institute for Sex Research Bloomington, Indiana. A microfilm collection of a thousand titles dating from 1700-1889

Leather Archives and Museum is collecting memorabilia of the fetish world, to fight isolation, invisibility & fragmentation 5015 N Clark St, Chicago IL 60640. ☎(312) 878 6360, fax 545 6753

Retrograph Archive is a picture archive specialising in erotica and pins-ups. They have a large collection of 1920's French sepia nudes, some of which include bondage and spanking. Run by Jilliana Ranicar-Breese from 164 Kensington Park Road, London W11 2ER fax ☎(0171) 229 3395

The Public Library on the corner of 5th Avenue and 42nd Street in New York has an Ephemera Department which keeps collections of old porn and related items. Once inside, the staff are helpful and fun

Spider Webb the internationally renowned tattoo artist has a gallery of tattoo art at 220 Main Street, Derby, Connecticut 06418, USA ☎(203) 732 4571

The Vatican Library in Rome holds hundreds of erotic books including the Register of Erotic Books published in 1936. Nobody from the outside world is allowed to view them.

the vatican library in Rome

The Victoria and Albert Museum houses John Wilmot's bawdy manuscripts, and erotic art books by the likes of Edward Fuch and more, all locked away

exhibitions

150 Ways of Loving was an exhibition put on at the Artspace on Auckland's waterfront in New Zealand to show that the boundaries between explicit pornography and other forms of expression are blurred. Defining something as "art" is no longer valid when "porn" is banned. It was a protest against forthcoming censorship legislation

The Akehurst Gallery was brave enough to put on an exhibition of all the things seized during the police's witch-hunt of Graham Ovenden, from which he was fortunately cleared. Called "The Obscene Publications versus Art" it demonstrated the radical intentions of this gallery. 1a Rede Place, London W2 ☎(0171) 243 8855

Apropos is America's first erotic art gallery. 701 East Las Olas Blvd, Ft Lauderdale, Florida 33301 ☎(305) 524 2100 fax 524 1817

Azzlo the spacious Japanese fetish and bizarre boutique in Tokyo has an art gallery which welcomes exhibitions of photographers, designers and artists of this genre. AZZLO/Discipline Gym, 21 Sakamachi, Shinjuku, Tokyo 160 ☎(3) 3356 9267 fax (3)3356 9810

Erotic Art Expo in Miami Beach, with big name judges from the art world and big cash prizes. Contact John Casey at *Sarasota Arts Review*, 1269 First Street, Suite 4, Sarasota Florida 34236 ☎(813) 364 5825

looking

211

The Exotic World Burlesque Historical Society and Museum is Dixie Evans' "Hubba Hubba Hall of Fame" with photos, shoes and G-strings from dancers going way back. She also runs the Diamonds in the Desert Exotic Dancers' Reunion and is president of the Exotic Dancers League of America. 29053 Wild Road, Helendale CA 92342, USA ☎(619) 243 5261

Gallerie Les Larmes d'Eros has great shows in Paris, showing their favourite local photographer Guy Lemaire as well as artists from abroad. 58 rue Amelot, 75011 Paris, France ☎ 43 38 33 43

Charles Gatewood's Forbidden Photographs exhibition was shown at the Morphos Gallery, San Francisco ☎(415 626 0368), and is often on tour

The Hamburg Erotic Art Museum is a four-storey warehouse housing old masters and contemporary masterpieces. They have a catalogue which can be purchased for 49DM from the museum Bernhardt Nochtstr 69, 2000 Hamburg 36, Germany fax ☎(40) 317 4758

The Lesbian and Gay Community Services Center in New York has a permanent erotic art show on all of its walls, which was done to celebrate the 20th Anniversary of the Stonewall riots. 208 West 13th Street, NY NY 10011 ☎(212) 620 7310

Michael Manning's fetishistic photos are shown as an exhibition called **Lumenagerie**, 3288 21st St, # 21, San Francisco CA 94110 ☎(415) 550 7640

Maryland Art Place's Teeny, Tint Press, Zimizdat & Other Propaganda 218 West Saratoga Street, Baltimore MD 21201 ☎(301) 962 8565. Travelling exhibition of zines

"Rated X" Exhibition annual erotic photo show at the Neikrug Photographica 244 East 68th St, New York 10021 ☎212) 288 7741 fax 737 3208

René "I am the Best Artist" Moncada's gallery in New York shows radical erotic art 147 Wooster Street, New York NY 10012 ☎(212) 982 1556

Secret Jewel Galleries are erotic art shows inside Japanese sex motels. The best are at Kokusai Hihokan at the Isawa Spa in Kofu b(0552) 625000; Kinugawa Hihiden, closer to Tokyo in Nikko ☎(0288) 770 564; and Sanzenin Inn in the Shinjuko area of Tokyo ☎(03) 200 3001

Sexart Salon sensual, erotic, outrageous and sexually radical art and writing forum organised by Mark I Chester. PO Box 422501 San Francisco CA 94142, USA ☎(415) 621 6294/544 1136

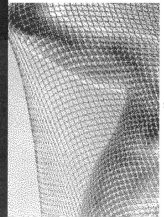

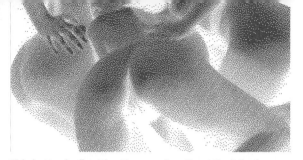

Nicholas Treadwell, a stalwart in the radical art movement has moved his gallery and exhibition space to London. Contact can be made on ☎ (0850) 221213

The Vibrator Museum is at the Good Vibrations store in San Francisco, with machines dating back to the turn of the century, helping women to see that their need for such things isn't new and the range enormous. You can view it any time at Good Vibrations, 3492 22nd Street, SF CA 94110 ☎ (315) 550 7399

What She Wants is an exhibition of photographs of sexy-looking men by female photographers which was first shown in Britain in 1994. The book under the same name, by the curator, Naomi Soloman, is published by Verso. Naomi can be contacted at PO Box 435 London SW9 OXE

those that show you the way

Exposures offers workshops on erotic photography in London, specifically women photographing men ☎ (0181) 341 6620

The Good Vibrations Guide to Sex how to have safe, fun sex in the 90's is now out, at $29 plus postage.Cleis Press PO Box 8933, Pittsburgh, PA 15221

Different Loving is a very well researched and compiled book offering in-depth interviews of people in the S/M scene. $50 from QSM, PO Box 882242 San Francisco 94188

The Other Side photographs by Nan Goldin paying tribute to people who have successfully scrambled gender lines to suit themselves, thus expressing gender euphoria. **(Cornerhouse)**

scrambled gender lines to suit themselves

Sexual Energy Ecstasy. A Practical Guide to Lovemaking Secrets of the East and West by David and Ellen Ramsdale. An excellent introduction to Tantric sex and sexual worship. Peak Skill Publishing, PO Box 5489 Plays del Ray, CA 90296.

Ties that Bind: The S/M Leather/Fetish Erotic Style — Issues, Commentary and Advice by Guy Baldwin, $14.95 Daedalus Publishing 4470 - 107 Sunset Blvd, #375, Los Angeles CA 90027

looking

213

Cupido is the leader in right-on sex. Now ten years old, with yet-to-be fulfilled promises of foreign editions (it's in Norwegian), it has lovely photos and stories about all kinds of sex involving all genders, races, ages and preferences. Postboks 9121 Gronland, 0133 Oslo, Norway

Marquis Peter Czernich's new fetish magazine which is even more adventurous and stunning-looking than << O >> was. Flensburgerstr 5, 42655 Solingen, Germany ☎(212) 586151 fax 586156

Libido — The Journal of Sex and Sensibility The thinking person's sex magazine with stylish photos. 5318 N Paulina Street, Chicago IL 60640, USA

Lust a new British magazine edited by Rosie Peake which crosses boundaries and provides erotic adventure. £2. Aurora Publishing PO Box 6556 London N13 4NY

On Our Backs Quite the best lesbian sex magazine for inspiration, information and hot stuff. Blush Entertainment Corp, 526 Castro, San Francisco, CA 94114, USA

Paramour the new 'literary and artistic erotica' mag, mostly in black & white. Sensual, trying to exploit and, unlike many of the other literary erotic mags, it doesn't lack humour. PO Box 949 Cambridge MA 02140, USA

Porn Free New kind of porn, female-made. PO Box 1365 Stuyvesant Station New York NY 10009, USA

Screw This New York tabloid has been published by Al Goldstein for over 25 years and still has the funniest and most informative sex journalism you can find. Milky Way Productions, 116 W 14th Street, New York NY 10011, USA ☎(212) 989 8001

The Spectator San Francisco's age-old tabloid with some of the most thought-provoking sexual fun you'll ever read or see. PO Box 1984 Berkeley, CA 94701-1984, USA

Verbal Abuse edited by Chi Chi Valenti is an arty, glitzy underground art mag with some erotic content from New York. 315 Park Avenue South, Rm 1611, New York NY 10010, USA. £25 sub incl post

funniest and most informative sex journalism

sex on telly

You can watch hard core sex on telly in many parts of the world but in Britain it's more problematic since they made the de-coders illegal. It's still not impossible for the determined. The Filmnet channel offers British viewers erotic films after midnight, mainly quality hard core, available also on Astra/Sky No 11. TV 1000 transmits hardcore some nights, and can also be seen through the D2-Mac decoder (you may need to keep changing your smartcard as the scrambling frequency changes) and Eurocrypt. Astra supplies the Adult Channel which can be viewed free of charge for fifteen minutes a night — just a saucy taster to tempt you to subscribe. RTL Plus on button No 1 of an Amstrad tuner is hard core German porn.

video guides

Adult Video News Yearly Adult Entertainment Guide $8.95 from AVN 8599 Venice Blvd. Suite J, Los Angeles, CA 90034, USA

The Amateur Eye reviews amateur videos PO Box 2503, Cincinnati OH 45202, USA

The Bare Facts Video Guide is constantly updated and covers just about every skin flick ever made, featuring 1,000 actresses and 500 actors who appear nude in films. £11.50 The Bare Facts PO Box 3255 Santa Clara CA 95055, USA

Batteries Not Included is the name of a newsletter devoted to fans of the hard core video world. $2 per issue Richard Freeman, 130 West Limestone St, Yellow Springs, Ohio 45387, USA

The Directory of Adult Films and the hard cord video review magazine, ***Porn Star*** from Adam, 8060 Melrose Ave, Los Angeles, CA 90046-7082

The Dirty Hacker is an American bulletin board reviewing X rated movies, whorehouses and mail order companies and showing an amazing variety of images. Modem ☎ (914) 794 1971

The Eve Fund a resource for women who are sexual with one another and wish to produce innovative, erotic, safer sex films and videos. c/o Frameline, 346 Ninth Street, San Francisco CA 94103, USA ☎ (415) 281 0292

Something Weird Catalogue PO Box 33664 Seattle WA 98133 manages to unearth all kinds of wonderful old films including the 1967 *Venus in Furs*, and sells them on video

Video XCitement a monthly tabloid specialising in amateur videos PO Box 187 Fraser, MI 48026, USA $45 US sub, $30 Canada/Mexico/$58 Europe. $70 Asia

The X-Rated Videotape Guide by Robert H Rimmer and Patrick Riley is published by Prometheus Books at £10 incl post. 59 John Glenn Drive, Amherst NY 14228-2197, USA

looking

215

specialist videos

Amateur – Video Alternatives 2317 Markoe Ave, Wentzville, MO 63385 sell hot Amateur tapes. Their vids get better and better. Almost as good is **Promotions Company** PO Box 1385 Greenville NC 27835-1385, USA. **Nasty Jacks** sells unscripted, uncensored, people-next-door videos 7210 Jordan Ave, Ste A-62, Canoga Park, CA 91393, USA; **Jani** provides loud

loud ass fucking and gang bangs

ass fucking and gang bangs in her vids PO Box 20213, Indianapolis IN 46220, USA. **Bear Cave BBS** are asking for amateur porn to swap on a one-to-one basis and advertise on Compuserve: from Modesto CA, USA ☎(209)577 6165; **Candida Royalle**'s *Lovers: An Intimate Portrait* excels with real-life experience sex from **Femme**, PO Box 268 Price Station, New York NY 10012; The Viewer's Wives series by Marcus Allen in vivid hardcore comes from **Your Choice** Postbus 2138, 1000 CC Amsterdam ☎(20) 620 4209

Banshee Productions sell high-quality specialist erotic videos including *Rapture*, the award-winning documentary about crossing the boundary between physical pain and religious ecstasy. PO Box 8844142 San Francisco, CA 94188-4142, USA

BR Creations have lots of wonderful videos which feature corsets. PO Box 4201 Mountain View, CA 94040

Bondage Videos are available from **B&D Pleasures** the best titles including *Shanna's Bondage Fantasy, Bondage Across the Border, Ariana's Bondage* and *Dream Caller Bondage. Dungeon Dykes 2* by **Fantastic Pictures** shows dildo-masked maidens with lovely natural tits engaged in domination of the hottest variety. ☎(0-800) 827 3787)

CD Roms with videos People who prefer to watch their videos on computer rather than on the VCR, can purchase these discs. **California Adult Software** POBox 50204 Long Beach, CA 90815, USA offers alternative lifestyle information & images, **The Interactive Adult Movie Almanac** produced by **New Machine** in the USA has an exhaustive coverage of stars, video and screen action analysis and **XCD** 137 S Vermont Ave, #195, LA CA 90004, USA ☎(213) 368 8940 contains the amateur erotic videos from California XCD Entertainment

dildo-masked maidens with lovely natural tits

Jennifer Clifford sells hardcore school uniform hetero-action with over-age teenage girls. Postbus 854 1440 AV Purnerend, Holland

Crossdressing videos PO Box 61263 King of Prussia, PA 19406, USA ☎(610) 640 9449 Self help and lessons in speaking, deportments, make-up and dressing

looking

216

Deep Throat Videos can be obtained from **Marlowe Sales** 11085 Olinda Street, Sun Valley CA 91352, USA

shows split penises, pussy piercings in progress

Flash Video Box 410052 San Francisco CA 94141, USA. Produce No Boundaries I and II, both X-rated, shows split penises, pussy piercings in progress and tattooed bad girls. Painless Steel features Mr Sebastian and pierced clits, cocks and nipples

Foreskins feature in the gay videos from **Tiger Media** 3808 Rosecrans Street, Suite 4000, San Diego CA 92110, USA

Girdles – Eric Kroll's stylish videos *Girdle Gulch* and *Girls from Girdleville*. Call to order from New York ☎ (212) 864 2465

Kings & Criminals, Expo '93 and Sink the Ink are three tattoo vids you can buy for £40 plus £1.50 p&p **Prayer Productions**, 61 Quantock Valley, Milton Keynes, MK4 2AQ

Kinky videos demonstrating S/M toys such as the violet wand, rope, whips etc **SandMutopia Supply Co** PO Box 11314 San Francisco CA 94101

Japanese Cartoon Porn at its best is seen in *Utotsukidojo: Legend of the Overfiend*

Masturbation — female: *Self Loving* is a video showing Betty Dodson's workshops which help women to come more easily and with more pleasure. PO Box 1933 Murray Hill, New York NY 19156 or from Blue Moon 89 London Lane, Bromley, Kent BR1 4HF

Masturbation — Male: *Fire on the Mountain: An Intimate Guide on Male Genital Massage* deals with Taoist eroticism between men,

taoist eroticism between men

made by Joseph Kramer. 45 minutes long, $60. **EroSpirit Research Institute,** PO Box 3893, Oakland CA 94609

Maximum Perversion is a pretty exciting range of videos from **Scala BV** in Amsterdam which include rubber, group sex and everything. You risk all kinds of crap from our HM Customs by requesting them, but here's the address: HPF NZ Voorburgwal 66, Suite 95 Amsterdam 1012SC Holland

Messy mud and cake fighting videos Aquantics Beach House, 2

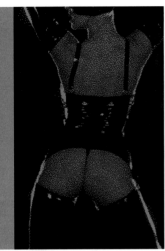

St Julian Terrace, Tenby Dyfed SA70 7BL, UK

Messy pie throwing and wrestling videos from **Video Vortex** 5699 Kanan Road Suite 320, Agoura, CA 91301, USA

Naturism The Naturist Video Club run by Susan Mayfield allows members to make and buy naturist videos. PO Box 65, Leighton Buzzard, Bedfordshire LUT 8TJ, UK

Necromantik & Necromantic 2 are to do with the relationship between sex and death. Necromantik shows Monika M having sex with a corpse. **Videomania** Suite 129 2520 N Lincoln, Chicago IL 60614, USA

Pumping Dick Videos Nyitray, PO Box 7181 Roselle, New Jersey 07203, USA

Safe Sex *Safe Is Desire* is aimed at lesbians and is hot and fun. **Fatale Video** 526 Castro Street, San Francisco CA 94114, USA. Videos aimed at gays, lesbians and straights are available from the **Terrence Higgins Trust** 52 Grays Inn Road, London WC1X 8LT ☎(0171) 831 0330 and **Gay Men's Health Crisis** Box 274, 132 W 24th Street, New York NY 10001 ☎(212) 807 6655

Scat videos c/o Martifoto, PO Box 669, 2501 CR Den Haag, Holland. Shot at the Master Shit Sanctuary at Palazzo della Merde at His Excellency, as well as some American tapes. All men

The Sex Maniac's Ball Video is out in the shops so please go along to your local videostore and make sure they've got copies stocked on their shelves after you've bought your own copy. £15 ($40 for NTSC) to The Leydig Trust, PO Box 4ZB, London W1A 4ZB

Shaving videos of men from **Golden Images** 1164 Ventura Blvd, Suite 655-D, Studio City CA 91604, USA

Sixties classics from Jezabel Films — lots of old fun plus *I am Curious — Yellow*. BCM Box 9235, London WC1N 3XX

Annie Sprinkle's range from *Sluts & Goddesses* to *Annie & Les* are available in all format from her at PO Box 435 Prince Street Station, New York 10012, USA

Swing videos are the craze in the USA and couples who want to perform on video to promote their local club, provide hot action. Sometimes they script the show, other times, when they've got some really flamboyant exhibitionists, it's spontaneous and

looking

218

uncut. Amongst the best are: **Zane Entertainments** at 21526 Osborne St, Canoga Park, CA 91304; **Glitz Video** at 942 Calle Amanecer Ste E, San Clemente CA 92673; **Odyssey Group** PO Box 77597 Los Angeles CA 90007; and **Positively Pagan** 5632 Van Vuys Blvd, Van Nuys CA 91401

Transvestite and Transsexual Crossdresser Videos from **Executive Imports International** 210 5th Avenue, Suite 1102, New York, NY 10010

Unusual Sexual Practices Brenda Love, authoress of the Encyclopedia of the same name, has made a video using slides and narration. It is available from the **Institute for the Advanced Study of Human Sexuality**, 1523 Franklin Street, San Francisco CA 94109, USA ☎(415) 928 1133

Vintage Video Porn can be obtained from **Filmfare Video Labs** 2508 Fifth Avenue, Suite 175, Seattle WA 98121 who specialise in video compilations of old stag and strippers' films. Catalogue $3. **Video Specialists** produce the *What Got Grandpa Hot* series of 20's and 30's silent porn, available from 182 Jackson Street, Dallas PA 18612, USA ☎(717) 675 0227. **The Lusty Lady sex theatre** in San Francisco has vintage porn in its video booths

Wrestling videos from **Festelle** PO Box 267 Windlesham, Surrey GU20 6AY, England. Catfighting, topless wrestling, medieval mud fighting, arm wrestling and female Thai boxing

erotic awards

looking

AVN Awards take place in January in Las Vegas c/o 8599 Venice Blvd. Suite J, Los Angeles, CA 90034, USA

The Erotic Oscars are presented at the Planet Sex Ball in March, to the best of many categories of performance, production and achievement

FOXE Awards for porno stars & fans 8231 DeLongepre Ave #1, West Hollywood, CA 90046, USA ☎(213) 650 7121

Hot D'Or Porno Awards at the Cannes Film Festival in the South of France Paris ☎ (14) 243 2222

US Erotic Film Festival UC Theater, 2036 University Avenue, Berkeley, California 94704, USA ☎(415) 843 6267

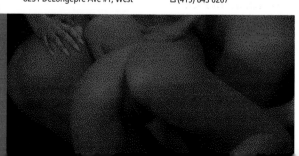

Here is a list of the best porno videos, compiled by Richard Freeman of **Batteries Not Included** specially for video fans reading this book:

Best Sex Videos ever

3AM (Cal Vista)
Georgina Spelvin in a true American tragedy

800 Fantasy Lane (Cal Vista)
Jamie Gillis tries to con Nancy Suiter, Hillary Summers, Serena, and Desiree Cousteau

Amanda By Night (Caballero)
Veronica Hart and R. Bolla as call girl and detective in a fine murder mystery

Baby Face (VCA)
Early and wonderful deRenzy romp

Bad Girls (Collector's)
Michelle Bauer and Anna Ventura meet Ron Jeremy as a boy scout

Barbara Broadcast (VCA)
Annette Haven helps Henry Paris turn food into sex

Butterflies (Caballero)
How are you gonna keep 'em down on the farm after they've seen Harry Reems?

Cafe Flesh (VCA)
Rinse Dream's midnight movie

Candy Strippers (Arrow)
Uncut, a porn classic. Cut, still the best nurses movie ever

Corruption (VCA)
Richard Mahler's remaking of Wagner's Das Rheingold

The Dancers (VCX)
John Leslie, Richard Pacheco, Joey Silvery and Randy West as male strippers

Dangerous Stuff (Command)
Eric Edwards tour de force with Angel

Desires Within Young Girls (Caballero)
Georgina Spelvin helps her daughters find husbands

Devil In Miss Jones (Arrow)
Damiano classic with Spelvin

Devil In Miss Jones Part 2 (VCA)
This time as a comedy with Spelvin and Jacqueline Lorians

Devil In Miss Jones Part 3 & 4 (VCA)
And this time as Dark Brothers with Lois Ayres

Dixie Ray—Hollywood Star (Caballero)
John Leslie in the best porno P.I. movie ever

Do Ya Wanna Be Loved? (AFV)
Rene Bond's last movie

Ecstasy Girls (Caballero)
Gillis, Leslie and Paul Thomas in classy Robert McCallum extravaganza

how are you gonna keep 'em down on the farm after they've seen Harry Reems?

Every Woman Has A Fantasy (VCA)
John Leslie in drag listens to women's fantasies

Exposed (VCA)
John Leslie tries to hide from Sharon Kane the fact that he was once in porn

F (Collector's)
John Leslie meets Seka in a house at the end of time

Felicia (Quality X)
  Fine European film of a young
  woman's sexual initiation

Firestorm (Command)
  Three part Cecil Howard drama of
  the lives of the rich and infamous

Her Name Was Lisa (VCA)
  Samantha Fox in Richard Mahler
  tragedy

Honeypie (VCA)
  Very hot loops with excellent S/M
  scene

Hot Dreams (Caballero)
  Sharon Mitchell in heat

Insatiable (Caballero)
  Marilyn Chambers' big budget
  special with John Holmes

Midnight Heat (VCA)
  Jamie Gillis as a killer on the run in
  Mahler classic

The Naughty Victorians (VCA)
  S&M set to Gilbert & Sullivan

Neon Nights (Command)
  Cecil Howard dreams with and of
  Lysa Thatcher

New Wave Hookers (VCA)
  Dark Brothers with Traci Lords as
  the devil

Nightdreams (Caballero)
  Dorothy LeMay's finest, Rinse
  Dream's best

Nothing To Hide (Cal Vista)
  Leslie & Pacheco redo Steinbeck.

The Opening Of Misty Beethoven
(VCA)
  Metzger's masterpiece with Gillis
  and Constance Money. Perhaps the
  best ever

Other Side Of Julie (Cal Vista)
  John Leslie charms everyone but
  his wife

Outlaw Ladies (VCA)
  Henri Pachard's women get
  revenge

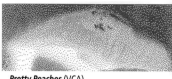

Pretty Peaches (VCA)
  Desiree Cousteau is on the loose

**The Private Afternoons of Pamela
Mann** (Quality X)
  Henry Paris comedy with Barbara
  Bourbon

Resurrection Of Eve (Mitchell
Brothers)
  Marilyn Chambers rises again

Satisfiers Of Alpha Blue (AFV)
  Damiano in sci-fi with Lysa
  Thatcher

Sensational Janine (Caballero)
  Patricia Rhomberg and a cast of
  thousands

Sensations (Caballero)
  Brigitte Maier as a young
  American meets such wonderfully
  decadent Europeans including
  Tuppy Owens

Sex World (Essex)
  Anthony Spinelli shows what Club
  Med should be

Story Of Joanna (AVC)
  Damiano directs Gillis in
  master/slave classic

Taboo American Style (VCA)
  Four part supersoap with Raven

Take Off (VXP)
  Leslie Bovee in a comic remake of
  The Picture Of Dorian Gray

Talk Dirty To Me (Caballero)
  Leslie and Pacheco in prequel to
  Nothing To Hide

V-The Hot One (Cal Vista)
  Annette Haven at her best

Wet Rainbow (AFV)
  Spelvin & Reems start a
  menage a trois

looking

221

Best Recent Videos

Anything That Moves (VCA)
Selena Steele and Tracy Winn in stylish John Leslie mystery about nude dancers

Behind Closed Doors (Vivid)
Barbara Dare retires to the country and finds her real life boyfriend

The Big Thrill (Vidco)
Hair Dressers serve an aphrodisiac in the coffee and all sex breaks out

Buttman Vs. Buttwoman (Elegant Angel)
Tianna takes off with Buttman's camera

Buttman's Revenge (Elegant Angel)
Buttman, cameraless, is down and out in LA

Buttman's Ultimate Workout (Evil Angel)
Buttman searches for Zara Whites while the women pump iron and sweat

Chameleons (VCA Platinum)
Deirdre Holland, Rocco Siffredi and Ashlyn Gere change identities and bodies in John Leslie's best film as a director

Cheerleader Nurses (VCA Platinum)
Jim Holliday leads us back to the days of Candy Stripers

Curse Of The Catwoman (VCA)
Raven and Selena Steele fight like cats over being leader of the pack.

Dirty Debutantes: The Series (4-Play)
Ed Powers adds to the art of the interview by having sex with the interviewee

Endlessly (Vivid)
Nikki Dial has endless sex with Marc Wallice after a night of partying and walking on the beach

Face Dance (Evil Angel)
John Stagliano's best film as Buttman meets Stanislavski. This two-part four-hour epic is the hottest film made in the last five years

Femme: The Series (Femme Productions)
Candida Royale has made a fine series of films that finally start to give us porno from a woman's view

Hidden Obsessions (Ultimate Video)
Janine and Julia Ann go at each other with a stylish ice dildo, adding heat to this Andrew Blake film

Justine: Nothing To Hide (Vivid)
Roxanne Blaze stars in Paul Thomas' finest work as a director. Excellent acting in a real story

Last Resort (VCA)
Madison and Joey Silvera speak a strange unknown language as they sexually wreck a bed & breakfast hotel

Last X-rated Movie (Command Video)
Four part Cecil Howard video of the life and loves of a videomaker. Tasha Voux and Stacy Donovan steal this movie

Loose Ends VI (4-Play Video)
Megan Leigh, in an incredible performance, battles Bionca with the devil as judge. We are the jury.

go at each other with a stylish ice dildo

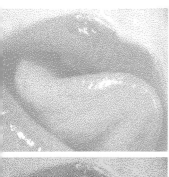

Mad Love (VCA)
Kendall Marx sees ghosts, murder and revenge

New Wave Hookers 3 (VCA Platinum)
Crystal Wilder incinerates the Dark Brothers, Rocco Siffredi, Jon Dough, Nikki Dial and anyone else who gets in her way

Only The Best: The Series (Cal Vista, VCA)
A great introduction, by Jim Holliday who knows more about the genre than anyone

Party Doll (VCA)
Kelly Royce learns about her sexuality as we learn about her

Sensual Exposure (Ultimate Video)
Kelly O'Dell cuts a sexual swathe through Andrew Blake's cool elegant settings

Sodo-Mania: The Series (Elegant Angel)
The best series of loops now being shot

Things Change (Cal Vista)
Nikki Dial falls out of love with Deidre Holland, who will do anything to get her back

Wild Goose Chase (Evil Angel)
Buttman, geese, women wrestling, private detectives— just your ordinary movie

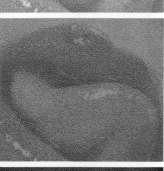

looking

223

we

are

the

jury

Astral Ocean Cinema PO Box 931753, Cherokee Avenue, Hollywood CA 90093, USA. Probably the most interesting porno catalogue selling the best range of books, mags and vids from all around the world, including Japanese porn: virgins taking a long time, keeping you in suspense, whilst losing their cherries

Belier Press collectors items and all the works of Stanton, Willie, Ward and Klaw. PO Box 1234, Old Chelsea Station, NY NY 10013, USA

Circlet Press produce hot sci-fi/fantasy alternative sexuality books and have a catalogue at $30 PO Box 15143, Boston Massachusetts 02215, USA

Delectus offers erotic books from the past, S/M, in catalogues. 27 Old Gloucester Street, London WC1N 3XX

Erotica Daisy Publications PO Box 2, Narborough, Leicester LE9 5XU, UK ☎(0553) 752925. Mostly S/M and specialist mags / books from the past

Forbidden Planet have some of the most beautiful erotic art and comic books on a special list. 71 New Oxford Street, London WC1A 1DG ☎(0171) 836 4179

Masquerade Books 801 Second Avenue, New York NY 10017, USA. They produce a newsletter which lists their range of paperbacks, some of which are classics and others are amongst the best of current erotic fiction. Aslo in-house articles on S/M and other topics of interest in the sex world

Midian Books Chestnut Cottage, 6 Deene End, Weldon, Nr Corby, Northants NN17 3JP, USA. Sells recent and not-so-recent erotica through their Erotica/Sexology supplements

Werner Pieper Media Xperimente, D-6941 Löhrbach, Germany. Sells books on nose-picking, shit, political porno and sacred subjects

The Private Case PO Box 23 Royston, Herts, UK. A comprehensive catalogue of all the best erotic books coming onto the market

QSM Their book and magazine catalogue is now growing, with all the best S/M and erotic books on sale. You have to write for a quote for shipping out of USA. Dept Q, PO Box 882242 San Francisco CA 94188, USA

C.J. Scheiner Books 275 Linden Blvd, Brooklyn, New York 11226, USA ☎(718) 469 1089. All kinds of old books on sexual topics.

Sussex Mailbox sell S/M and fetish books and magazines by mail or callers by appointment. PO Box 314 Haywards Heath, West Sussex RH16 2FH, UK ☎(0444) 482443

Synergy Book Service POB Eight, Flemington NJ 08822, USA. Intelligent service offering all kinds of porn including reprints, with *Sexual Perspectives* newsletter which reviews new stuff, and is welcoming to people with all kinds of tastes. Classifieds too

Sonrista Vertical (The Vertical Smile) is a range of erotic books from Celesta C/ Justinaiano 9, 28004 Madrid, Spain ☎ 410 11 01 fax 319 53 08

Vintage erotic postcards from ARS 24307 Magic Mountain Parkway, #124, Valencia CA 91355. $3 for catalogue

Flesh

adult swingers contact magazine

Every Page in Full Colour

Flesh GPO 3000 Darwin, NT 0900 Australia

< *chances are*
old Dame Nature
has invented all these
squillions **of** *funny fetishes*
to add
a little *spice* **and** *seasoning*
to the average marriage >

Dame Edna Everage

7 REACHING

reaching *others*

When writing off to these organisations, always enclose an SAE or an International Reply Coupon (IRC) - available from all post offices. Don't send a cheque abroad because they usually cost more to cash than they are worth. Eurocheques in Europe, or travellers cheques anywhere, are OK.

adult babies *(Infantilists)*

Carolyn's Kids
PO Box 183 Melhouse, MA 02176, USA.
Clothing, toys and babytalk

Diaper Pail Friends
38 Miller Ave # 127, Mill Valley CA 94965, USA.
Mail order and events

Mummy Hazel's Hush-a-bye Baby Club
c/o 43 South Hill Road, Gravesend, Kent DA12, UK ☎0898 520 539.
Tea parties, baby clothes, easy alphabet newsletter and playpens made to order and exciting outings to the Planet Sex Ball crêche

Infantae Press
PO Box 12466 Seattle, WA 98111, USA

age of consent discussion
and people who think the laws should be changed / abolished

NAMBLA
POB 174 Midtown Station, New York NY 10018, USA.
Strong political group for the rights and sexual dignity of gay men who like boys, with its own bulletin and campaigns

Paidika
PO Box 2377, New York, NY 10185.
A journal which tackles its subject seriously, discussing laws. Edited by Dr John DeCecco, Professor of Psychology at the University of San Francisco State University.
The journal costs $13.50

Uncommon Desires
Postbox 408 100 AK Amsterdam, Holland & PO Box 2377 New York NY 10023, USA.
A serious magazine which gives news items and articles on entrapment and unfair hounding of artists, etc.

Vereniging vor Acceptatie van Pedofilie
Vereniging Martijn, Postbus 43548, 1009 NA Amsterdam, Holland ☎(20) 693 47 93

Youth Connection
c/o Terry Inan, 3910 Nara Drive, Florissant, MO 63033.
Covers news and reviews from the Libertarian Student Network in the USA, featuring reviews and views, sometimes discussing age of consent

androgeny

Androgeny
PO Box 480740 Los Angeles CA
90048, USA ☎(213) 858 4867.
*Holds weekly discussion groups &
offers contacts for MtoF, FtoM, TV,
TS & TG & partners*

animal fantasies

Trained Pets Possy
PO Box 501539, 50975 Cologne,
Germany.
*For people who get in touch about
their animal fantasies*

The Wild Animal
Farm News, PO Box 608039 Orlando
FL 32860, USA.
*An erotic art publication dealing
with "the beauty and the beast"
subjects*

Zoo
Send 2 IRCs to PC PO Box 898, Carl
Junction, Missouri 64834, USA.
A professionally run self-help group

bisexuals

Anything That Moves
c/o BABN 2404 California St, San
Francisco CA 94115, USA
☎(415) 564 BABN.
Mag to give everybody a good time

Bi Academic Intervention
Ann Kaloski, Centre for Women's
Studies, University of York,
Heslington, York YO1 5DD, UK
e-Mail eaknl@york.ac.uk.
A network for bisexuals in academia

The Bisexual Resource Centre
58a Broughton Street, Edinburgh
EH1 3SA, Scotland.
*Open Tuesday 10.30-4.30, Thursdays
12 noon-7pm and Saturday 11am-
5pm. Publishes* Bifrost *which has
listings of groups and runs a penpal
scheme. The Bisexual Phoneline
operates on Thursdays 7.30-9.30pm,*
☎(031) 557 3620

**North American Multicultural
Bisexual Network (NAMBN)**
584 Castro St # 441, San Francisco
CA 94114, USA

SM-Bi's
c/o Central Station, 37 Wharfdale
Road, London N1 9SE.
*Networks bisexuals who are into
S/M. Newsletter, contacts and
campaigning*

Switch Hitter
955 Massachusetts Ave, #148,
Cambridge MA 02139, USA.
*A new bisexual zine with interesting
essays. $2*

body decoration

Body Art
PO Box 32 Great Yarmouth
NR29 5RD, UK.
*Glossy British quarterly with events
and personal ad section*

Body Play
PO Box 2575 Menlo Park,
CA 94206-2575, USA.
*Fakir Musafar's magazine & school of
professional body piercing*

Center for the Rainbow
47 W 25th St, New York City
☎(212) 222 9299
*Lessons in piercing, branding,
cutting & scarification*

Centrepunch
65 Acorn Ave, Cowfold,
W Sussex, UK.
*Friendly group with events, trips and
newsletter*

reaching

E.N.I.G.M.A.
LaFargewerks, 2329 N Leavitt,
Chicago Illinois 60647, USA.
Genital modification, fantasy or fact

Gauntlet
2215-R Market St #801, SF CA 94114.
☎ (415) 252 1404 / fax 415 252 1407.
*Needs an "over 21" statement to
reply. Magnificent catalogue of
piercing jewellery and incredible
Piercing Fans International Quarterly
magazine, sub: $40*

In The Eye of the Needle
PAUK at 153 Tompkinson Road,
Nuneaton, Warcs CV10 SDP, UK.
*Pauline Clarke's book on body
piercing, full of black and white
photos and chatty, unpretentious,
interesting text. Horny if you like
metal in holes .
£15 + £2 postage (UK)*

Piercing Fans International
PO Box 2646 Oxford OX3 9UD, UK

TatMag
PO Box 24058 Postal Outlet, 900
Dufferin St, Toronto Ont M6H 4H6,
Canada.
*Happy home-made mag of ideas,
designs and bodies, with reviews of
events and publications*

Tattoo Expo
c/o 118 Shirley Road, Southampton,
England SO1 3FD ☎ (01703) 230325.
*Holds an annual weekend of
tattooing and revelry in Dunstable
every September*

Wildcat International
16 Preston Street, Brighton, UK.
☎ (01273) 323758.
*A service for pierced people, which
also puts on wonderful low-price
Stainless Steel events*

bondage enthusiasts

Fantasy of Gord
HG Publications PO Box 27
Welshpool, SY21 OZZ, UK.
*Inventive ways of containing people,
demonstrated in magazines*

bum enthusiasts

Anal Banal
c/o 28 Colbery Place, London N16.
Anus fanzine

cigar fetishists

Hot Ash
PO Box 20147 London Terrace Stn,
NY 10011, USA.
*Postal and social club open to male &
female cigar fetishists.
Age statement required to make
sure you are over 18*

communes

and sexually free communities

Aquarian Research Foundation
5620 Morton Street, Philadelphia
PA 19144, USA.
*Germantown Peace Factory, a
community for peace and social
change. Publishes newsletter with
communal living news (send
donation)*

**ZEGG — The Center for Experimental
Cultural Design**
PO Box 14183 Scottsdale Arizona
85267-4183 Germany
☎ (phone/fax) (49) 33841 59565
*With a sister community in Berlin
and a club in Lanzerote, they aim to
establish a world of love, without
fear or violence. Have a
summercamp in Germany and
publish Compersion*

computer sex buffs

The Adult BBS Guidebook
Keyhole Publications, PO Box 35,
Sycamore Illinois 60178, USA.
*Produced to help people choose
which bulletin boards to belong to.
Send £10*

corsets & wasp waists

BRCreations
PO Box 4201 Mountain View,
California 94040, USA.
Newsletter for enthusiasts

Corset Digest
CD 4514 Chambless-Dunwoody
Road, Atlanta, GA 30338, USA.
*Informative and entertaining
newsletter*

Les Gracieuses Modernes
LGM Conderstr 30, D-5400, Germany.
*The big international event where
everybody meets up. Usually held in
London or central Germany*

London Life League
PO Box 1319 Place Bonaventure,
Montreal H5A 1H1 Canada.
*Delightful newsletter with fascina-
ting information and news on where
to get the best corsets. Friendly
correspondence and useful archive*

Romantasy
199 Moulton St, San Francisco 94123,
USA ☎(415) 673 3137.
*Celebrates National Lingerie Week
with vintage show*

Vampyre Society
PO Box 68 Keighley, W Yorks
BD22 6RU, UK.
*Events for corsetted vampirellas and
men in costume*

cybersex freaks

CyberSM
Cologne University, Kirk Woolford,
KHM Köln, Peter-Welter-Platz 2,
50676 Cologne.
Fax ☎ (221) 201 8917.
*Produced the first experimental suits
linking and activating bodies
through computer/telephone or
Internet*

Future Sex
60 Federal Street, Suite 502 San
Francisco CA 94107, USA
☎ (415) 541 7725 fax 451 9860
*Adventurous magazine combining
new sexual thought with new
technology*

VNS Matrix
22 Dunks St, Parkside
South Australia 5063. e-mail: 9401
489L@levels.unisa.edu.au.
*Four Australian girls hijacking the
toys from the technocowboys and
remapping cyberculture with a
feminist bent, undermining the
"chromo-phallic patriarchal code".
Password: aberrant, host network:
RAMpage. Sociopathic cybersluts*

disabled people

It's Okay
One Spring Bank Drive, St
Catherines, Ontario, Canada L2S 2K1.
*A magazine covering sexuality, self-
esteem and disability*

**National Leather Association
Deaf Intl.** PO Box 30286 Columbus
OH 43230, USA.
*Publishes Deaf Leather Reporter
$7 per year*

reaching

230

Outsiders
PO Box 4ZB, London W1A 4ZB
☎(0171) 739 3193.
*A self help group for people who've
become isolated because of
disabilities and want to find friends
and partners. Publishes* Practical
Suggestions

Overground
c/o 11 Church Lane, Stockport,
SK6 6DE, UK.
British mag for amputee seekers

Fascination
3949 West Irving Park Road, Chicago
Illinois 60618, USA.
*Club for amputees and amputee
seekers, with annual convention,
newsletter and videos*

doms & subs

Bizarre
Bizarre Publishing, PO Box 429
Orange California 92666, USA.
*Sparticus' new magazine which is
arty and intelligent, informative and
interesting.* $60 sub

Le Circle d'Omphale
F.A., PO Box 260, 33012 Bordeaux
Cedex, France.
*For female doms, for elaborating on
rituals and international contacts*

Ebony Goddess Society
6709 La Tijera Blvd, # 418,
Los Angeles CA 90045, USA.
*Dominant black women and
submissive black men belong for
support, workshops and parties*

**Esemian Sanctuary of the Goddess
Service of Mankind Church**
PO Box 1335 El Cerrito, CA 94530,
USA ☎(510) 874 4974 and
☎(415) 550 9098
*to find local BBS. Males worship
females on their knees*

Eulenspiegel Society
Box 2783 New York 10163, USA
☎(212) 388 7022.
*Long-standing gentle get togethers
and wild parties for S/M folk,
however extreme. Newsletter with
listings and contacts*

Femina Society
c/o Miss C. Deering, PO Box 1873
Haverhill, Massachusetts 01831
*For dominas only, dedicated to
female authority, with local
branches*

Fetish Times
BCM Box 9253, London WC1N 3XX.
*British magazine with listings,
articles on clubs and political stance*

Greenery
3739 Balboa Ave, #195, San Francisco
CA 94121, USA.
*Lady Green's newsletter for women
and men exploring female
domination, noting workshops in
the Bay area and offering tips on
torture techniques*

Gemini
PO Box 282719, SF CA 94128, USA.
*Club for couples where men are
dominant*

Gynarchy Club
NCJ, PO Box 343, CH 1211 Geneva 26
Switzerland.
*International circle of female
domination devotees*

Kink Pages
Dominant Publications, 601-1755
Robson Street, Vancouver BC
Canada V6G 3B7.
*Twice yearly magazine giving local
and international listings*

Lady O Society
Ryder Publishing, BCM 3406,
London WC1N 3XX.
*Articles, reviews and ads for and by
female submissives*

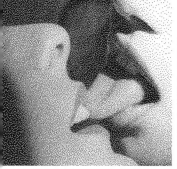

Lifestyles Directory
$5 to Winter Publishing, PO Box 80099, S. Dartmouth MA 02748, USA.
A directory of hard-to-find publications from mind to wild, mainstream to taboo

MSR (Master/Slave Relationships)
PO Box 191211 San Francisco 94119-1211 ☎ fax (415) 386 4692.
Debbie Jaffe's tapes, CDs and stuff

National Leather Association
NLA HQ PO Box 17463 Seattle, WA 98107, USA ☎ (206) 789 8900.
Info on local chapters around the states. Large gay membership

Offrande
APMC BP No 75462 Paris Cedex 10, France.
Wild S/M mag in French with details of parties

Outcasts
PO Box 31266 San Francisco, CA 94131-0266, USA.
Support & social group for fetishistic women including transsexuals. They publish an excellent leaflet on safety for AIDS awareness, bondage, clamps, clips, cutting, electricity, enemas, penetration with objects, piercings, shaving, slapping, wax, whipping, spanking and cropping.

Pamela Young's Dominique
154-160 Bedminster Down Road, Bristol BS13 7AF.
A straight-forward honest contact magazine for the scene. £6

People Exchanging Power
Events info line in the States is ☎ (505) 764 5711
Local groups around America which provide caring support and social events are listed in Travelling sections

Roissy Master Trainers
PO Box 14546, Chicago, IL 60614, USA.
Male dominants

SandMutopia Guardian
Desmodus Inc, 24 Shotwell St, San Francisco CA 94103, USA.
Excellent resource & mine of information edited by Pat Califia $24/$34 abroad

Schlagzeilen
Postfach 30 63 52, 20329 Hamburg, Germany ☎ (40) 432 2299.
Elegant and fascinating magazine in German, with contact ads, parties and meetings also held

S/M Depesche
Holstenstr 5, D24534 Numünster, Germany.
An extensive calendar of German S/M events — both non-commercial and in night clubs, commenting on trends

S&M News
Carter Stevens Presents, PO Box 551, Pocono Summit, PA 18346, USA.
Lively newspaper, they run Hellfire in New York and put on S/M weekends in the Poconos

The SM Gays Resource Books
SM Gays, BM SM Gays, London WC1N 3XX.
Excellent little books with features like 'What to do if the Police raid your home.' and lists groups for cigar smokers, and men interested in uniforms, messy, special clothing, hair-cropping & shaving.
They also list clubs and shops all over Europe. £2/$8

Strictly Speaking
PO Box 8006 Palm Springs, CA 92263,
USA. Fax ☎ (619) 363 6030
*Publish magazines featuring the top
doms around the world*

Taste of Latex
PO Box 460122 San Francisco
CA 94146, USA. ($19.95/$24.95
Canada/$34.95 overseas)
*Porn zine for pervs of all persuasions,
started by Lily Burana but may change
now she's moved to Future Sex*

dyke decadence

Bad Attitude
POB 390110 Cambridge
MA 02139 USA.
The lesbian mag with attitude

Brat Attack
POB 40754 San Francisco
CA 94140-0754
*The zine for leatherdykes and
other bad girls, with US &
international listings*

Dyke Mommies & Daddies
c/o Mr S, 1779 Boulton St,
San Francisco, CA 94103.
☎ (415) 863 7764
Has groups in various US cities

Girls' Own
BM Princess, London WC1N 3XX.
*A quaint British lesbian mag with
contacts.*

Lesbian S/M Mafia
SASE to LSM, Box 993, Murray Hill
Station, New York NY 10156

On Our Backs
Blush Entertainment Corp
526 Castro, San Francisco,
CA 94114, USA.
*The fun & ferociously caring lesbian
sex mag*

Oysters
Austern, Lachmannstr 4, D-10967
Berlin, Germany.
Lesbian lechery

Places for Women
Ferrari Publications PO Box 37887
Phoenix AZ 85069
The world travel guide for lesbians

Quim
BM 2182 London WC1N 3XX.
*Hot stories & pics, with news
on the pulse*

Wicked Women
PO Box 1349 Strawberry Hills.
New South Wales, Australia 2012.
*Glossy sexy lesbian mag, pro S/M,
with news & views, no personals but
plenty of ideas about meeting others*

Wildfire Club
BM Labry London WC1N 3XX.
For dashing ladies into S/M

Seattle Madness
1202 East Pike, #819, Seattle,
WA 98122, USA ☎ (206) 233 8429.
*Powersurge Women's SM
Leatherdyke conference, auction,
ball and show*

Wildside
Rozenstraat 14, 1016 NX
Amsterdam, Holland.
Lesbian S/M group

Venus Infers
VI 2215-R Market St, Suite 294,
San Francisco CA 94114, USA.
*Aimed at women interested in
having S/M with other women. Has
classifieds*

reaching

enema enthusiasts

Nozzle Talk
PO Box 618 Ansonia Station,
New York NY 10023-0618, USA.
*Discusses equipment and techniques,
with some contacts*

extremes

The Common Denominator
BM Box 2182, London WC1N 3XX.
*For diesel dykes, dirty daddies, toy
boys, baby dolls, drag things and
camp queens*

Fetish Times
B&D Company POB 7109 Van Nuys,
CA 91409, USA.
*The original mag under this name,
catering to special interest fetishists
such as feet, enemas, calipers, with
plenty of reader input.
$3 sample issue*

Toilet Mouth
PO Box 102, Clifton New Jersey
07011-0102, USA.
*An intense new zine which
celebrates extreme fetishism.
£4 from Deron Slapin
(send age statement)*

**The Center for the Academic Study
of Extremes in Human Experience**
POB 28760 Seattle WA 98118, USA.
*Non-profit archival resource for
people dedicated to understanding
weird and normally suspect
behaviour such as sacrifice, trance
states and snake handling*

fat people

**The National Association to Advance
Fat Acceptance**
PO Box 188620 Sacramento
CA 94818, USA ☎ (916) 443 0303,
fax 443 2281.
*Has a journal for men who admire
fat women and many other
worthwhile ventures*

female power

Amazon Sisterhood of America
TASHA PO Box 634 Wilmington
NC 28401, USA.
*For people who believe in the
natural superiority of women*

The Female Power Club
Pb 63128, 1005LC Amsterdam,
Holland.
*For powerful, dominant and
confident women over 25. They hold
a hot (masked) Female Power Ball
for women who are in control, and
their guests. Send stamp/IRC*

fighting femmes

Executive Boxing Club
PO Box 1298 Grand Rapids
MI 49501-1298.

Festelle
PO Box 267 Windlesham,
Surrey GU20 6AY, UK.
*Specialise in fighting females
and will send you their video
catalogue free*

HEW
Longetivity Books, Westowan, Truro,
Cornwall TR4 8AX, UK.
Glossy and fun magazine

**Women's International Sports Club
& Women's Combat Sports**
WCS PO Box 187, E Dereham,
Norfolk NR20 4SY UK and FWFC,
PO Box 24081, Ft Lauderdale,
Florida 33307 USA.
*Topless wrestling matches, boxing,
fantasy matches*

foot/shoe fetishists

Footlovers Admiration Society
LAS PO Box 867 Stanford Le Hope,
Essex SS17 7JJ, UK.
*Publishes Footsy for the foot-shoe
fetishist*

Foot Fetish & Fantasy Society
FFF Soc PO Box 24866 Cleveland
OH 44124, USA.
Dedicated to women's feet

In Step
Tri D enterprises, PO Box 386
Walnut, CA 91788, USA.
*$5 incl post. A paper devoted to the
foot fetishist, with photos and ads*

Gossamer Productions
PO Box 94193 1090 GD Amsterdam,
Holland.
*An international association for
people who appreciate feet —
especially when they are in
beautiful fully-fashioned stockings
and high heels*

Seamed Stockings and Stiletto Heels
SSSH, PO Box 122, West Haddon,
Northampton NN6 7DS, UK.
*A group devoted to fully-fashioned
nylons and stilettos. Membership £10*

gays

Alternative Dateline
☎(1-900)420 8686, ext 433.
US Nationwide voice mailbox

The Alyson Almanac
*lists and describes the best and worst
gay plays, books and movies, with a
dictionary of slang and historical
terms, and examines laws and
attitudes in various countries. A bit
like this book, only gay. ($9.95)*

Holy Titclamps
(including Queer Zine Explosion)
PO B 591275 SF CA 94159-1275, USA.
*Larry-bob's fine resource for queer
zines, places and videos. Profound
articles and meticulous listings.
$10 sub*

Gay Pride
BM Trust, London WC1N 3XX
☎(0l71)738 7644.
*Celebratory marches in various
major cities*

Lesbian & Gay Freedom Movement
LGFM BM Box 207
London WC1N 3XX.
*Anarchist movement to support
oppressed groups and bring freedom
to all ages, so that everyone can
enjoy their own lives without
exploitation, harassment, abuse or
control. They produced a "Handy
Guide to Sex and the Law" which
shows how totally irrational British
sex laws are*

The Pink Paper
77 City Garden Row, London N1 8EZ.
*National free paper with listings for
gays and lesbians*

**London Lesbian And Gay
Switchboard**
☎(0171)837 7324

Sydney Gay & Lesbian Mardi Gras
PO Box 1064, Darlinghust NSW 2010
Australia ☎(02)332 4088
*These huge parades, parties & Sleaze
Balls have become tourist-boosters
for Australia*

giantess lovers
and people who want to be
trampled

Mr Carpet
PO Box 1097 Pocono Summit,
PA 18345, USA.
*Male carpet available for hire.
Also interested in correspondence*

Giantess
E.L. Publications, Suite 138, 306
Nassau Road Roosevelt,
New York 11575, USA.
*Books, picture sets & mags, including
The Shrinking Pill, on gigantic
women with enormous boobs
crushing and interacting with wimps*

Squish
Bigtime Productions, 308 E Base Line Street, # 167, San Bernadino, California 92410, USA.
e-mail: Bigtime 1 @ aol.com.
Stories and beautiful drawings in mags and videos of huge women (and men) and tiny adventurers and crush lovers who like to dream of big bare-foot ladies trampling them

group marriage
and people into polyfidelity

Expanded Family Network
PO Box 12762 Berkeley CA 94701, USA ☎ (510) 644 4276.
For people who wish to explore the polycommitted lifestyle

IntiNet Resource Center
PO Box 150474 San Rafael California 94915, USA ☎ (415) 507 1739.
Working towards changing the belief that monogamy and the nuclear family are the only normal healthy moral choices you can make

PEP
PO Box 6306 Captain Cook, Hawaii 96704-6306, USA.
Produce newsletter Loving More *with news of group marriage and personal ads, and hold a terrific annual conference in San Francisco*

handballing

Trust: The Handbook
by Bert Hermann Alamo Square Press, POB 14543 San Francisco CA 94114, USA.
The definitive guide to arse fisting, step by step with love.
Sadly, no personals!

hair enthusiasts
and hairy people

Daughters of Hirsuitism
203 North La Salle St, # 2100-S, Chicago IL 60601, USA.
For women who have lots of hair and may be unhappy about it

Hair Apparent
Bob & Deb at 123 West Wallen Road, Fort Wayne, IN 46825, USA.
A newsletter for those who like unshaved women. They offer films and photos of hairy women. Send a few bucks

R. Hughes
PO Box 25, Harbor City, California 90710-0025, USA.
A network of long haired ladies and their admirers — the "Rapunzels" of the world. They trade information, photos, videos and have members worldwide

hedonists

The Bast Journal
PO Box 1361 Tustin CA 92681, USA.
For worshippers of Bast, the ancient Egyptian goddess of sex, drugs and rock'n'roll. Covers a wide range of topics to transvestitism through politics to music. $45 sub

HIV positive people
and help groups

Helplines have been set up in all cities now, where you can ask about support of all kinds, including social. Should you wish to consult a book to find a group, ask at your library for the National AIDS Manual or their UK AIDS Directory. They have the most comprehensive listing of AIDS and HIV groups anywhere

Bob's Bar
at the Anvil, 88 Tooley Street,
London EC1 ☎ (0171) 407 0371.
*Europe's first bar for people with
AIDS, HIV and their friends.
Call for the dates*

Body Positive
51 Philbeach Gardens London SW5
☎ (0171) 835 1045.
Britain's national network

The Prisoner's Helpline
at the Terrence Higgins Trust
☎ (0800) 212 529 (no charge)

Body Positive
2095 Broadway #306, New York
NY 10023, USA.
*Monthly magazine full of
testimonies, listings, and informative
articles on positive people around
the globe. $1*

Diseased Pariah News
c/o Men's Support Center PO Box
30564 Oakland CA 94604, USA.
*Stylish zine done with humour,
imagination and care. $3*

Positive Image
PO Box 1501 Pomona, California
91769, USA ☎ (909) 622 6312.
*A social/sexual communications
network for persons who have
HIV/AIDS. Sub: $25 / $30 overseas
18+ statement required*

POZ
PO Box 1279 New York 10113-1279,
USA. $19.95 sub, free to
impoverished PWA.
*An American magazine about life
with AIDS which is powerful,
courageous and beautifully written*

mac & rainwear lovers

International Mackintosh Society
Box 202 Folkestone,
Kent CT20 3EY, UK.
*Put on an annual weekend &
events abroad*

masturbation

Bodysex Groups
PO Box 1933 Murray Hill,
New York NY 19156.
*Workshops run by Betty Dodson to
help women achieve orgasm
through masturbation. The video is
listed in the Looking section*

Factor Press
*PO Box 8888 Mobile, Alabama
36689, USA.*
Publishes Celebrate the Self
*newsletter and books on the joys
of wanking*

My Own Cum —
 a masturbatory zine
c/o Terminal Products Group, 1573 N
Milwaukee #422, Chicago
IL 60622, USA.
*Stories and analysis about wanking,
seeking contributions*

Club Relate
PO Box 478 Gainsville FL 32602, USA.
*Sharing interests in masturbation
at monthly parties and through
newsletter*

alt.sex,masturbation
#3537 an 322222@anon.penet.fi
(Wee Will) on Internet

men's feelings

Body Electric School
6527 A Telegraph Avenue Oakland,
CA 94609-1113, USA
☎ (510) 653 1594, fax 653 4991.
*Workshops for men to gain a deeper
connection with their bodies*

Lifeworks
2205 40th Place NW, Apt #1,
Washington DC 20007-1681, USA
Put on Healing the Inner Warrior
*programmes with Celtic influences
and massage*

Men & Masculinity Conference
PO Box 24159 St Louis MI 63130

Men Talk
The Men's Center, 3255 Hennepin
Ave S, Suite 45, Minneapolis
Minnesota 55408, USA.
☎(612)822 5892

messy fun friends

Messy News
PO Box 181030 Austin, Texas
78718-1030, USA.
*Also on CompuServe & Internet.
Bimonthly for lovers of wet and
messy fun, wetlook, mud, food,
paint, etc. News, lists of feature films
with messy scenes, personals and
club listings*

Mudbathing Cooperative
818 Truman, Arlington,
Texas 76011, USA.
*For sensualists into slippery mud
massage & floatation adventures*

The Mud Club
MM PO Box 7, Seascale, Cumbria
CA20 1JE, UK.
*For mud lovers all over the world
and membership provides a
quarterly newsletter and free
personal ad. It is mostly gay but not
exclusively so. £12 membership
I£13 Europe and $25 USA*

Mud Puddle Visuals
Sysop Dave Lodoski
☎0101 818 246 2498.
Computer bulletin board

Pie Mafia
PO Box 721027 Orlando
FL 32872 USA.
*A group devoted to tracking down
hard-to find clips of women being
pied. The newsletter is*
The Magnum Report

Pumping Water
1223 Wilshire Blvd, Suite 215, Santa
Monica, S California 90403, USA.
*(SASE) Erotic getting wet with
clothes on*

Jay Richardson Enterprises
Box 26002, 72 Robertson Road,
Nepean, ONT K2H 9RO, Canada.

Splosh
PO Box 70 St Leonards on Sea, East
Sussex TN38 OPX, UK.
*Glossy photos with lively girls, news
of events and personals*

Tonyo Boeki Shokai
PO Box 150, Shinjuku, Tokyo, Japan.

Wet & Messy
WMD PO Box 37 MDA Knoxfield,
Victoria Australia 3180.

Wet-T
Boschetsriederstr 51a,
8000 Munich 70, Germany.

mummification

CEO Summum Corporation
*Salt Lake City is the only company
dedicated to mummifying you (or
your pet) but you have to be dead*

naturists

Naturist Leisure, *Nudist Update* **and
the Naturist Video Club**
Susan Mayfield, PO Box 65, Leighton
Buzzard, Bedfordshire LU7 8TJ, UK.
*Saucy yet serious information and
listings, holidays and fun*

*Nude and Natural - The Quarterly
Journal of Clothes-Optional Living*
PO Box 132 Oshkosh, WI 54902,USA.
*Not sexy but a lovely magazine with
news from all over the world, club
listings and campaigning attitude*

Coast and County Guide Books to Britain
3 Mayfield Avenue, Scarborough
North Yorks YO12 6DF.
cover every known beach & resort.
£17 for the pair

Tahanga Research
PO Box 8714 La Jolla, CA 92038
(SASE/SAE $1)
Nudist guide books on Asia, Mexico
and all parts of the globe

necrophile & vampire

Blue Blood
Cyber Junk BLT, 3 Calabar Court,
Gaithersburg, Maryland 20877, USA.
A mag for people into Vampirism,
erotic cutting, counterculture,
rock'n'roll and fetishism. $24 sub

Cemetery Dance
PO Box 16372 Baltimore
MD 21210, USA.
Shuddery stories and reviews

Temple of the Vampire
Box 3582 Lacey, Washington
98502, USA.
Complete information on the living
cult of the Undead

The Vampyre Society
PO Box 68, Keighley, West Workshire
BD22 6RU, UK.
Put on lavish events where ladies
wear corsets, and produce a
newsletter listing new members

NecronomicoN
15 Jubilee Road, Newton Abbot,
Devon TQ12 1LB, UK.
Erotic-horror magazine £4.99
/£7 Europe/$10 USA

new age enthusiasts

Ecstasy — the Journal of
Divine Eroticism
POB 862 Ojai, CA 93024, USA.
Articles on mind/body disciplines,
music & passion, erotic dreams, etc.
$20 sub

obscure & old porn

Desert Moon Periodicals
1031 Agua Fria, Santa Fe, New
Mexico 87501, USA
☎(505) 984 8448, fax 989 3713.
Obscure, peerless, sometimes
bizarre and always eclectic
magazines and books

Kinematics
61 37th Street, New York City, USA
☎(212) 944 7561.
Every strange and obscure book,
video, item or mag that is legal to
sell, including imports

The Redeemer
BCM Box 9235, London WC1 3XX.
Gloriously grotesque

Tease
88 Lexington, Suite 2E, New York
City 10016, USA. ☎(212) 686 0652.
Sexy fun from days gone by till now

pagan/magickal groups

Larry Cornett
9527 Blake Lane, Apt 102, Fairfax
VA 22031, USA.
Produces a regular international
calendar of events. $4.50 US, $5
Canada, $8 other

Draconis Nest
Box 408 Woden ACT 2606, Australia.
Holds pagan summer gathering in
Australia

Hoblink Network
13 Merrivale Rd, Stafford,
ST179EB, UK.
Support & info for gay, lesbian &
bisexual pagans

The Luna Calendar
Luna Press Box 511 Kenmore Station, Boston MA 02215, USA.
Pretty calendar is produced every year

Pagan Link Network
c/o J. Male, 25 East Hill, Dartford, Kent, UK.
Links individuals & groups for support & info. Send SAE

Pagan Voice
17 Blethwin Close, Henbury, Bristol BS10 7BH, UK ☎ (0117) 2506895.
The monthly newspaper of paganism and magick. Paths, political info and monthly update on events

Sub-Cultures Alternative Freedom Foundation
SAFF 6-8 Burley Lodge Road, Leeds LS61QP, UK.
Counteracting power and nonsense of fundamentalists.

Wiccan/Pagan Press Alliance
PO Box 1392, Mechanicsburg, PA 17055, USA.

penis talk

Acorn
Tony Acorn, PO Box 113 Weston-Super-Mare, Avon BS23 2ED, UK.
A smart little publication about cocks, women pissing standing up, cock shape and foreskins. Members meet for a get-together in Bournemouth on a weekend at the end of March

Added Dimensions
Gary Griffin, 4216 Beverly Blvd, Los Angeles, CA 90004, USA.
Books on large endowments, penis enlargement, autofellatio, and Penis Power Quarterly on the same topics. Sub $19.95

The Hung Jury
PO Box 417, Los Angeles, CA 90078, USA ☎ (213) 850 3618.
Hetero men with giant dicks (10 inches and over) and women who want to meet them. Publishes Measuring Up. Enclose $6

National Organization of Circumcision Information Resource Centers
PO Box 2512 San Anselmo, CA 94979-2512 ☎ (415) 488 9883.
Hold conferences and provides info.

Peanuts
PUK PO Box 31 Aldridge, Walsall WS9 8RH, UK.
For gay and bisexual men who are worried that their penis is smaller than average. The British version of the Dutch group called Pinkeltjes

Pump It Up
MIRZA, 139 West 4th Avenue, Roselle, New Jersey 07203, USA.
A magazine about thick, meaty pumped-up dicks, penile pumping, with free "Pump Personals". £15 per issue. They also sell penile pumps

Uncircumcised Society of America
Bud Berkeley, PO Box 26011 San Francisco CA 94126, USA.
Events, ads, books

RECAP
c/o R. Wayne Griffiths, 3205 Northwood Drive, Suite 209, Concord CA 94520, USA.
Provides technical and moral support to men seeking foreskin restoration, with local contacts

Small Etc
PO Box 610294, Bayside, NY 11361, USA. *In praise of cute dicks*

Penis Mightier
SF Jacks 2236 Market St, Suite 127, San Francisco CA 94114, USA ☎ (415)979 0537.
Magazine and club who meet for meating. $6 donation

reaching

240

piss/ shit enthusiasts

AVI
7 rue M-Berthelot,
92700 Colombes, France.
*For exhibitionists into pissing
in public places*

Jack's Number Two
PO Box 543353 Houston, Texas
77254-2253, USA.
*Sub of $30 / $45 overseas pays for
your personal ad and three issues of
The Shitlist which features ads and
lists of vendors. You must be over 21*

Urolo-gnisten
Collector's Shop, Boks 301, 7001
Trondheim, Norway.
*Small piss club with members all over
Norway, mostly communicating by
post*

pornography

Caress Newsletter
The Write Solution Flat 1, 11 Holland
Road, Hove BN3 1JF, England.
*News of what publishers want in the
way of sexy stories and novels,
reviews of new books and info about
booksellers*

Pornowriter
Robert Carr, Box 2761, Borah Station,
Idaho 83701, USA.
*Produce a floppy Mac disc which
helps you write naughty stories and
supplies sound effects etc. $10*

porn stars

5-k Sales
9420 Reseda Boulevard, Suite 836
Northridge CA 91324, USA.
*Handles most of the Hollywood porn
actresses' fan clubs.*

FOXE
8231 DeLongpre Ave #1,
West Hollywood, CA 90046, USA.
*Has a newsletter listing the fan clubs
of all the porno stars*

The Madonna Fan Club
8491 Sunset Blvd #8491 West
Hollywood, CA 90069, USA

Nina Hartley Fan Club
1442 Walnut #242 Berkeley CA
94709, USA

prostitutes

*British law forbids me to list our
brothels or sex services but luckily,
many of the magazines and
newspapers I list are risking the
law by taking ads*

Finding a prostitute is difficult for
some people. Here are some places
to try:

Bars —
*Whores hang out in particular bars,
waiting to be chosen. They flirt with
you, and then take you into back
rooms or to nearby pads for sex*

Massage Parlours —
*Some offer sex. You can book the
person of your choice ('aquaria' is
the name for the type where they all
stand on display in a window) and
have a massage. This could be by
hand or the entire body with the
masseur/se sometimes being naked
or sexily dressed. Then your arousal
is dealt with. In good parlours, this
may happen many times*

Saunas —
*Where the professionals drape
themselves around the pool or
Jacuzzi and you can sit and relax,
read the paper or flirt with them,
until one takes your fancy, when you
retire to a cubicle or bedroom. In
New Zealand they are called Spas*

Sex Shows —
*Where the performers and other
professionals who might play with
you while you watch the show, are
available for sex either on the
premises or elsewhere*

Fantasy Booths —
Where you talk to each other, usually through a window and each plays with themselves

Cinemas —
Like those in Berlin, where you can watch hardcore while getting sucked on the plush seats. Alternatively, go into a booth, choose from a selection of hundreds of videos, and get laid

Fantasy Parlours —
Where your fantasy is acted out and you get a wank at the end. Alternatively, where you're put in a fantasy situation like the school class or gymkhana which the Muir Academy provides in Britain

Houses with windows —
Red light districts such as in Amsterdam, The Hague, Southampton's Derby Road, Birmingham's Cheddar Road, and the Miari area of Soeul, where you can choose your whore as she sits in the window. Once inside, the curtain in drawn and you get on with it

Dungeons —
Where S/M or other fetish activities are administered either by or to you

Orgy Clubs —
Where professional girls will perform in groups with male clients and couples sometimes join in the fun. Common in Switzerland

The Brothel —
Houses specially designed for selling sex. Giving the professionals a proper work place, company and protection, and offering the clients a choice of partner in comfort and safety is ideal. A decadent ambiance inspires adventure and a liberal attitude inspires boldness, so any sexual favour can be requested without embarrassment or humiliation. Decadent ones still survive in Central and South America. Germany, Holland and a few Asian countries like Korea and Japan have meticulously run houses. However, there are also soul-less State-run brothels in Germany called Eros Centres and labour-camp style legal brothels in Nevada. The latter make professionals wary of legalisation because, run without flair or humour, they can turn into dreary places where the hookers have no sense of freedom and the clients little joy. What most professionals want is simply to be decriminalised

Street Hookers —
Can be found in most cities but you should be warned that in the UK and US, the police will arrest you for kerb-crawling and female police sometimes pose as whores on the most popular streets to entrap you. I have attempted to list the safest streets for you to look in each section of the Travelling section

By Letter, Video or Phone —
Ads for this can be found in the backs of sex magazines. Video services that are sometimes in video magazines, offer you the chance to say what you want to see, and they sell you a video with your fantasies enacted specially for you. **Adam** *(8060 Melrose Ave, Los Angeles CA 90046-7082, USA $8), has a column which advises readers on phonesex and* **The Phoneman** *2421 West Pratt Blvd, Suite 1334, Chicago IL 60645 offers advice. There is no such service elsewhere*

Asia File
c/o Orient X Press, POB 2908 Standford CA 94309 or c/o Europ Video 183/31 Soi Post Office, S. Pattaya, Chonburi 20260, Thailand. Newsletters on recommended places to find commercial sex in Asia $60 for 5 issues. MO's to Orient X Press.

Third World International Traveller
c/o Excogitations PO Box 6260
Pasadena TX 77506
offers news sent in by travellers

Hustling. A Gentleman's Guide to the Fine Art of Homosexual Prostitution
by John Preston is a Richard Kasak book available for $12.95 through Masquerade, 801 Second Avenue, New York 10017, USA.

Male Prostitutes for Women
The few brothels that exist are listed in the Travelling Section (specifically in Germany, Korea and Thailand). Sex magazines for women such as For Women and The Australian Women's Forum feature ads. Escort agencies sometimes have men on their books. In general, there are many more men on offer than women who want to buy sex. The lesbian commercial scene, however is more active and lesbian hookers can be found through the lesbian scene and their magazines.

prostitute self-help

and support

AIDS Preventive Centre Of Lithuania
Molettu Pl. 40, 232021 Vilnius
Lithuania.

Asamblea Feminista de Madrid
M. Cruz Fernandez & C. Garaszabel,
c/Barguillo No.44 2 Izda, 28004
Madrid Spain.

Associaçao De Prostitutes-Brazil
F.Bollho Reis, Rua Miquel de Frias
71-B, Estacio RJ Cep 20-211-190,
Rio de Janiero, Brazil.

Brazil's National Network of Prostitutes
Beijo da rua, Largo do Machado 21-cobertura, CEP 22221, Rio de Janeiro, Brazil ☎ (21) 265 5747.

Buklod-Phillipines
Glenda Tuazon/Linda Cunanan
1 Davis St, New Banic Ain,
Olangpago City Phillipines.

Le Bus de Femmes
Lydia, 47 rue de Rivoli,
75001 Paris France.

Centre de Documentation Internationale sur la Prostitution
CDIP Griselidis Real,
24 Rue de Neuchatel, CH-1201,
Geneva Switzerland.

Committee for the Civil Rights of Prostitutes
Pia Covre & Carla Corso, Casalle
Postale 67, 33170 Pordenone, Italy
☎ (39-344) 625 940.

Com. Per I Diritti Civili
Pia Covre, Casa Postale 67 38170,
33087 Pordenone Italy.

CORP — Canadian Organisation for the Rights of Prostitutes
Box 1143, Station F, Toronto
Ont M4Y 2T8 ☎ (416) 964 0150.
Publishes Stiletto which gives news on police corruption and other strong legal stuff

COYOTE
2269 Chestnut Street, Suite 452,
San Francisco CA 94123 (SAE for info)
☎ (415) 435 7850.
Probably the most active Prostitute's organisation outside Australia, with news on groups worldwide. Works for the rights of all sex workers, strippers and phone operators. Is currently negotiating on laws at the local Mayor's Office

Empower Bangkok
Noi Apusuk, PO Box 1065 - 9/12
Soi Pipat, Silom PostOff - Silom Rd
1065 Bangkok Thailand.

Enda Tiers-Monde Senegal
Marie-Helene Mottin Sylla, BP 3370,
Dakar Senegal.

Ghana School Of Medicine
Matilda Papoe, Box 4236
Accra Ghana.
Runs a prostitute health and support group

Hydra
Rigaerstr 3, (Friedrichshain) O-1035
Berlin, Germany ☎(30) 312 8061.
Support and campaigning, holding European congresses

Ilana Malinova
c/o Res. Inst Of Labour & Social
Affairs, Palackeho Nam 4 Prague 2
Czech Republic.

Mr A. de Graaf Stichting
1016 DK Amsterdam, Holland.
A government-funded group which aims to further public discussion on prostitution, encourage decriminalisation, empower prostitutes and provide information to interested parties through its library

New Zealand Prostitutes Collective
Clair Hill PO Box 68509 Auckland
New Zealand.

New Zealand Sex Workers' Rights
PO Box 68-509 Newton Auckland NZ
☎(09) 366 6106.

Oldest Profession Times
c/o '90's Ladies & Friends, PO Box
26610, Suite 298, Sacramento CA
95826, USA ☎(213) 382 6445.
Covers health, free speech, sex education, drugs and news, updating on people in prison for prostitution-related "crimes". Bimonthly

PANTHER
PO Box 2826 Darwin NT 0801
Australia ☎(089) 41 1711.

PASA
PO Box 7020 Hutt Street, South
Australia 5000 ☎(08) 362 5775.

PION-NORWAY
Postboks 527, Sentrum,
0105 Oslo 1 Norway.

PONY (Prostitutes of New York)
PONY 25 West 45th Street,
Suite 1401, New York 10036, USA.
Publishes Pony Express *with inspiring articles and warnings, like accounts of aggressive hotel security staff*

POW (Prostitute Outreach Workers)
1st Floor, Forest Mills, Alfreton Rd,
Nottingham NG7 3JQ
☎(0602) 249992.

Praed Street Project
at St Mary's Hospital, Paddington,
London W2 ☎(0171) 725 1549).
offers advice on health

Prostitutes And Civil Rights
Instituto de Estudes Da Reliligia,
Ladeira de Gloria 98, RJ 22 211,
Rio De Janiero, Brazil.

Prostitute Collective of Victoria
10 Inkerman Street, St Kilda Vic
3182, Australia ☎(03) 534 8319.
Its slogan is "No bad women, just bad laws" and they produce a good magazine called Working Girl

Red Thread
Postbus 16422, 1001 RM Amsterdam
☎(20) 243366.
Campaigns for improvements in the law and can supply you with an up-to-date list of other groups

Self Help Center Israel
Linda Smith c/o King George 37/11,
Tel Aviv Israel.

Sex Industry Survivors
San Francisco ☎(415) 883 0736.
Therapy group for women adjusting to life after leaving the business

Scot PEP
26a Torphican Street, Edinburgh
EH3 8HX ☎(0131) 229 8269.

SIERRA
70 Brewer Street, East Perth Western
Australia 6000 ☎(06) 227 6935.

SQUISI
PO Box 689 West End, Queensland
4101 Australia ☎ (07) 844 4565.
*Their magazine has an "Ugly Mug"
list of all the obnoxious/abusive
johns and how to spot them*

SWOP
PO Box 1453 Darlinghurst NSW 2010
Australia ☎ (02) 212 2600.

US Prostitutes Collective
PO Box 14512 San Francisco,
CA 94114, USA ☎ (415) 558 9628.

WISE in the ACT
PO Box 229, Canberra ACT 2601
Australia ☎ (062) 57 2855.

public sex enthusiasts

Steam
PDA Press Inc, Rte 2, Box 1215
Cazenovia WI 53924, USA.
*Quarterly journal devoted to public
sex, mainly aimed at men. It lists
baths, parks and back rooms around
the world and offers tips. Send age-
statement and pledge safer sex
when sending £10 sub*

AVI
(7 rue M-Berthelot, 92700 Colombes,
Paris, France)
*For exhibitionists into pissing in
public places*

Exposure
BM Exposure London WC1N 3XX.
*Club for voyeurs and exhibitionists
in London and Essex*

riot grrrls

Real Grrrl
Fantagraphics Books 7563 Lake City
Way NE, Seattle WA 98115, USA.
*Lists the zines produced by
Riot Grrrl groups*

Action Grrrl Newsletter
Sara, 543 Van Duzer St, Staten Island,
NY 10304, USA.
*Attempts to network
women/girls/grrrls everywhere.
Reviews and listings*

ritual

Ritual
29 Brewer Street, London W1.
*Fetish magazine covering rituals at
clubs and elsewhere*

OV
Temple of Psychic Youth,
PO Box 1455 London N4 1JT.
Occulture magazine £1.50

romantics

The Simply Sexy Softly Erotic
Source Guide
Niche, PO Box 71887, Las Vegas,
NV 89170, USA.
*Mail order guide for naturists,
couples, singles and women*

rubber enthusiasts

Ataraxia
PO Box 222-B Gotham, New York
14461-0222, USA.
*An International database of
rubber/leather resources*

Marquis
Flensburgerst 5, 42655 Solingen,
Germany.
*Beautiful magazine devoted to
rubber fashions and promoting the
clubs where they are worn*

Latex Seduction Club· BP 651,
44018 Nantes, Cedex 01, France.
French club for rubber fetishists

science fiction fantasy

SF Convention Register
$1.50 from Erwin Strauss
PO Box 3343 Fairfax VA 22038, USA.
Incredibly comprehensive with every attempt at accuracy and help you to plan, and find what you want

schooling and dressage

The Muir Academy
PO Box 135 Hereford, HR2.
Holds courses for boys and girls in an authentic schoolroom. They also put on Pony Express, a grand pony boys / girls event. Competitions take place for the best pony turn-out, dressage and racing. Dress code: fetish and riding gear

Halcyon Days
Nottingham, UK ☎ 0604 811320.
Put out Apron Strings about maid training and other re-hashed stuff

Shades 2
PO Box 8 Romford, Essex
RM3 8EY, UK.
Pony girl racing in countryside & female sub activities

sex therapy

Don't answer adverts, as professionals don't advertise. Get referred by your own doctor. If you daren't talk to your own doctor about sex, get another doctor

shaved people

Bushwackers
614 Fairglen, Annapolis MD 21401, USA

Colorful People
PO Box 617 Sentrum,
0106 Oslo Norway.
Genital depilation, tattooing & piercing

Smoothie Club
TSC PO Box 1409 Worthing,
W Sussex BN14 8PE, UK.
People who like smooth bodies

singles interested in sex

Susan Block
USA ☎ (213) 654 7727.
Radio shows with introductions on air

Beautiful Girls from Eastern Europe
PO Box 1137, W-7737
Bad Duerrheim, Germany. $10.
Marriage-minded and horny girls, and other world-wide friendship zines too

Meeting & Attracting
LGL Productions, PO Box 224, Ojai,
CA 93024-0224, USA.
Cassettes that help to dissolve fears which keep you from meeting others

MTV
has ads for singles all over Europe

Teletext
(also on Sky) now has one-to-one advertising

spanking

Domestic Discipline Digest
BB Publications, PO Box 1033
Grover Beach, CA 93483, USA.
Stories about warmly remembered childhood episodes, with illustrations

No-Nonsense Ladies
CD Publishing, 213 Valley Street,
Suite 228-SP, South Orange,
NJ 07079, USA.
A forum free to women and couples for men and women who want their spankings from women. Devoted to "strong women behind great men"

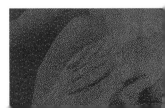

The North East Spanking Society
c/o TEP PO Box 441, Waltham
MA 02254-0441, USA.
*Have an annual get-together and
a newsletter with reviews &
personal ads*

Private Quarters
Arachne Press, PO Box 262116,
San Diego, CA 92196, USA.
*Fiction by professional spankers and
readers, with personal ads and free
mail forwarding. Formally called
Spankads*

Privilege Club
40 Old Compton St,
London W1V 5BP.
*Spanking/caning afternoons for male
doms*

Spankee's Club
6750 Shadybrook Lane, #110, Dallas
TX 75231, USA ☎ (214) 739 4760.
Postal club run by Randie & Priscilla

Stand Corrected
Shadow Lane, PO Box 1910, Studio
City, CA 91604-0910, USA.
*Glossy spanking, paddling and
caning stories with photos. Holds an
annual Halloween spanking event*

The Thunderbolt Book Club
BCM Thunderbolt,
London WC1N 3XX.
*Offers books on erotic spanking
bottoms — sexual literature written
by bottom-sexuals for bottom-
sexuals. £5 to join, then you get the
list of books to buy by post*

The Upper Hand
Calbrat Enterprises, PO Box 637,
Capitola, CA 95010, USA.
*Newsletter containing advice, stories
and personals*

Martin Cole
40 School Road, Mosely,
Birmingham, UK.
*Surrogate therapy for which you can
sometimes get BUPA to pay. He
seeks male surrogates who can really
teach women and help them, rather
that men who just fancy themselves*

**International Professional
Surrogate Assn**
PO Box 74156 Los Angeles 90004,
USA ☎ (213) 469 4720.
*A group which has been going for
over twenty years, for mutual
training, support and conferences*

*Most towns have local contact
magazines stocked in their sex shops
or newsagents and phonelines, and
these are listed in the Travelling
Section*

Adam
Knight Publishing, 8060 Melrose
Ave, Los Angeles CA 90046, USA.
*A fun tit mag which runs swing ads,
reviews of clubs & club listed state-
by-state and by country.
Sub $36/$46 abroad*

For 2
CP Berner, Postfach 32, Schloss
Wackerstein D-85102, Germany.
*Magazine listing swingers clubs in
Europe, as well as swing tours*

Lifestyles
2641 W La Palma, Suite A, Anaheim,
CA 92801, USA ☎ (714) 821 0030.
*Hold a vast convention in San Diego
with seminars and balls. Also
publishes an international directory
of clubs ($10) & organises trips to
Mexico, Caribbean, Japan and
Europe*

Desire
Red Sky Publishing 192 Clapham
High Street, London SW4 7UD
☎(0171) 627 5155.
*Britain's new magazine for couples
which has personal ads in the back*

Loisirs 2000
BP 3032 , 30002 Nimes,
Cedex, France.
*Wonderful magazine & BBS with its
own guide book (40F) covering
everything in the South of France
from cycling to swinging, singles &
S/M*

National Connection
$42 PO Box 603549, Cleveland Ohio
44103, USA ☎(216) 431 3355.
*Regular swingers mag edited by Patti
Thomas who visits clubs personally.
They also make swingers videos
and run a BBS*

Swingers Update
Contact Advertising POB 3431
Ft Pierce, Florida 34948-3431, USA.
*Recently improved swing magazine
with reviews of clubs and up-to-date
articles on swinging by authoritative
participants*

Unreal People
Sundance Assoc CPCH, PO Box 77817
Los Angeles CA 90007, USA.
*Sample $10. Hard core photos mean
that you can see what you're getting*

Taloned Women

Nails Talons and Claws
NTC PO Box 1081 Bedford Park, IL
60499, USA.
*Non-commercial newsletter on
women with long nails and
scratching, with reader-written
stories, contacts and videos to buy.
Women are classified into ten
categories, depending on the length
of their nails and their passion*

tickling enthusiasts

The Feather
WWT, PO Box 1829 Homestead,
Florida 33090-1829, USA.
*Published 6 times a year and
contains articles, photos and news
on tickling, with classifieds. £20*

Tobias Hackner
1349 South Hudson Ave, Los
Angeles,CA 90019, USA.
Tickling postal club

transsexuals
Man-to-Woman and
Woman-to-Man

The Australian Transgenderists
Support Assoc of Queensland
PO Box 212, New Farm,
QLD 4005, Australia.
Support, penfriends & newsletter

ETVC
POB 6486 San Francisco CA 94101,
USA. ☎(415) 763 3959.
Pansexual group for transsexuals

Gendys
BM Gentrust, London WC1N 3XX.
*Organise the Gender Dysphoria
Conference*

FTM Female to Male
Transsexual Group
5337 College Ave #142 Oakland
California 94618, USA.
Have local groups around The States

F2M
c/o Johnny Armstrong
☎(212) 7251289
*Holds the Drag King Club & Pageant
in New York*

Internet
*Now has a Transgender Board for
people who wish to discuss their
progress of breaking the traditional
boundaries of their own gender*

Press for Change
BM Network, London WC1N 3XX.
A pressure group trying to get

transsexuals the right to live as their re-assigned gender with proper civil rights

San Francisco Gender Information SFGI
PO Box 423602 San Francisco CA 94142, USA.
Referrals and networking for transsexuals

transvestites

Crosstalk
c/o Jenny Baker The Northern Concord, PO Box 258 Manchester M60 1LN, UK.
Personal magazine with local and relevant listings

International TV Repartee
Rose's, Roundel Street, Sheffield S9 3LE, UK ☎ (0114) 261 9444.
Glossy mag with a calendar of international TV events, articles on make-up, dealing with the police, sex and marriage and personal ads. £6 per issue or £18 sub

Kentucky Woman
Charnwood House, Heathway, Camberly, Surrey GU15 2EL, UK ☎ (01276)67898.
Dressing service with huge range of petticoats, bridal gowns and uniforms

Landelijke Kontakt Groep T&T
c/o PO Box 11575, 1001 GN Amsterdam, Holland.
Monthly meetings in several Dutch cities

Phoenix Society
c/o P. Pine, PO Box 58 Wits 2050 South Africa.
SA's largest, oldest and most influential TV/TS support organisation

Tapestry
Journal of the International Foundation for Gender Information
IFGE PO Box 367 Wayland MA 01778, USA ☎ (617) 899 2212.
The most upfront attitude and best international listings magazine

Taffeta
G&M Fashions, PO Box 42 Romford Essex RM1 2ED £10 per copy.
Appeals to the fun trannies and women who enjoy being with them

Transvestites Guide to London
PO Box 941 London SW5 9UT. Tranny Line ☎ (0181) 363 0948.
Excellent guide to everything. They also put on regular nights of unpretentious fun

Texas T Party
PO Box 170042 San Antonio, Texas 78270, USA ☎ (210)980 7788.
Raucous weekend of classes, events and frivolity

underground magazines

Apogee — a guide to unlimited possibilities
Dag Haslemo, Skogstua, 1560 Larkollen, Norway.
Long lists of mags and organisations all over the world, some political, some liberal, others just plain obscure

ByPass
Free on Fastbreeder BBS ☎ (0171) 501 9126 or £1.20/£3 abroad from Box B, 111 Magdalen Road, Oxford OX4, UK.

reaching

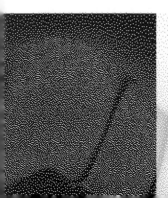

Entertaining and critical reviews of thousands of mags, a few of them erotic, tempting you to send off for and swap

Factsheet Five
PO Box 170099 San Francisco CA 94117-0099, USA.
International listings with reviews of thousands of alternative publications. $6 or $9 by air

Sexzine
BM Uplift, London WC1N 3XX
Taking some of the most relevant articles from around the world and putting them together for British people to read

uniforms

Patrol Uniform Club
of Texas 313 Arkansas Avenue, Texas 78210, USA ☎ (210) 533 6001.
State-wide club for men into uniforms $ 5 per month

uninhibited people

ApaEros
c/o Burt, 960 SW Jefferson Ave, Corvallis, Oregon 9733, USA.
Unedited reader-written forum on sex, relationships, erotica et cetera. An apa is an Amateur Press Association / Assured Publication. If you subscribe, you get to express yourself in the mag, whatever you write, no censorship. With sex,

obviously, this is explosive. The Burts (John & Cath) have been wonderful clerks for many years but are hoping to hand it over to new blood. You? You get sent lots of other sexzines to review, and your subscribers are some of the sexiest people on this planet

Apapa Freer
Pat Underhill, PO Box 759 Veneta, Oregan 97487, USA.
An aberrant apa. Pat prints everything she can fit in/considers worthy, to find more freedom, changing feelings, whilst trying to avoid the attention of the authorities

Odyssey
USA Modem ☎ (818) 358 6968.
A fun way to "meet" people and enjoy uncensored sex talk

Planet Sex Ball
PO Box 4ZB London W1A 4ZB UK.
Fun charity event for people of all persuasions, promoting the mutual acceptance of sexual expression. People come from all over the world

women-only sex stores

Good Vibrations
Joanni Blank, Open Enterprises, 938 Howard Street, San Francisco, CA 94103, USA
☎ (415) 947 8990, fax 974 8989.
This store has been going for almost two decades and offers apprenticeships to women who want to start their own stores. Two weeks training costs $500

want more?

The Organ
acts as an quarterly update to the Handbook, letting you know about new organisations, as they emerge. £20/£25 UK/Europe - $45 elsewhere, incl p&p, from The Leydig Trust, PO Box 4ZB, London W1A 4ZB

reaching

250

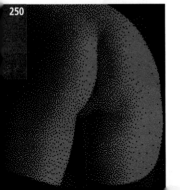

< **language**
is the **dress**
of *thought*>

Samuel Johnson

< *true love: an injection with affection*
to the midsection from a projection
without objection >

8 TALKING

A	=	North American
Au	=	Australian
AG	=	American Gay
B	=	Berkshire
C	=	Cockney
F	=	French Origin
G	=	Geordie
H	=	Hell's Angels
I	=	Irish
K	=	Kosher
O	=	Old English
R	=	Regimental
S	=	Scottish
SA	=	South African
Y	=	Yorkshire

armpit Fuck

bagpipe, coitus in axilla, pit job, huffle.

androgynous

android, he-she, ambi, he-she cup cake, fluff, effeminist (A).

andrologist

cock surgeon, urologist.

arse

ass (A), anus, rectum, tail, rear, backside, bum, baked plum (C), butt (A), ring (SA), ringpiece (SA), fugo (O), roby douglas (O), brother round mouth (O), spice island (O), dilberry creek (O), wrong door (O), feak (O), Holloway Middlesex (O), ers (S), toadum (S), dowp (S), back passage, Khyber (C), bottle and glass (C), the low countries, prat, tush, fanny (A), derriere (F), chunk (A), fesses (F), bunghole, Grand Canyon (AG), Hollywood uterus (AG), exhaust pipe (AG), biscuit (AG), bun (AG), keister (AG), dirt road, dinger (Au), Cadbury canal (A), Hershey highway (A).

arse-licking

rimming, reaming, feuille de rose (F), postillionage (F), analingus, pearl diving (A), chew my ass (A), trip round the world, brown nose (Au), ring round the moon, kiss my arse, black kiss (Spanish), cleaning up the kitchen (AG) .

auto fellation

suck yourself off, self service.

balls

gonads, testes, bollocks, flowers and frolics (C), ghoulies, goolies, knackers, pills, cojones, cods (A), family jewels (A), marbles (A), rocks, stones, stanes (S), nuts, orchestra stalls (C), cobblers' awls (C), ballokes (O), culls (O), scrotum cod (O), codlings (O), coillons (O), dusters (O), leerodies (S), nerts (A), ding dongs (AG), kanakas (Au).

bestiality

animal training, chicken-fucker, sheep dip, any merino in a snowstorm (Au), farmyard fucker, Bodil, 'roo rooting (Au - as in Kanga), zoo queen (AG), animal husbandry, into dogs, pet lover.

big

hung (A), well endowed, shlonger (K), kingsize, hung like a bull, donkey-dick, donkey dong, dollar an inch man (AG), stallion, muckle (S), muckle greet (G), cunt like a horse collar (Y), hit in the ass with a scoop shovel (A), yodling up the canyon, heavyweight.

bisexual

AC/DC, bi, switch-hitter (A), zig-zag (SA), double adaptor (SA), bicycle, dabbler, versatile, caught between the pointers and the setters, ambidextrous, ambisexuals, fruit fly, fly bi, ambi, adaptable, two-way.

bondage

B&D, restraint, straps, chains, corset, gag, ballgag, shackles, fetters, body bag, encasement, strapped, bound & gagged, pony girl/boy, trammel, manacle, tyve, hobble, harness, yoke, collar, bilboes, bridle, tether, handcuffs, ankle-cuffs, clamps, straitjacket, butt-plug (A), gas mask, boots, stocks, whipping, crucifix, pillory, blindfold, cage, fetish.

breasts

bosoms, tits, boobs, boobies, boovies (O), bubbies (A), knockers, coconuts, titties, tom tits (C), Toms (C), Mae Wests (C), Bristols (C), Manchesters (C), cat and kitties (C), tale of two cities (C), cabman's rests (C), norks, jugs, bust, peccaries, udders, bells (A), nay-nay (K), head lights (A), maracas (A), a pair, mammaries, melons, twins, nompers (Y), buns, nipples, nips, bee stings, gnat bites, fried eggs, threepenny bits, dumplings (A), chuggers (A), orbs, lilies, founts (O), dugs (O), cherrylets (O), rosebuds, ruby jewels (O), strawberries (O), milky way (O), baby's public house (O), dairy arrangement (O), kettledrums (O), heavers, panters (O), cleavage.

brothel

cathouse, maison clande (F), whorehouse, massage parlour, sauna, rap parlour, sex palace, bawdy hause, academy, finishing school, maison joie (F), bordello, slut hut (AG), lingerie studio, tanning salon, health parlour, home situations (Au).

buggery

anal intercourse, sodomy, cornholing (A), back door, bit of brown, Greek, Russian wrestling, butt fucking (A), Syrian side of life, chocolate speedway (G), up her jacksy (C), up the Nile, back scuttling, dirt track (A), tailgate driver, fluter (A), meat hound (A), go Hollywood goose (A), take a trip to the moon, kneel at the altar (A), ride the deck (A), snag (A), arse bandit (AG), goosing, turd packer, pumpkin pie (AG), wreck a rectum, pile driver (A), booty jones (A), Socrates' pleasure, butt darts (A).

buttocks

rump, fanny (A), behind, posterior, butt (A), can (A), bottom, fife and drum (C), fud (S&Y), bum, prat, tuckus (K), bucket (A), derrière (F), dutch dumplings (AG), droddum (O), white cliffs (O), western end (O), nates.

254 < Come nudge me, Tam, come nudge me, Tam,
Come nudge me over the nyvel!
Come lowse and lug your battering ram,
And thrash him at my gyvel! >

Robert Burns

buxom

well stacked, fleshy, sonsie (SA), stacked like a brick shithouse (A), torsilu (B), zaftig (K), busty, big ones, D-Cup.

circumcised

clipped, pruned, halfskin fusilier, Nova Scotia (C), Roundhead, acorn.

clitoris

clit, clitty, cloot (S), little bud, pleasure stud, pink bud, little man in the canoe, goalkeeper, panic button, bell, love button.

cock

prick, dong, penis, winkle, phallus, John Thomas (A), rod, tool, generating tool, plonker, willy, organ, dick, peter, percy (Au), one eyed trouser snake, jilogo (SA), joint, weapon, rig, the unit (A), dang (A), whang (S), knob, shatt, head, glans, dork, member, stick, spear, stroupie (S), schlong (K), weenie, welt, the bishop, meat, middle leg (A), pole, wire, bald-headed hermit (O), girl-o-meter, ice cream machine (A), Roger, mutton cudgel, chopper, accoutrements, pork sword (B), sucker (I), langolee (I), gooser, corey (O), rooster (O), lizard (R), golden rivet (R), cod (S), pizel (S), quim stick, dolly (AG), cherry-splitter (AG), giggle stick (C), Pego, lingam (Indian).

condom

rubber, prophylactic, French letter, johnny, Durex, sheath, (love) love glove (Au) Jimmy hat (A), plonker, envelope, bubble gum (A), dunky, Femidom, Reality.

coprophalia

dingleberry nibbling, nugget munching, scatology, the wind the rain & the lava (A), shitfeast, scat.

crutch watcher

bulge detector, basket picnic (AG), bikini inspector (A).

cunnilingus

Frenching, plating, gamming (Y), blowjob, chew out (A), head job (A), go down on, muff munching, licking out, muff-diving, tonguing, mouth music, sit on my face, cunt lapping, hot dinner (A), eating at the Y (A), yodling in the canyon (A), downtown to lunch (A), honey potting (R), kissing the pink, clitlick, fress, dive in the bushes, sneeze into the cabbage, yaffle, nunga munch (Au).

cunt

see **vulva** and **vagina**.

dildo

winger-dinger (A), penis-shaped sex aid, phantom phallus, rubber bullet (R), olisbos consolateur (F), godemiche, cucumber.

dogging

car park sex, putting out, back-seat job, voyeur, exhibitionist, gangbang, car-wash (AG), joining.

doggy-fashion

on her knees, from behind, en levrette (F), like a lioness on a cheese-scraper, up in the hat rack.

dominant

Master, Mistress, control. M/S, D/S, B&D, correction, training, English, corporal punishment, CP, dungeon master, dom, governess, schoolmistress/master, top.

ecstasy

pleasure, turned on, cloud nine, seventh heaven, hellbender, euphoria, rapture, bliss, hot ziggety!

ejaculate

shoot your load, spunk, shoot your wad, fire a shot, jet the juice(A), dump the ashes(A), empty the trash(A), spend (O), fetch (O), Female ejaculation, G-Spot, squirting, shooting. See Premature Ejaculation.

enema

colonic irrigation, enema bag, bardex nozzle, high colonic, clyster, clyso pompe (F), wash the egg out, konni (K).

erect

hard-on, bone on, the horn, stiff, stiffy, stonker, a stand, crack-a-fat (Au), long arm (A), a stay (A), a heart (A), blue veiner, a jack up, rampant Hampton (C), leaning tower of pisser, angle of dangle, raise a beam (A), raise a gallop, heat of meat.

exhibitionist

flasher, expose yourself, lasher-mack, streaker, mooner, orgiast, stripper, madel, showgirl, show-off, dangle queen (AG), raincoat brigade, whakapohane (NZ Maori).

felch

kiss with sucked out come (AG), exchanging loads, snowdropping, snowballing, White Russian.

fellatio

blowjob, B.J., give head (A), plate, gam, 'French', gobbling, deep throat, irrumate, pipe, suck off, face fucking, dick drinking (AG), zipper dinner (A), meat sandwich (A), gnawing the 'nana (Au), derby (A), service, go down on, smoke, play the magic flute (I), play the organ (AG), kiss the worm, whomp it up, garden gate (C), puffing in the percy (Au), take it in the mouth, peter eater, jaw queen (AG), severe scorcher (AG), donkey serenade (AG), stick face.

fist fucking

hand balling, wrist wrestling, hand sandwich, shaking hands with the baby (A), F.F.A.

flirt

give the eye, the come on, petting, seduce, yucking it up (SA), chatting up

frotteur

rub against, commuter creamer, cushion your jewels (A), bumping pussies (AG), la mano morta (Italian).

fuck

screw, ball (A), poke, shag, roger, get some nookie, rooting (Au), houghmagandie (S), have it off/up/away, get it on, on the job, bunk up, in and out, knock, score, make it/out/love, swive, hump, jump (SA), crawl (A), tip (A), smoke (A), sleep with, sauté my monkey (A), bonk, curl the tail (A), give her the barrel (Y), lay, get laid, sexual intercourse, fornicate, shoft, grind, bang, touch of the rod, tango, get your leg over, Friar Tuck (C), a serve (Au), slam (Au), ham slammer (Au), sink the sausage (Au), go all the way, knee trembler, go for gold, grab a piece (A), get a piece of ass, greasing the steer (A), noggin', dip the wick, pop (A), shtup (K), give a pork swording (B), taste (A), TCB (A), deep plumbing, fur burger (SA), wool pudding (SA), get your oats, tear the back aff (Scouse), ball bashing, jumm (O), pizzle (O), plug (O), prick the garter (O), peste (O), wag one's tail (O), Mount Pleasant (O), empty the bag (I), tumble (O), pushpin (O), bang (O), big J (AG), High Russian

(AG), GB (AG), good seeing to, laying pipe (A), American Culture.

gangbang

gang shay (A), pull a train (H), airtight (AG), onion (Au) .

gerontosexuality

sugar daddy, dyke daddy, alter kocker (K), gerontophile.

good sex

earth mover, cloud nine, shooting the rapids, plunging through the mattress (A), bomber hanger (A), get tucked into it (A), stuck in, Monica moving-hips, bonzer (Au), royal, rum, ace-high, tops, princess of the bed, A-one, exquisite, ecstasy.

g roping

grappling, Octopus, touch up, fondling, petting.

homosexual

endless vocabulary - as listed in *The Queen's Vernacular* which has the richest gay slang imaginable. Compiled by Bruce Rogers, published by Blond & Briggs, England and Arrow Press, USA, 1972.

irrumate

fuck in the mouth, singe someone's face (AG).

kinky

round the world, pervert, perv, way out, spicy, numbers game (A), freaky, adventurous, degenerate, PG (AG), animal, outrageous, bizarre, sexobatics, trisexual, wild thing.

kiss

french kiss, deep tongue, peck, sixty nine, brush your lips over, press your lips to, love bite, soul kiss (A), swapping spit (A).

liberation

politico, sexually right on, radical, rad, cool, sex-marcher, politically correct lifestyle, sex-freedom, libertine, sex-pol (German).

love bite

strawberry (A), double dracula, papillons d'amour (F), monkey bite (A), bubble gum (AG), rose tattoo, passion purpura, hickey (A).

lunchtime fuck

nooner (A), funch, appetizer, matinee (O), LV leg-up.

lusty

randy, horny, lecherous, juicy, cream your jeans, rooty (A), a rush (A), hand trouble (A), hat pants, wet, drooling, sex maniac, jacked up (A), geared up (A), wired up (A), hungry, raunchy, hornbag, goer, fucker, raging hormones.

masturbate

wank, frig, jerk off, jack off (A), beat off (A), toss, jerkin' the gherkin (Au), Mrs. Palm and her five daughters (Au), meet four sisters on Thumb Street, beat your meat (Au), flong your dong (A), gallop the maggot, play with yourself, pump, nifty-fifty, five knuckle shuffle, rub yourself, jilling off, twang the wang, milk (A), five tackle one (SA), J. Arthur (C), Jodrell (C), dousing the hankie (Au), bashing the bishop, pocket pool (A), roll your own, flog your dolphin, dishonourable discharge, keep down the census, manual exercises, housewife's honour.

mutual masturbation

Swedish, Skeet shooting (catching ejaculate in mouth) (AG), tossing bean bags (AG), petting, tossing each other off, hand jobs, Jack-off, Jack 'n' Jill party.

necrophilia

mortuary love, pork packing (A), dead boring, it takes some pluck to have a cold fuck - but look at the money it saves, necrofellow, Miss Vampira.

nipples

cherries, teats, big browneyes, strawberries, rosebuds, areola, half inch bolts, radia dials, bee bites (AG), nubes, nubs, nubbins.

nymphophilia

DOM, jailbait (A), cherry-picker (A), San Quentin quail (A), short eyes (A), paedo, school girl fan.

one-timer

oncer (AG), one night stand, Romeo, Casanova, local bike, never come back for seconds.

orgasm

cum (A), banners & drums (C), come off, light up, the big O, satisfy, le petit mort (F), spasm, ejaculate, spunk, pop the cork, pocket the red, earth mover, the sneeze in the loins (F), get there, reach it, clitoral orgasms, G-Spot orgasm, prostate orgasm, vaginal orgasm, spasm, sympathetic orgasm, multiple orgasm.

orgy

group sex, daisy-chain, wifeswapping, partouze (F), swinging, Roman, synergy, Forum-minded, like-minded, lifestyles (A), group grind (SA), cluster fuck, moresomes (A), gangbang, freak scene (AG), polaroid party, flesh picnic, love feast, pajama party, poke party, circus, pig pile (AG), line up, lamma hutching (when all the mouths are full) (AG), tan cream (A), Mazola oil party (A).

orgy-master/mistress

make the plank (AG), plug them in, orchestrator, master of ceremonies, le main officieuse (F).

perineum

tant (AG), guiche, groin, t'ain't.

petting

snogging, necking, fondling, flirt, prime it (AG), caressing, groping, hanky panky, homework (A), canoodling, spooning (O), fooling around, upstairs and downstairs, pashing (Au).

piercing

infibulation, ring, ear, nose, eyebrow, nipple, navel, clitoris, frenum, foreskin, ampallang, dydoe, Prince Albert, apadravya, hafada, guiche, body jewellery.

< reality is not limited to the familiar, the commonplace, for it consists in huge part of a latent, yet unspoken future word >

Dostoevsky

premature ejaculation

PE, Easter Queen (AG), come too fast, come in your pants.

promiscuous

fucks anything, anybody's, open, free, liberal, needy, greedy, local bicycle, go trashin' (AG), out to get laid, fucks more people than you do.

prostitution

whore, hooker, call girl, concubine, street-walker, rent, cracking it, bordello, trade, brothel, crib (A), cage (India), night butterfly (Indonesia), lady of the evening, red light, brass nail (C), demi-mondaine (F), mistress, white slavery, traffic in women, pimp, amateur, away-day girl, window girl, massage parlour, sauna, hostess, pro, professional, prossy, tart, ferry (Au), rent boy. gigolo, geisha, Oiran (Japanese), harlot, trick, John, client, customer .

pubic hair

muff, pubes, fuz, bush, fur, thatch, short & curlies, woolies, beaver (A), jungle, map of Tasmania (Au), twat rug (O), cunt curtain (O), kitten's ear (O), fleece (O), Bushy Park (O), Fort Bushy (A), gorilla salad (A).

quickie

quick poke, wham, bam, thank you ma'am, shortcake (AG).

rampant

passionate, lusty, raunchy, wild, debauched, hound dog (A); *Women*: banger. eager beaver (A), goer, spunky, foxy, whicky woman (A), nympho, corker, hot honey (A), brazen, red hot, hip chicken (A), cool (A), bombshell, insatiable, doxy (O), hussy (O), groupie, good time girl, loose, another slice off the cut loaf (I), promiscuous, easy, local bike, bangs like a dunny door on a windy night (Au), sports model (A), high voltage mama (A), raw piece (A); *Men*: Casanova, Don Juan, bonar, beefcake (AG), wolf, cake eater (A), stud, ladies' man, cuntsman (A), virile, bull, campus butcher (A), horny, knicker-ripper, all-nighter, smutty piece (AG), stuff (AG).

S & M

S/M, sadomasochism, sadomaso, sadism, masochism, algolagnia, dominant, submissive, D&S, slavist, torture ritual, corporal punishment, CP, bondage & discipline, B&D, bondage, slave, master, mistress, spanking, caning, discipline, deprivation, correction, flogging, whipping, restriction, punishment, purge, English, the English vice (F).

scrotum

ballbag, sack, Mephistopheles' purse, cod (O), the wrinkled retainer, lust cluster, jewel box, catcher's mitt (A).

seduce

flirt, woo, charm, chat-up, give the come on, turn you on, titillate, titivate, make eyes at, vamp, lead on, pull, copping off (Scouse), tempt, make out (A), scare, hats on (A), yucking it up (A), pluck some feathers (AG), ravage, snog, give the eye, make a pass at, do the moves.

sensuous

sybarite, epicurist, gentle, touch, focus, tender, intuitive, receptive, responsive, music lessons, sensualist.

shaved

depilation, penny reel (O), bald beaver (A), smooth pussy, the last chicken at Sainsburys, bikini-waxing (A), smoothie.

sixty-nine

soixante-neuf (F), go down on each other, tête beche (F), zigzagging (A), cunnilingus and fellatio, boating, nose to tail.

small cock

dinky dick (AG), hung like a stud fieldmouse (A), biteful, minnow, yoyo, pinkie, smetana, stump, wagette, petite.

smegma

dick cheese, smentana (K), crusty.

spanking

schoolboy/girl, nurse, caning, rulers, paddle, smarting botty, naughty boy/girl, teacher's kicks, corporal punishment, nun's fun.

spread legs

split beaver (A), open heart surgery, tunnel-shot, pelvic exam, speculum.

spunk

semen, juice, cum, load, jism, seed, ejaculate, fetch (O), slime, smeddum (S), melts (S), gurr (S), jollies, jizz, dream whip (AG), doll spit, love juice, french fried ice cream (AG), mushroom soup.

submissive

slave, servile, obedient, humiliation, domestic training, kennel training.

swinging

open marriage, sex club, swapping, wife swapping, closed and open swinging, recreational swinging, utopian swinging, indoor sports, key clubs, group sex, orgy, threesome, sexual freedom, soft & hard swinging, social swinging, polyfidelity, group marriage.

threesome

sex sandwich, twos-up, slurpy seconds, la main officieuse (F), plug them in, accomplice, ménage à trois (F), troilism, double entry, couple freak, triad, face-to-face-to-face

tossing

(a French word meaning finding a mutual attraction to a stranger and fucking on the spot, be it in the cinema, aeroplane, on the beach or in the dole queue).

talking

260

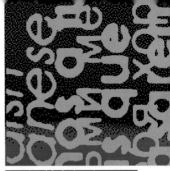

transsexual

TS, sex change, he she, she-man, danish pastry, Copenhagen capon, phalloplasty, big surprise, transectional, tronny, transy, intersexual, hermaphrodite (morphodite), transgenderism, girl-boy, girl with a dick, pre-op, post-op.

transvestite

TV, drag queen, dressing up, gender-bender (SA), pantie queen, transgenderism, girl boy, tranny.

turned on

stimulated, erect, seduced, lusty, feel the sap rising, drove up (A), cream your jeans.

uncircumcised

uncut, prepuced, tref (K), wear a turtle sweater (AG), Bologna, does it wink? (AG), draped (AG), draw-drapers (AG), cavalier, Roman roll (A).

urolagnia

watersports, golden showers, piss play.

vagina

cunt, slit, crack, hole (A), cooze, cuzzy, crack, fitz (A), cock (Dixie), flue (Y), yoni (India), nookie, fanny, pussy, honeypot (O), golden doughnut, toosh (K), gash, sharp and blunt (C), growl and grunt (C), happy valley (A), vage (A), box (A),love lane (O), cupid's highway (O), artichoke, pipkin (O), chalice (O), mantrap (O), pokehole, gully hole (O), rattle snake canyon (A), mute (AG), papaya (AG), dead-end street, gate of Hell.

vaginal clenching

snapping pussy (A), snapping turtle (A), pompoir (F / Tamil, S. India).

vaginal lubrication

wet, pussy juice, love juice, sloshy, sopping, dripping, gushing, french dip (A), cyprine (F).

vanilla sex

straight, missionary, mundane, bambi, pagan, cuddlies.

voyeur

peeping tom, watch queen (AG), Bo Peep (AG), peek freak (AG), Knee Pad Associates, playing doctor, looky-loo.

vulva

snatch, twat, quim, blit, beaver (A), gash, pumpum, pussy lips, lips, labia, piss flaps, coral sheath (O), oyster, mystic grotto (O), love's pavilion (O), clitoris. mons, crotch (A), squack, curtains of beef, cumquat, minge, box, matt.

vulva-to-vulva

bumper to bumper (A), flat fuck, troilism.

wifeswapping

swapping, key games, trade off (A), 2+2 (F), M/C seeks couples.

withdrawal

get off at (Haymarket - or any penultimate station before a city centre), pulling out.

english	french portuguese	german welsh
Take me home, I'll show you a good time	Viens chez moi, on va prendre du bons temps *Vamos para casa, passaremos bons momentos*	Komm mit nach Hause und wir werden viel Spass haben *Cym fi adre ac fe gawn ni amser da*
We simply must have a double bed	Nous avons absolument besoin d'un lit à deux places *Tem que ser una cama de casal*	Wir müssen einfach ein Doppelbett haben *Mae'n rhaid i ni gael gwely dwbwl*
My wife and I would like to make it with you	Ma femme et moi amérions le faire avec toi *Eu e minha mulher gostariamos deo fazercontigo*	Meine Frau und ich wollen es mit dir treiben *Fe hoffai'r wraig a finnau wneud cyfathrach rywiol a chi*
Please hold my cock/pussy	Je t'en prie, prends ma bite/ma chatte *Por favour segura on meu pau/ minha buceta*	Bitte halte meinem schwanz/fotse *Daliwch fy ngwialen/nghotsen*
I/We only want to have safer sex	Je/Nous ne veux/voulons que de Sex Sans Risque *E melhor para voce, e melhor para me*	Ich will/Wir wollen nur sicheren Sex *Rydw i eisiau rhyw diogel yn unig*
Please direct me to the red light district	S'il vous plait, pouvez-vous m'indiquer le quartier des filles? *Conduza-me a das putas*	Wo gehts zum nuttenviertel? *A wnewch chi fy nghyfeiro i ardal y golau coch os gwelwch yn dda*
I would like to order a prostitute	Je voudrais me payer une pute *Eu quero uma puta*	Ich möchte eine hure bestellen *Gwelwch yn dda fe hoffwn archebu putain os gwelch yn dda*
I am gay/I am not gay/I am bisexual	Je suis/je ne suis pas gouine/pédé/je suis bisexuel: je fais les deux *Estou homosexual; nao sou bicha/ sou bisexual*	Ich bin schwul/ nicht schwul/bin bisexuell *Rwy'n gyfunrhywiol/nid wy'n gyfunrhywiol/ rwy'n ddeurywiol*
I am a masochist; I need a sadist	Je suis masochiste; j'ai besoin d'un(e) sadique *Sou masoquista; preuso dum sádico*	Ich bin masochist; ich brauche einen sadisten *Rwy'n hoffi poen; rhaid i mi gael rhywun cealon*

talking

< I would rather have all the risks which come from free discussion of sex than the great risks we run by conspiracy of silence >

Dr C. G. Lang - former Archbishop of Canterbury

english	french *portuguese*	dutch *italian*
Have you come? / Are you satisfied?	**Tu as joui? Tu as satisfait(e)?** *Já te vieste? Estás satisfeito(a)?*	**Bist du gekommen?** **Bist du befriedigt?** *Wyt ti wedi soethu dy liwyth?*
Do you have syphilis/gonorrhoea/crabs/AIDS?*	**As-tu la syphilis/la blennoragie/des morpions/SIDA?** *Tens sifilis/gonorreia/chatos/SIDA?*	**Hast du syphillis/gonorrhea/flöhe/AIDS?** *Oes gennyt ti syphillis/gonorrhea/grancod/AIDS?*
Where is the local VD clinic?	**Où est le centre prophilactique?** *Onde estao clinica de doencas venereas?*	**Wo ist der örtliche Hautarzt?** *Ble mae canolfan lleol am glefyd gwenerol?*
Are you body positive?	**Es tu sero positif?** *Eu sou serro positivo?*	**Sind sie HIV-positiv?** *Wyt ti corff cadarnhaol?*
I enjoy spanking/ being spanked/ being tied up	**J'aime frapper/ être frappé(e)/ être attaché(e)** *Eu gosto de bater/ de apanhar/ de ser atado*	**Ich schlage gem/ ich lass mich gem/ ich mag gern gefesselt sein** *Rwy'n hoffi chwipio tin cael chwip din/cael fy rhwymo i fyny*
Are you on the Pill? Have you got a contraceptive?	**Tu prends la pillule? Est-ce que tu as un contraceptif?** *Usa a pilula? Vocs ten luva?*	**Nimmst du die Pille?Hast du ein Kondom?** *Wyt ti ar y bilsen? Oes gennyt ti declyn i arbed fy feichiogi?*
I can't understand a word you are saying: let's just make love	**Je ne comprends pas un mot de ce que tu dis: faisons simplement l'amour** *Nao entendo nada do que estas dizendo: vamos so fazer amor*	**Ich verstehe kein wort von dem was du sagst. Lass uns nur bumsen** *Fedra, i ddim deall yr gair: gad i ni wneud cyfathra-chrywiol*
I can't take any more!	**Je n'en peux vraiment plus** *Nao posso mais*	**Mir reichts** *Fedra'i ddim cymryd dim mwy!*
Thank you: that was wonderful	**Merci: c'était merveilleux** *Obrigado: foi maravilhoso*	**Danke: das war herrlich** *Diolch yn fawr. Roedd hwna'n rhyfeddol*
I love you	**Je t'aime** *Amo-te*	**Ich liebe dich** *Rwyn dy garu di*
I don't love you, but you're great	**Je t'aime pas, mais tu es merveilleux(se)** *Não te amo, mas és boa*	**Ich liebe dich nicht,aber du bist grossartig** *Dydw i ddim yn dy garu di, ond wyt fin rhagoral*

talking

* **N B.** Herpes being the generic name is international

english	arabic *hebrew*	dutch *italian*
Take me home, I'll show you a good time	**Hudni i biet; lowrtik al mutar** *Khi oti habajta ve lah tou*	**Laten we naar jouw huis gaan en een lekker ritje maken** *Portami a casa, e ti far ò vedere come divertirci*
We simply must have a double bed	**Ana aw kabir** *Anahnu zkukim lemita kfula*	**We moeten absoluut een tweepersoonsbed hebben** *Dobbiamo avere un letto matrimoniale*
My wife and I would like to make it with you	**Ana ow murati anez ien nik-nak mahbat surng chong wan ha** *Isti vani rozim liskav ithem*	**Mijn vrouw en ik zouden graag een triootje met je maken** *Mia moglie (mio matito) ed io vorremmo divertici con te*
Please hold my cock/pussy	**Isa samti m siki subri/cuss** *Ahazi li bazajin/kus*	**Pak alsjeblieft mijn pik/poesje vast** *Per favore, prendi il mio cazzo/la mia figa*
I/We only want to have safer sex	**La urid sauf ilakatun aslam jinsian** *Anee ruc rotsch/Anach noo rotsin min batuach*	**Ik wil/Wij willen alleen veilig vrijen** *Vorrei fare del sesso ma senza rischio per la mia salude*
Please direct me to the red light district	**Fien hetet el sharamet?** *Ejfo ezor hazonot*	**Kunt u me de weg naar de walletjes wijzen** *Per favore, indicarni la via delle luci rosse*
I would like to order a prostitute	**Ana awez sharmuta** *Ani roze lehazmin zona*	**Ik wil graag een hoer bestellen** *Vorrei avere una prostituta*
I am gay/I am not gay/I am bisexual	**Ana beta áerial/ ana mush/ beta coulo** *Ani homoseksuali/ lo homoksuali/ ani bisekuali*	**Ik ben homo/Ik ben geen homo/Ik ben biseksueel** *Sono omosessuale/ non sono omosessuale/ sono bisessuale*
I am a masochist; I need a sadist	**Ana beta masochist: ana awez sádist** *Ani mazochist: ani zakuk lesadist*	**Ik ben masochist: ik zoek een sadist** *Sono masochista: ho bisogno d'un(a) sadico (sadica)*
Have you come? / Are you satisfied?	**Enti khalasti/ mabsouta?** *Haim baat al sipukeh?*	**Ben je klaar gekomen? Ben je bevredigd?** *Sei venuto? Sei soddisfatto?*
Do you have syphilis/gonorrhoea/crabs/ AIDS ? *	**Enti andek shohary/ shiblan/ crabs/ Naks al Manaah?** *Jes lah sifilis/ ziva/ mandevoskees/ AIDS?*	**Heb je syfilis/ gonorreu/ schaamluis/ AIDS?** *Hai la sifilide/ lo scolo/ le piattole/ AIDS?(pronounced Aiuyds)*

264

* N B. Herpes being the generic name is international

english	arabic / hebrew	dutch / italian
Where is the local VD clinic?	**Fien el mostasfa?** *Ejfo hamerpaa lemahalot medabkot?*	**Waar is de poli-kliniek voor geslachtsziekten?** *Dov'è la clinica delle malattie veneree?*
Are you body positive?	**Hal fahsak mudil?** *Yesh lecha goof positivi?*	**Ben je sero-positief?** *Sei siero positivo?*
I enjoy spanking/ being spanked/ being tied up	**Ana b, hebt lel darb wa el tasieb** *Ani ochev leanot/ ani nehene chshmarbitzimli/ lihiot cashur*	**Ik vind het leuk om billekoek te geven/ krijgen/ vastge-bonden te worden** *Mi piace frustare/ essere frustato (frustata)/ essere legato*
Are you on the Pill? Have you got a contraceptive?	**Enti khati el habub/ ana maia kabut** *Haim at al haglula*	**Gebruik je de pil? Heb je een condoom?** *Prendi la pillola? Hai un contra-ccettivo?*
I can't understand a word you are saying: let's just make love	**Ana mush araf betuli a thala l nik** *Ani lo meuin ma at omerat, achanu osim ahaveh*	**Ik begrijp je niet: laten we gewoon vrijen** *Non capisco niente di quel che dici: facciamo semplice mente all' amore*
I can't take any more!	**Khfiea keda** *Ani lo jahol joter*	**Ik kan niet meer** *Non ce la faccio più*
Thank you: that was wonderful	**Shukran: kan-modish** *Toda ze haja nehedas*	**Dank je: het was heerlijk** *Grazie: é stato bellissimo*
I love you	**Ana b hebek** *Ani ochev otach*	**Ik hou van je** *Ti amo*
I don't love you, but you're great	**Ana mush b hebek, enti quisea** *Ani lo ochev otach aval at tova meod*	**Ik hou niet van je: maar je bent fantastisch** *Non ti amo, ma sei meraviglioso(mera-vigliosa)*
Show me what turns you on	**Wa rini enti aweza fien** *Tari li ma at ohevet*	**Waar word je geil van** *Fammi vedere che cosa ti fa eccitare*

talking

265

english	spanish (s. american) / swedish	russian / japanese
Take me home, I'll show you a good time	**Vamos a tu casa y verás que bien nos lo pasaremos** / *Ta med mig hem, så ska vi ha det trevligt*	Возьми меня домой. Я тебя хорошенько развлеку. / *Anata no uchi ni tsurettete, tano- shimaseru kara*
We simply must have a double bed	**Necesitamos una cama grande** / *Vi måste ha en dubbelsäng*	Нам необходима двойная кровать. / *Daburu bed ga shituyo desu*
My wife and I would like to make it with you	**Mi m ujer y yo queremos follar contigo** / *Min fru och jag vill knulla dig*	Моя жена и я хотели бы развлечься с тобой. / *Kanai to watashi to issho ni shitai*
Please hold my cock/pussy	**Por favor acarici- ame la polla/ el coño** / *Känn min kuk/ fitta*	Возьми меня за хуй/ пизду. / *Ole-no ochinchin tsukande/watashi-no omanko ni sawasute*
I/We only want to have safer sex	**Solo quiero/ queremos hacer el amor con preser- vativo** / *Jag vi vill bara-ha säkrare sex*	Я/мы хотим только безопасный секс. / *Watashi/Watashit- achi wa anzen na seikõ o shitai*
Please direct me to the red light district	**Por favor, dígame dónde está el barrio de putas** / *Var får 'red light' området*	Скажите, пожалуйста, где находится квартал красных фонарей? / *Akasen wa dokoka oshiete kudasai*
I would like to order a prostitute	**Quisiera contratar una prostituta** / *Jag vill ha en hora*	Я желал бы заказать девочку. / *Baishunfu o ödá shitai*
I am gay/I am not gay/I am bisexual	**Soy homosexual/ No soy homosexual/ Soy bisexual** / *Jag är homo- sexuell/ jag är inte homosexuell/ jag är bisexuell*	Я гомосексуалист/я не гомосексуалист/я бисексуален. / *Watashi wa gei desu/watashi wa gei dewa nai/watashi wa ryoto tsukai desu*
I am a masochist; I need a sadist	**Soy masoquista y, busco a un sadico/a** / *Jag är en maso- chist: jag behöver en sadist*	Я мазохист: мне нужен садист. / *Watashi wa mazo- hisuto desu, sadisuto ga hoshii*
Have you come? / Are you satisfied?	**¿Te has corrido ya? ¿Estas satis- fecho/a?** / *Gick det för dig? Har du fått nog?*	Ты готов/готова? Ты довлен/довльна? / *Kurai makkusu ni tasshi taka?/ Man zoku shita ka*
Do you have syphilis/gonorrhoea/crabs/ AIDS ? *	**¿Tienes la sífilis/gon- orrea/ladillas/el SIDA?** / *Har du syfilis/ gon- orre/ flat löss/ AIDS?*	У тебя сифилис/ гонорея/ СПИД? / *Baidoku/rinbyo/ke- jirami/ AIDS o motteruka?*

talking

* **N B.** Herpes being the generic name is international

english	spanish (s. american) / *swedish*	russian / *japanese*
Where is the local VD clinic?	**Fien el mostafa?** *Var är näraste VD klinik?*	диспансер? Где находится венерический *Chi kakuno VD clinic wa dokodesuka?*
Are you body positive?	**¿Das positivo?** *Är ni kropps positiv?*	Ты серопозитивный/ная? *Anata-wa AIDS desuka?*
I enjoy spanking/ being spanked/ being tied up	**Me gusta dar azotainas/recibir azotainas. Me gusta que me aten** *Jag tycker om att sla dig/ bli slagen/ bunden*	Я люблю мучить/ мучиться/быть связанным. *Tataku no ga suki/ tatakareru no ga suki/shibarareru no ga suki*
Are you on the Pill? Have you got a contraceptive?	**¿Tomas la pildora? ¿Tienes un condón?** *Tar dy p-piller? Har du något skydd?*	Ты принимаешь противозачаточные таблетки? У тебя есть презерватив? *Hinin yaku nonder-uka? Hiningu o motte ruka?*
I can't understand a word you are saying: let's just make love	**No entiendo ni una palabra de lo que dices, ¿y Sí hiciéramos el amor?** *Jag förstår inte ett ord du säer: låt oss alska i alla fall*	Я не понимаю ни слова: давай лучше трахаться. *Nani o yutteru ka wakarimasen: love make o shiyö*
I can't take any more!	**No aguanto ya más** *Jag har haft nog*	Я больше не могу. *Koreijö muridesu!*
Thank you: that was wonderful	**Gracias, ha sido maraviloso** *Tack: det var underbart*	Спасибо, это было замечательно. *Dömo arigatö: suba rashikatta*
I love you	**Te amo** *Jag älskar dig (dej)*	Я люблю тебя. *Aishite masu*
I don't love you, but you're great	**!No te amo, pero eres increíble** *Jag älsker dig inte men du är toppen!*	Я не люблю тебя, но ты замечательный/ замечательна! *Aishite naikedo anata wa subara shi*
Show me what turns you on	**Dime lo que gusta hacer** *Visa mig vad du gillar*	Покажи мне, что тебе доставляет удовольствие. *Naniga anata o köfun saseruka oshiete*

talking

computer *sex*

< I think lust motivates technology.
the first personal robots, let's face it,
are not going to be made to bring people drinks >
Mike Saenz

Computers are bringing us incredible opportunities to enjoy more sex (safely) and expand our sexual imaginations and fantasies. The best toys are the Bulletin Boards, the Internet, and interactive CD Roms. If you have a computer, telephone and modem, you can talk to people through computer networks, homing in on specialised sexual topics. Affairs are conducted and views shared throughout the day and night between anonymous people. You can pretend to be a fantasy character or be yourself, and nobody knows where you are in the whole world. The French use **Minitel**, supplied free by the French National telephone company, and the Americans have thousands of systems available to them. Perhaps the most significant advance for many people is that they talk to each other about their sexual tastes and needs before they ever meet. Thus, love stems from the excitement of sharing the same sexual mentality rather than from the initial impressions of looks and physical chemistry.

The biggest network in the world is The **Internet**. The Internet is millions of computers joined by full-time fibre-optic lines, a spider's web which nobody owns, and nobody controls. The Net is divided into

three key areas: mail, remote access and Usenet. Mail is the electronic mail of e-mail, and you can mail anything: text, pictures, video, sounds, all in a matter of seconds. On the Internet, you can subscribe to magazines, use Telnet to drive other people's computer programmes, use ftp to copy files and, perhaps most exciting, find images, sounds and videos through the easy-to-use WorldWide Webb (www). "Talk" is used for chatting, and one-to-one conversations can be conducted with your screens divided in two, showing what you are both saying simultaneously. Multiple conversations are also possible on screen, although these are usually less interesting. Usenet is for hard news and is an anarchic collection of news-groups, some of which are sexually oriented. 'alt.sex', for example, is subdivided into a huge number of sub sections like alt.sex. watersports, alt.sex.enemas, alt.sex.stripclubs, etc.The Internet has become the world supersex-highway. Time-wasters and commercial hawkers get flamed (rudely criticised).

It's easy to see (download) pictures from the Net, but to put your own pictures into the system (uploading), you need a scanner (costing as little as £100).

Before you can plug into the Internet, you need a service provider and the best in Britain is **Demon**, who supply some free access software, and charge under £12 a month *(See addresses, below)*. Once installed, for the cost of a local call, you can be in touch with the entire world, and the sixteen million other people on the Net.

Multi-User Dungeons exist on the Net — these are imaginary cafés you can enter as a certain type of creature and have encounters with others.

Because the Net is so big, it's extremely complicated to use. Other systems are simpler, like **Compuserve** and **Cix**. Cix is a British bulletin board which has a lively sexuality conference. There is a guide to adult bulletin boards in the Reaching section under Computer Sex Buffs.

You can also find your own type of bulletin board by looking in the quality magazines that cater to your own sexual taste, although the scope in Britain is very limited. *Penthouse*'s **Pleasure Dome** has just begun and will hopefully supply more than reproductions of their pin-ups. They have also produced *Digital Dreams*, a magazine devoted to computer sex. The most interesting magazine is the American *Future Sex*.

Getting into adult bulletin boards is not as easy as it was. You need to prove you are old enough and if you misbehave you will be banned everywhere. Part of the British Criminal Justice Bill aims to control these boards, as they fear what might happen if we all plug and talk to each other(!).

Interactive computer sex began with the American discs **Virtual Valerie** and **Donna Matrix** created by Mike

Cyber/SM

Saenz but now his interactive techno trollops are on CD Roms and have taken a leap forward with **VV2**. The Japanese have a huge range of interactive porn on the 3DO system. Because CD Roms are so easy to pirate, many companies are holding back on releasing some of their most adventurous material.

Touch typists may wonder how you can enjoy all these sexual treats on the screen while your fingers are busy tapping into the keyboard, but the good news is that one-handed keyboards are now available from Miscrosoft!

CD Roms with libraries of porn and sex videos are listed in the Looking section.

talking

269

Cybersex has been hyped up in the media. The potential is exciting: you might one day be able to have simulated sex inside a kind of space suit which you can programme to give you your ideal visual, sound and tactile experiences. Already, **CyberSM** has made a pair of prototypes for use by couples. Wearing these suits, using two computers and a phoneline or the Internet, you can stimulate your partner (and vice versa), the two of you sitting on opposite sides of the globe! You spell out what feels good and what you want, which makes you very aware of which specific parts of your body enjoys which kinds of sensations, and how hard or soft. Such exercises in erotic communication can be quite illuminating.The colour images used in the title pages of this book are from some of the three-dimensional body scans which Kirk Woolford made for the virtual bodies to be manipulated via computer screens in his CyberSM programme. ◀

computer sex addresses

Cix
☎(0181)390 1244 for bauds up to 2,400 and ☎(0181) 390 1255 for faster modems.

Cyberotica
The Internet's erotic magazine with personals, contact Kyle Shannon
e-mail: doggie@echonyc.com

CyberSM
Kirk Woolford at Cologne University, KHM Köln, Peter-Welter-Platz 2, 50676 Cologne
Fax ☎(49) 221 201 8917.
e-mail: kwolf@obelix.khm.uni-koeln.de

Demon Internet
42 Hendon Lane, London N3 1TT.
☎(0181)349 0063, fax ☎349 0309.

Future Sex
Kundalini Publishing 60 Federal Street, Suite 502, San Francisco 94107.

Pleasure Dome
☎(0181) 742 7676 (settings are 8-n-1).

Virtual Valerie, Donna Matrix, VV2
Reactor Inc, 445 West Erie, Chicago Il 60610
Fax ☎(312) 573 0891 USA.